Confirmation
and
First Communion

CONFIRMATION
and
FIRST COMMUNION

A Study Book

Frank W. Klos

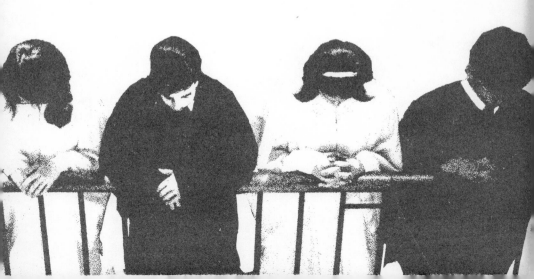

CONFIRMATION AND FIRST COMMUNION

A STUDY BOOK

By Frank W. Klos

Copyright © 1968

AUGSBURG PUBLISHING HOUSE

BOARD OF PUBLICATION OF THE
LUTHERAN CHURCH IN AMERICA

CONCORDIA PUBLISHING HOUSE

Prepared for the Boards of Parish Education of the
Lutheran Church in America, The Lutheran Church —
Missouri Synod, and The American Lutheran Church.

Scripture quotations from the *Revised Standard Version of the Bible,* copyrighted 1946 and 1952 by the Division of Christian Education, National Council of Churches, are used by permission.

Acknowledgment is made for permission to reprint various material:

The last lines from Stanza 4 of "Onward Christian Soldiers," by Sabine Baring-Gould, published by J. Curwen & Sons, Ltd., London.

Quotation on page 120 from *Youth: The Years from Ten to Sixteen* by A. Gesell, F. Ilg, and L. B. Ames; copyrighted 1964. Published by Harper and Row, Inc., New York.

Quotation on page 124 from *Religious Thinking from Childhood to Adolescence* by Ronald Goldman, copyrighted 1964. Humanities Press Inc., New York, publisher in the U.S.A. and Routledge & Kegan Paul, Ltd., London, world publisher.

A line from Stan Freeberg's record album *The United States of America,* copyright 1966 by Capitol Records, Hollywood, California.

407 G68   Printed in U.S.A.   2-3

A Word of Introduction

Responding to an invitation from the Lutheran Church in America to undertake a joint study on the theology and practice of confirmation, The American Lutheran Church and The Lutheran Church—Missouri Synod agreed to participate in this important task. A fifteen-man commission was established to pursue the study. The commission represented broad areas of church life in its membership, including theologians, parish pastors, laymen educators, liturgiologists, and administrators.

Because of the mobility of the population and the growing cooperation among the three major Lutheran bodies, the commission felt it was highly desirable to plan joint action to meet a common problem for Lutherans in North America. However, commission members agreed that any long-standing practice of the church, such as confirmation, deserved careful study before any modifications were proposed. Since its initial meeting in September, 1964, the commission has held eleven two-day plenary sessions and innumerable committee meetings. The first stage of its work is now completed. The report for study by the three cooperating churches is bound in the back of this book.

During 1970 and 1971, the three Lutheran churches will be asked to consider the report, revised following the study program, at their national conventions. The recommendations, if adopted, will have a profound effect on the life of the church. Therefore, it was considered mandatory that everyone interested in the theology and practice of confirmation should study the report and its implications. The study program is planned for 1969 to equip convention delegates, congregational leaders, and pastors to deal effectively with the issues involved.

This study book is your personal guide to the report and the crucial areas of confirmation and first Communion. It is a tool designed to help you probe the significance of these experiences in the lives of adults, children, and youth.

We invite you to explore with us the important issues involved. May we encourage you to avoid coming to conclusions prematurely. Let the facts and the insights of the study stimulate your thinking. Then you can help us formulate the final report to the three churches by sharing your reactions to the commission's recommendations with us. What should the church do?

THE EDITORIAL COMMITTEE

C. Richard Evenson
W. Kent Gilbert
Arthur L. Miller

Table of Contents

A New Definition of Confirmation

Confirmation is
    a pastoral and educational ministry
    of the church
that is designed to help baptized children
    identify with the life and mission
    of the adult Christian community,
and that is celebrated in a public rite.

1

Spotlight on Confirmation

"Confirmation is a time when you take the vows of loyalty to Christ and his church that your parents took for you when you were baptized."

"I really became a Christian when I was confirmed. Publicly, I had to accept Jesus Christ as my personal Lord and Savior."

"You asked when I joined the church. Well, I was confirmed when I was about twelve years old."

"Sure I remember my confirmation. That was when I got my first pair of long pants and a real wrist watch and a Bible with my name stamped on the cover in gold. My grandparents had a big dinner in my honor; all my uncles and aunts came and brought me presents."

"I'd like to forget confirmation. The pastor made us all stand up in front of everyone at church and answer questions on the catechism. My mind went blank; I couldn't think of anything we studied. My father was so angry."

"Sure I knew I had to be confirmed if I wanted to take Holy Communion with all the grownups in our congregation."

"Confirmation was exciting. We all wore white robes. The girls carried corsages and the boys wore white roses pinned to their robes. Each of us recited a verse we intended to live by. It was just like graduation at school."

What Is Confirmation?

What exactly is confirmation? A poll-taker going door to door among Lutheran families is apt to come away with almost as many varied answers as the number of people he questions. This is rather odd when you realize that confirmation has been an integral part of Lutheran church life in North America as far back as anyone can remember. Surely, somewhere in the official documents of the churches there is a clear, concise explanation of what confirmation is all about. Yes? Try to find that simple statement somewhere.

Church constitutions have a way of speaking about "confirmed members" or even "confirmed members in good standing" without spelling out what these terms mean. Service books contain liturgical orders for confirmation but the rubrics neglect to explain the nature of confirmation. If you analyze carefully the parts of the confirmation services the churches have used, you are apt to come up with more questions than answers. Even theological texts that presumably have the last word on matters of doctrine and policy either bypass a direct study of confirmation or else word their comments in such ambiguous terms that you can drive a bulldozer through the loopholes. Trying to define confirmation without solid footing is frustrating.

Let's try an experiment. Shut your eyes and recall your own confirmation. Do you remember the day? What happened? What attitudes did you have. Were you scared? Thrilled? Bored? Relieved? Inspired? Be honest now! What did being confirmed mean in your development as a person or, to be more specific, as a Christian person? How did you react to your catechetical studies? What did you feel when you knelt at the altar for the first time to receive Holy Communion? Through the mists and fogs of memory, some things come through clearly, don't they? Perhaps your feelings and insights may not be what you think the church would like to hear. That's all right. We are not interested at this point in what the church wants us to say about confirmation and first Communion. We only want to know what these high-water marks in your growing years meant and continue to mean to you now that you are an adult.

Now, let's take a second step. Suppose you were in a position in the church to determine exactly what admission to the Lord's Supper and what confirmation should be in the lives of children and youth on their way to maturity. What would you decide? Don't get too academic in your way of thinking. Think in terms of your own children or grandchildren or young friends and relatives. Here they are parading across your inner vision, bubbling with vitality, full of joyful expectancy and potentiality, standing on tiptoe to catch a glimpse of the tomorrow toward which they are heading. What do you want for them? How can the church best groom them for significant participation in the life of the congregation? How does confirmation fit into the picture of the church's ministry to their needs? At what age do you think they are capable of understanding the reality of sin in their lives and their need for God's forgiveness? This question is particularly related to their participation in the Sacrament of the Altar.

Your recollections of your own experiences and your wishes for the well-being of the youth of your parish are vital factors in examining the theology and practices of confirmation. Now is the time to express convictions, to air lingering doubts, to ask probing questions. In short, now is the time to throw the spotlight on confirmation. In careful and critical study, we should explore its genuine usefulness to the ongoing life of the church. What it now *is* in current practice and what it *can be* are perhaps two different things. Let us see.

Taken for Granted

The most amazing fact about confirmation is that it is generally taken for granted in most congregations. In fact, those who from time to time question its validity or the effectiveness of some of its shaky practices (many of which have grown up around confirmation silently and slowly like moss covering a woodland boulder) are considered troublemakers. They are apt to be classified in the same category as those who challenge the sanctity of motherhood or who suggest mistreatment of the nation's flag.

Why do we get so upset when someone wants to update or improve confirmation. Well, for one thing confirmation has been, traditionally, a standard part of church life for a long time. Second, it has become a fairly effective way of processing children through a series of ecclesiastical puberty rites. Like an old, comfortable pair of shoes that may look worn out but feel pretty good at the end of a long day's work, confirmation is appealing. In the minds of some it may look antique in the twentieth century, but it has worked reasonably well in the past. Why shouldn't it work just as well now? Often parents are heard to say something like this: "I had to go through catechetical classes and confirmation to join the church. It didn't hurt me and it won't hurt my kids to do the same thing."

Conditioned

It may be that confirmation has been taken for granted so long in many Lutheran parishes, that people have been conditioned to react to it automatically.

Conditioning describes an interesting process that directs the formation of some of our behavior patterns. It simply means that we associate one thing with another in a more or less permanent bond and respond accordingly, often without thinking about it. For instance, we associate the ringing of the telephone with answering it. We may be on a stepladder painting; we may be taking a shower; we may be doing numerous things that make it inconvenient to stop for conversation; but when that phone rings we run to pick it up. Similarly, have you ever noticed how the sight of a police cruiser on a freeway suddenly causes drivers to slow down to the legal speed limits?

Say the word "confirmation" in many congregations and see what happens. Church councils make sure that catechetical classes are held in prime educational time in the parish calendar. Pastors are willing to make whatever adjustments in their schedules are necessary to reach the maximum number of pupils through these classes. Even parents who may have been lackadaisical about seeing that their youngsters participated regularly in the congregation's educational program make sure that they do not miss any of the required preconfirmation classes. Whatever else may be going on in Lutheran congregations, you can rest assured that in an overwhelming majority, pastors and people, are building programs around confirmation as one of the "givens" of parish life.

There is nothing wrong with having some of our behavior conditioned. It enables us to take care of a lot of routine tasks automatically. However, conditioning discourages thoughtful evaluation of what we are doing and why we are doing it. The problem word here is "automatically." It is healthy every so often to examine carefully some of our automatic procedures and assumptions. This we should do with even a time-honored, important rite of the church, such as confirmation.

Assumptions

Let's take a look at what we know about confirmation based on the assumptions people have about this particular rite of the church. The assumptions, of course, come from observation of present practices, which vary a great deal in many respects as you move about the Lutheran communities in North America.

Many of the variations are due to our European ancestry, the traditions fostered by Old World cultural customs. Often we tend to explain the nature of confirmation as would Norwegians or Swedes or Danes or one of the many different groups of Germans that immigrated to this continent. Yet, in the midst of this variety, there is some common core of assumptions that we can identify.

Prerequisite for Communion

First of all, most people assume that confirmation is basically a way of preparing youth to receive their first Communion. We want to assure ourselves, as custodians of one of the great liturgical mysteries of the forgiving presence of God in human lives, that our young people know exactly what is happening in the sacrament. Otherwise, they would not be able to receive the bread and the wine meaningfully to their own spiritual strengthening.

Generally, in The ALC and the LCA when pastors say to the confirmands that their confirmation now admits them to "the fellowship of the Lord's Table, and to participation in all the spiritual privileges of the Church" (*Service Book and Hymnal*, p. 246), the emphasis is on the first part of the statement. Actually what other "spiritual privileges" do these confirmands not now enjoy as baptized children of God? The rite of confirmation in The Lutheran Church—Missouri Synod is even more ambiguous: "[We] invite and welcome you, as a member of the Evangelical Lutheran Church and of this congregation to participate with us in all the rights and privileges of the Evangelical Lutheran Church" (*The Lutheran Agenda*, p. 26).

Climax of Study

The second assumption is that confirmation provides a fitting climax to an intensive period of study based on Luther's *Small Catechism*. The time involved may range from a six-month cram course in Christian doctrine to a three-year or more broad-based educational program that covers many elements of Christian faith and life. In a great many parishes the emphasis is on the content of the courses rather than on the developmental needs of youth. Insistence on memorization of Luther's brief explanations to the Ten Commandments, to the articles of the Apostles' Creed, to the petitions of the Lord's Prayer is revealing. This insistence suggests

11

that the young person's ability to repeat the "right" answers to theological questions without too many mistakes is equated with his readiness to be considered as an adult member of the congregation. The converse is usually also accepted: If you don't know the catechism, you are not ready.

How far churches should go in planning courses based on the catechism is a matter for debate, especially among those parents, church councilmen, and pastors who feel that catechetical "training" should be kept to the minimum. "Why make it so tough for young people to become Christians?" demanded one irate father when he heard that his son was expected to attend a catechetical class for several years. "It is easier," he went on, "for an East German to escape over the wall to the West than it is for our kids to get into church."

Compared to the old Berlin Wall with its dirty grey cinder blocks and barbed wire, the new wall now being built looks like a tourist attraction. Although the new wall is three- to six-feet higher and is neatly whitewashed, it actually hides a most diabolical, practically escape-proof obstacle course. There are alarm fences, trip wires to set off flares, hidden six-inch steel spikes, nine-foot anti-tank ditches. Some sections of the 300-foot approach to the wall are patrolled by German Shepherd dogs, other sections by armored cars. East German government officials are determined that no more of their countrymen will find freedom in the welcoming West.

It is interesting that recently when the three major Lutheran denominations in North America each developed an educationally sound three-year catechetical curriculum, many parents reacted as though a new Berlin Wall complete with obstacle course were being erected across the road to confirmation. Why, some asked, must you make the requirements for confirmation so difficult? Naturally, if you think of preconfirmation instruction in any form as a kind of "hair shirt" that a child must endure in order to achieve recognition of his spiritual maturity, any expansion of hours of study seems odious.

Actually, most of the complaints parents expressed to the three new catechetical curricula could be classified under two headings: "I never had to go through all that in order to be confirmed," and "My son's friend Jimmy who goes to the Presbyterian (read Methodist, Baptist, or whatever) church doesn't have to go through all that in order to join the church."

12

Full Membership

That brings us to the third assumption: confirmation is for all practical purposes a form of becoming a full member of the church. It marks the transition from childhood to adulthood. Regardless of how often we as Lutherans affirm that Baptism is the doorway into church fellowship, there persists among many an uneasy feeling that those who are baptized as children are really only Christians junior-grade. Something that is lacking must be supplied.

But what is lacking? Those who are baptized as adults take their own vows, accept Christ as their personal Lord, express their loyalty to his church. At Baptism, infants have their parents or sponsors answering in their stead. It is an easy step then to assume that the child must someday take those vows for himself before he can be regarded as a full member of the Christian community. Once he undergoes that experience, then it is another easy mental step to assume that he has graduated from spiritual childhood.

Small wonder why the dropout problem among our youth coincides very closely with the time of their confirmation. Up to this time, they felt concentrated parental and pastoral pressure to complete their catechetical studies, to be confirmed. Now the pressures are off. Many find themselves not much different from the way they were before, except now they have the freedom not to get involved in Sunday school, or for that matter, in any church activities that demand time and interest.

Underlying many of these assumptions is the unspoken confidence that the whole catechetical-confirmation complex punches out dedicated young church members bearing the portrait of Christ emblazoned on their hearts as effectively as the United States mint stamps out slugs of metal alloys into nickels with the bas-relief of Thomas Jefferson on their surfaces. Unfortunately, the process doesn't always work out that way.

One pastor was impressed with Edwin Abbey's painting of a medieval youth kneeling in a chapel for a night-long prayer vigil as preparation for the coming morning when he would be knighted. The pastor decided to add a similar vigil to his confirmation practices. He gathered his confirmands in the sanctuary on the Saturday evening before Pentecost and told them that they were to be "on silence." For the next four hours they were to meditate on what their commitment to Christ really meant to them, on the sacred vows they were about to take, on their life-

13

long loyalty to the church. They could use their Bibles or the service books as resources, but above all they were to engage in prayer and serious thought. At the end of that period the pastor spoke to each one, releasing him from his silence and asking, "What do you want most?" The first three answers he received were: "To go home and get some sleep," "I'm hungry," and "To get out of here."

Opinion Survey

As part of its examination of confirmation and first Communion, the Joint Commission on the Theology and Practice of Confirmation conducted a survey in the three Lutheran churches participating in the study. Those invited to participate were in three categories: pastors serving parishes, pastors in other church positions, and laymen. The purpose of the survey was to ascertain with some degree of reliability what Lutherans were thinking about these matters.

One question dealt with the role of the confirmand in the confirmation rite. Those who completed the survey were asked what roles they considered to be most important. Laymen from all three churches agreed closely that the confirmand's primary role was to "promise lifelong allegiance to Christ." Pastors, on the other hand, ranked "renewal of the baptismal covenant" first. This was particularly true of younger pastors. Older pastors tended to give more status to promising life-long allegiance than did their younger co-workers. It was interesting that the reverse differentiation was true among laymen; laymen under twenty saw the role of promising loyalty as essential more often than did laymen in older age groups.

Another question in the survey asked only the pastors what procedures in the Order for Confirmation they considered to be most important. This was a good question because it revealed much about the pastors' concepts of confirmation. Their three top choices in a list of possible procedures were: "confession of faith by class as a body," "confession of faith by each catechumen separately," and "private examination of the catechumens prior to the rite." It may be significant that the pastors did not consider such procedures as "authorization for catechumens to participate in the Lord's Supper" or "administration of the Lord's Supper" to be of primary importance. For most pastors involved in the survey, confirmation is evidently the time for renewing in public the baptismal covenant, for confessing faith, and for promising lifelong allegiance to Christ.

What Do You Think?

Are you confused? Has our spotlight on confirmation clouded the issues rather than clarified them? Perhaps you can understand why the joint commission stated that "confirmation is one place where the Lutheran Church is most vulnerable theologically," and that "a number of major revisions are necessary to meet present day needs."

Confirmation as it exists in present practice is a curious mixture of feelings, assumptions, hunches, and traditions liberally blended into both a process and a rite that is hard to explain. If confirmation is as important to the life of the growing child as we Lutherans claim it is, then we ought to know exactly what we are talking about. This is the time to ask why and how and what and when—and to insist on useful answers.

What you think is important. You can help the commission prepare its final report to the churches. In your congregational study program on confirmation you will have an opportunity to react to the commission's proposals and to share your opinions with them. Are you willing to keep an open mind as you work through the study? You will be generally following the investigative trail followed by the members of the commission. They were determined to gather all the facts, analyze all the pertinent factors, and test all proposed theories in the light of biblical witness and theological convictions before submitting a series of recommendations. Let's take the same path; then we will be in a position to evaluate their recommendations on the same solid foundations on which they were formulated.

2

Climate for Change

In a small rough-stone chapel nestled cozily in an Austrian valley, worshipers paused before a blank grey-painted wall as they entered and bowed solemnly. Visitors to the chapel were puzzled by this act of reverence; the wall was perfectly bare and, with its peeling paint, far from attractive. No one in the chapel knew why the people bowed their heads toward the wall except that their parents and grandparents had always done so. The mystery was finally solved when the villagers decided to renovate their beloved chapel. Underneath alternate layers of paint and dirt dating from as far back as the sixteenth century, there was on the wall a fresco of the Virgin Mary holding the Christ child in her arms. The custom of reverence, begun with intelligent motivation, continued on through the years by the sheer momentum of habit.

Sometimes confirmation practices carried on diligently from generation to generation are equally obscure. There may have been a good reason at one time for the introduction of certain standards. Take the matter of age of confirmation. In one parish in the South, children are confirmed at the age of twelve. A search of the church records indicated that this had been the customary procedure for almost seventy years, although nowhere was there discovered any rationale for its being followed. Finally, during an anniversary celebration in the parish, a sermon by one of the earliest pastors in the congregation was discovered in a pile of old books. The pastor had encouraged the establishment of the age of twelve because as he put it, "Our Lord went to the

Temple when he was twelve years old and answered questions. Our children should follow Jesus' example."

A man who grew up in a midwestern parish recalled that his grandfather had told him that there were good sociological reasons for being confirmed at twelve. When the grandfather was confirmed, the local community recognized him as a potential apprentice. He was free to leave school and learn a trade. He was now considered part of the productive side of society. Since he would be earning his own money, he would also be taxed just like any adult in the community. "And what is more," added the grandfather, "I now had the privilege of smoking and swearing."

Where Are Congregations Now?

Before we proceed any farther, it might be helpful to take a long look at where congregations are in their present practice of confirmation. In the recent survey pastors were asked at what grade level youth were confirmed in their congregations. The average grade reported by three groups of pastors participating in the survey was 8.4. At the present time, the study showed that American Lutheran congregations have the highest average confirmation grade (8.65) with Lutheran Church in America congregations only slightly lower (8.55). The Lutheran Church—Missouri Synod averages about one-half grade less (8.05).

There are some interesting variations in the survey that are worth noting. The number of years a pastor has been in the ministry is a factor. Older pastors tend to favor earlier confirmation than do younger pastors. Larger congregations have a slightly higher grade for confirmation than do smaller congregations. Then there is definitely a regional influence. Congregations in Canada have the highest grade for confirmations with congregations in the West North Central region not far behind. These are closely followed by congregations in New England and in the Mid-Atlantic regions. The lowest grade for confirmation is in the South Atlantic, East, West and South Central regions.

Let's make one point clear: Finding out the average grade level for confirmation in our churches really doesn't tell us much unless we go on to ask why. Why was this particular grade level selected? What were the reasons for choosing it above other grades? In some areas of the church, for instance, the critical factor is the local school system. Communities with four-year high schools are more apt to encourage congregations to confirm in the eighth grade than are communities which offer separate junior high schools for grades seven to nine.

What about your congregation? What factors could you identify as the most influential in establishing the grade level at which the youth of your parish are confirmed? Local customs, parental preference, constitutional edict, pastoral choice, economics?

Consider what your congregation seems to regard as the purpose of confirmation. This, in effect, becomes the operating definition of confirmation in your parish.

Here is a good experiment: Write down on these lines or on a separate piece of paper all the factors you think are important in establishing the grade level of confirmation in your situation.

FACTORS   INSIGHTS

_____   _____

_____   _____

_____   _____

_____   _____

_____   _____

When you have the list completed, read over each item and beside it jot down what biblical or theological insights make that factor crucial. Chances are you will soon discover that some practices are the results of parish concerns having little to do with biblical and theological reasoning. The factors involved in selecting a certain grade level are more often based on sociological conditions, the psychological needs of youth themselves, and the educational philosophy of the congregation.

A Time for Experimentation

Partly because many people feel that present confirmation practices are inadequate to meet the needs of today's youth, a ground swell of experimentation has been moving through the churches. This is true in Europe and in some of the newly developing nations as well as in Canada and in the United States. One form of this experimentation has moved in the direction of separating admission to first Communion from confirmation. Where this is done, children are generally admitted to the Sacrament of the Altar following some specialized instruction around the time they are ten to twelve years old. They are confirmed later when they are in the fourteen- to sixteen-year age bracket and are more capable of identifying with the adult Christian community.

Some Latvian congregations have moved the confirmation age as high as seventeen and eighteen.

Another form of experimentation has been conducted on a far wider scale. The three major Lutheran churches in North America with their broadened and intensified three-year catechetical programs have converged on the developing needs of growing children, seeking to guide them more adequately in their spiritual growth. The educational emphasis focuses on youth where they collide with their environments. There is no attempt to make adult Christians out of them, using textbooks like some gigantic cookie-cutters to turn them all out looking alike. Instead, modern education is much more concerned with helping seventh- eighth- and ninth-graders cope as Christians with their involvements in their shifting, changing world. The distinction may seem subtle but it profoundly separates the new catechetical materials from the old.

Incidentally, these three-year programs have had an effect upon both the grade for confirmation and the day of confirmation. If you would look over congregational statistical reports from the past twenty years for all three churches, you would discover that the age for confirmation has been slowly climbing. There has also been a gradual shift from Palm Sunday to Pente- ✗ cost as the time for confirmation. The latter change is coming about for several reasons. Among them, a growing number of pastors feel that the church's birthday celebration on Pentecost is a far more meaningful occasion for confirmation than Palm Sunday. The day of palms echoes the jubilant cries of those who welcomed Christ to Jerusalem with "Hosannas" only to turn against him with vicious cries of "Crucify Him" five days later. Then, too, Pentecost coincides more closely with the end of the public schools' academic year in the spring.

Looking Ahead

Let's go back to the survey again. There are some other significant questions that merit our attention. For instance, pastors were not only asked about current confirmation practices, they were invited to suggest at what grade the church *should* confirm. Almost without exception every group of pastors suggested a higher grade for confirmation than they now have. However, it should be pointed out that urban pastors tended toward a slightly lower grade than did those in small towns, suburban, and rural areas. Laymen were also asked this question. Their preferences were not quite as high as the pastors, but both groups markedly thought of higher grade levels than present practices observe.

What about a uniform age for confirmation? About 70 percent of the laymen and over 60 percent of the pastors surveyed favored a uniform age. There was little variation among the respondents from the three churches. Nonparish pastors were somewhat less favorable than parish pastors. This was an exception for the group which throughout the survey generally supported the most fundamental changes.

A related question asked respondents to suggest a uniform age if one were to be established. The average age that pastors chose was 14.87 or translated into grade level: 8.87. Laymen were only slightly behind. Their choice of average age was 14.50 with 8.50 as the corresponding grade level.

It becomes increasingly obvious that generally most pastors and lay leaders are looking forward to a unified confirmation age among all Lutheran churches. And for the most part they are setting their sights higher than ever before. This raises questions concerning the reasons behind a growing desire for uniformity of confirmation practices in the three churches, for experimenting with change, for seeking more effective catechetical-confirmation experiences for children and youth.

Growing Together

One obvious reason for changing ideas about confirmation is that Lutherans in North America are gradually growing closer in their working relationships. A decade ago, eight Lutheran churches jointly produced the *Service Book and Hymnal;* today as a result of mergers, those eight churches are now two. The newly founded Lutheran Council in the United States of America provided a common venture for the vast majority of Lutherans in a variety of activities, from providing a ministry for servicemen to producing motion pictures.

It's a funny thing about Lutherans; we tend to reflect our nationalistic origins. Actually, we have been divided more on the basis of Old World traditions than on theology. The period of immigration explains a lot about the reasons for this situation. Lutherans came to the New World from Norway, Sweden, Denmark, Latvia, Iceland, Finland, Estonia, Slovakia, Hungary, and from many differing sections of Germany. They came at different times and therefore reflected changing customs. It was only natural that, in the areas where they settled in Canada and the United States, they should try to preserve the customs and traditions of their homelands as they remembered them.

It has taken a long, slow process of acculturation (Canadianization or Americanization) until these Lutheran immigrants could feel secure in their new homes. "At-homeness" gave them the courage to branch out and become immersed with other citizens in building a pluralistic society to serve the best interests of all. Frequently it has meant sacrifice and also holding a clear vision. In the early days of Pennsylvania, a German Lutheran legislator from Philadelphia made a valuable contribution to the commonwealth. He got up out of his sick bed and rode on horseback to the state capitol at Harrisburg to cast a deciding vote on a delicate issue. The ¡uestion was: Shall the official language of Pennsylvania be German or English? Because of one man's determination and vision, Pennsylvanians now speak English (officially) with the rest of their countrymen.

Time also has dimmed the differences in European backgrounds. Cooperative efforts among the Lutherans in many areas, from establishing a common English translation of Luther's *Small Catechism* to planning a joint celebration of the 450th Anniversary of the Reformation, have broken down a number of existing barriers. Some of the shaky reasons for separation in the light of the fierce challenges to Christianity in the modern world seem to be dissipating. Lutherans are now emphasizing their common gospel, their common faith in Jesus Christ as the Lord of all life. This suggests that they build on this foundation by establishing a common theology of confirmation and a common series of confirmation practices. ˣ

A Mobile Population

Throughout North America, people are on the move. Many families are uprooted every two or three years. Business firms transfer their employees about their sprawling enterprises to learn all the phases of the operations. Government offices, military services, and research foundations send their personnel from one assignment to another. Add to this the temper of the times, a general feeling that a better job awaits in another city or another section of the country, and you can understand why about a fourth of our population is looking for new homes annually. Even

21

within a city and its suburbs, the population shifts about. Apartment-dwellers find that newer buildings may offer more attractive quarters than the ones they occupy. Rising young executives feel compelled to move with each promotion to an address more commensurate with their station. Many are forced to move as big sections of the metropolitan areas are gobbled up in the insatiable hunger of freeway construction and urban renewal.

The church has a vital concern for people and the problems they face as they move about. It is not only a question of making sure that they transfer from one congregation to another but also a matter of helping them keep their interest stimulated in the mission of the church. A person who knows that his family will be in this particular locality for only two years may be reluctant to build any strong friendships or to sink any roots. The future upheaval will be painful enough. Then there are those who feel that if their own denomination is not represented in the new locality, they are free from any obligation to seek out a new church home. How can the church minister to people who are on the move?

This is a point where, cooperatively, Lutheran churches regardless of their background can turn more attention to the needs of people and put less emphasis upon exclusive concerns for denominational systems. For instance, it would be fine if a child who had two years of catechetical instruction before moving to a new community could move right into his third-year class without any serious difficulties. Every attempt should be made to help him feel at home in his new congregation. Currently, in many instances, a child-on-the-move feels out of place in his new surroundings. In some cases he may find that while he has been confirmed, his new agemates may have one or two more years of catechetical classes to attend. In other cases the reverse may be true. Neither situation encourages the newcomer to assume that the church knows what it is doing; he is more apt to chalk up this phenomenon as one more example of congregational idiosyncrasy. Far too often children grow into youths with the notion that their congregations are involved in gameplaying with themselves as pawns. The system seems to be more important than they are. If you doubt these rather harsh comments, have a serious chat with the teen-age dropouts in your parish. The big question is: How can we help our youth identify with the adult Christian community meaningfully so that they feel they are important to its life. The answers we give will have to stand the test of the individual's moving.

The Walt Disney glamorized small-town America, where people were born, went to school, got a job, married, raised their families, and died in the same community, exists today only on the wide screen of your local drive-in. The familiar village church no longer can count on a stable population nor on a stable pastorate. Pastors are moving about almost as rapidly from one parish to another as the people to whom they minister. It is seldom possible for a pastor to baptize children and eventually grandchildren in the same family. As a matter of fact, the average pastor today doesn't often confirm those children he has baptized as infants. In some high mobility areas, such as communities near research centers, military bases, and managerial training schools, you frequently have strangers ministering to strangers.

If the church is to offer some sense of stability in a mobile age, this stability will have to come from its sense of mission, from its carefully planned and usable programs. A common gospel, a common catechism, a common liturgy point the direction. (Lutherans in North America are now at work in the critical area of developing a new common worship book of services and hymns.)

Megalopolis

If the small town is fast disappearing, megalopolis is rapidly appearing. Population experts predict that within the near future there will be continuous cities from Boston to Richmond, from Chicago to Milwaukee, from Dallas to Fort Worth, from Los Angeles to San Diego. As the freeways extend into virginal farming country, new housing developments along its sides spring up like steel filings attracted to a magnet. Scientific advances in agriculture coupled with mechanization of farm equipment make it possible to feed a burgeoning population with less land devoted to farming and with fewer farm workers needed to make it productive.

The sprawling metropolitan areas and their equally sprawling main-route links with the hinterlands make it possible for many to commute to industrial or business jobs within the city complex. Many cities find that inadvertently they have grown in a series of concentric rings. The center commercial and artistic hub is surrounded by the poverty ghettos, the racial enclaves, the once prominent neighborhoods of gentility now turned into stopping places for transients. Each additional ring that moves out from the center represents a higher level of affluence. Some recent developments, however, have complicated the picture as builders leapfrog the neat divisions and erect high-rise apartment houses in the center city areas where people with more than adequate incomes can live protected lives only a stone's throw away from rat-infested tenements. Similarly, middle-class apartments and housing units may be built up around each station along the right-of-way of commuter rail lines.

One problem that faces a congregation anywhere within the amorphous urban sprawl is defining the community it serves. Parishes may overlap like shingles covering a roof. Parishioners may work in one area, live in another, and go to the church of their choice in still a third. It is not unusual for any given urban-oriented congregation to have its children and youth spread out among a variety of different schools in different parts of the city and in some instances among several different school districts. The onus of developing a rich, meaningful program that will attract people and inspire their loyal participation is squarely on each congregation.

The church is no longer the community social center with dictatorial privileges over community mores and customs. Ease of transportation and a plethora of other places where people can spend their time (fill in your preferences) and which shape their behavior accordingly offer stiff competition. The church's fervent aspiration to be the central influence in the lives of its constituency needs solid support in a genuine sense of ministering to people. It may well be that we will have to revise radically our concept of the institutional church if we are to make it effective in our swiftly changing society. A strong emphasis on its basic pastoral and educational ministry (of which confirmation is a vital part) can turn the church into a fellowship of the concerned, a magnet for the wanderers. Perhaps the cutting edge of this ministry has to be where people are—and they are everywhere.

Another serious problem in urbanization is reaching people who desire anonymity. It is easy to get lost deliberately (or accidentally) in the city's crowds. Getting past the doorman in an exclusive apartment-house complex is only one of an urban pastor's difficulties. How does he know or make contact with the hundreds of persons living jammed into blocks of substandard housing? How does he reach the children of indifferent parents or minister to the lonely, the frightened, the desperate who live behind the invisible shields of noninvolvement?

This might be a good time to pause and think about your congregation. How do you fit into the picture we have sketched of our mobile, urban-oriented country? What do you think your community will look like ten years from now, twenty years from now? What kind of relationship with the church do you want for your children or grandchildren, your young relatives and friends who will by then be the leaders of both the community and the church? Isn't this all related to what we can do for them during their catechetical-confirmation years? The sense of mission and ministry we foster right now in our congregational life will determine how well we plan ahead.

Leisure

Add to your picture of the future the increasing leisure time that most people have. There is no need here to go into the changes in work schedules from the days of our fathers and our grandfathers. There may be a time coming to some of our science fiction writers when technological advances will dictate that governments will pay people not to work at all. Don't laugh! Right now, farmers are paid not to plant corn in the south forty or not to grow potatoes in the patch behind the barn.

Added hours of free time have generally pushed many people into a more frantic search for pleasure. Longer weekends are an invitation to get away from the workaday world to the mountains, the seashore, the recreation areas. A check of consumer statistics reveals that the sales of boats, camping equipment, and "second houses" is at an all time high. Admittedly, part of the drive that lies behind these purchases is generated by the desire to get out of the "rat race" for a brief while. Another part, though, may be linked with the curious Puritan heritage that has so shaped men that they feel guilty unless they are doing something at all times.

Planning a congregation's program realistically to make it flexible enough to fit into the parishioners' widely disparate schedules is far from an easy task. You know all this. But how do we go about dealing with the complications? Perhaps, on one hand, we do need the special services held at the ski slopes and the shore resorts, in the national and state parks. Perhaps, we also

25

need confirmation programs that are solid and yet flexible enough to include a family camping program, that will equip our increasingly vacation-minded populace to enjoy their leisure and at the same time to take their sense of Christian community with them wherever they go.

Pressures on Youth

One element in the leisure picture deserves special mention. While adults are experiencing a shorter workweek, their children are moving in the opposite direction. With the heavy emphasis on cramming more information in the pupil's head in these days of the knowledge explosion, public schools are demanding more and more educational time. Some sections of the country are experimenting with eleven-month school years. In addition, numerous and varied extra-curricular activities absorb a fantastic number of hours in the student's week. He is pressured: by his school to make good grades so he will be accepted by a college; by his parents to be a success in everything he does from sports to dramatics to studies; by his friends to be "where the action is"; by himself to be popular, well-liked, and proficient in his chosen skills.

You can readily understand why young people today often see the church's educational and liturgical opportunities as just another series of demanding pressures competing for his limited time. Somehow the church must convince them that it is primarily on their side and interested in their welfare, that its programs and rites are designed to help them be themselves as efficiently as possible. This suggests that the church had better examine the validity of its time-honored insistence on meeting requirements. New ways must be found to implement its genuine concern for helping children and youth utilize their dynamic relationship with God as well as their own capacities to meet the challenges they must face.

The Changing Family

Probably no single sociological unit comes in for as much brow-beating today as does the family. Of course, older family patterns are changing. Where once the father of the house was truly its head whose word was law, modern families have become more democratic. Where fathers are away from home a lot, mothers find themselves forced to make decisions and to act as disciplinarians. The growing number of working mothers has caused many adjustments in family living.

Much of modern advertising tends to play down the family in order to focus on the teen-age market "where the money is." Community patterns often siphon off family members into their little subgroups, discouraging family togetherness. If there is an exclusive teen-age culture today that refuses to "trust anyone over thirty," it is because adults have willingly created this Frankenstein monster by shutting teen-agers out of their adult world. Instead of seeing the adolescent as an apprentice adult, the temptation is to see him as an overgrown child not yet ready for adult experiences. Consequently, when he has the opportunity he often takes those experiences gluttonously and on his own terms instead of gradually, according to the guidance of elders.

Unfortunately some of the current family crisis is fostered by congregations. This seems a terrible accusation. But what about the congregation that provides little if any opportunities for family participation in the life and mission of the church? Some congregations, for example, insist that children have no place in the public worship. As one man put it quite succinctly at a council meeting, "Keep the children in the children's church where they belong. I don't want to go to services and be disturbed by noisy children." (By the way, aren't adults ever noisy?) Shades of the disciples rebuking the parents who brought their children to Christ for his blessing! Perhaps, we need to hear against from Jesus that children are model candidates for the kingdom of God. Another congregation may feel it encourages its youthful members best by treating them as a generation of envelope-stuffers and bulletin-folders without giving them any real sense of participation in the vital work of the parish. Youth power could be harnessed more effectively on the parish social ministry committee or in community outreach programs.

Strengthen the Family

Martin Luther considered catechetical instruction to be a basic part of the family's responsibility. He presented his *Small Catechism,* for instance, "in the form in which it is to be taught by the head of the family." He saw the congregation as a collection of families coming together for additional worship, education, and service. By strengthening and promoting family life, he was convinced that he was similarly building up the church of Jesus

Christ. If he could speak today, what he would say about the present practices of continually splitting up the family in church activities is best left untranslated. He could use some mighty salty invectives when he grew angry.

We know from both biological and psychological sciences that human life is a continuum, a process in a social context. Is it possible that the church can begin to see that confirmation recognizes the process of youth's moving gradually into adulthood in relation to his human family ties as well as his church family associations? If it does, some radical changes might be made in our present practices. We need to strengthen the family for its all important share in the church's ministry.

Educators, basing their insights on research data, tell us that attitudes are more often caught than taught. Psychiatrists point out the overwhelming influences on the individual of his early home experiences. This is where he gets his basic identification with the adult world. Here he forms images of the kind of adult he wants to become. Here he shapes his impressions of community groups outside the family, such as the church, that seem to be significant to his parents. Whether parents accept the fact or not, they are always teaching in the family circle. And it is true that what they do often speaks so loudly that what they say cannot be heard.

From every side you get supporting evidence to highlight the importance of the family and its interrelationships to the growing life of each person. "What a father says to his children is not heard by the world," wrote Jean Paul Richter, "but it will be heard by posterity."

Amalgamation

Another important sociological factor to take into account as we talk about changing patterns of confirmation is directly related to the people who make up our congregations. There was a time not too long ago when the typical Lutheran surname was Peterson or Schmidt or Holmquist or Zimmerman. Now you meet Lutherans named O'Leary and Martinez and Wichinski and Bernini. This welcoming of others than those who came from Northern European Lutheran stock has been healthy for the church.

A church executive commented once that he didn't think that the melting-pot idea was an adequate description of the United States. He said, "It's more like fruit cake where each fruit is bound with the next but each retains its identity." Then he added wryly, "And there's always room for a few nuts." He could say this equally well about Lutheran churches today.

Mid-twentieth century realities make us realize that people of all nationalities and backgrounds are living in the vicinity of our church buildings and needing the power of the gospel. Does it matter how much money they have in the bank or what color skin they have? More and more congregations are destroying the man-built barriers that keep them safe in a nice, quiet, private-club-like atmosphere. They are willing to open up their hearts as well as their facilities in the true New Testament sense of evangelism to all who would come to Christ.

There was a serious conflict in Jerusalem in the early days of the fledgling Christian church. Peter felt that all converts to Christianity must first become Jews, with all males being circumcized, with both males and females undergoing the traditional ritualistic purification rites. Paul objected strenuously. In his opinion, every person came to his faith in Christ directly and therefore became a member of Christ's church by Baptism without any intervening steps. Ultimately, the council presided over by James, the brother of Jesus, reached a decision. While the council's final position was more of a compromise than a clear-cut decision, it did approve Paul's point of view. You can read this council's proceedings in Acts 15.

If we as Lutherans are to take this decision seriously, then we are forced to reevaluate some of the prerequisites for church membership that have developed with our confirmation customs, particularly those that stem from our German or Norwegian or Swedish ancestry. There is nothing wrong with traditional customs that are voluntary; it is when customs become mandatory that we distort their importance. Again, whatever procedures, rites, practices the church adopts should have pertinent meaning and application for all.

Concern

In this sketchy treatment of our changing society in which the Lutheran churches seek to carry out their mission, there are many other identifiable factors that impinge on the role of confirmation in our church life. The ones we have discussed seem critical and should form the backdrop before we investigate possibilities of reshaping both the rite and the practices of confirmation.

29

Let it be said outright: No responsible group within the church promotes change for the sake of change. There is little to be gained by modernistic expediencies as some suggest, such as simply switching all those "thous" in the rite to "yous." However, there is much to be accomplished by seriously studying the basic purposes of confirmation in the lives of children and youth. What ought it to be?

A lot of people are wondering just what confirmation means. Church leaders and parents alike have experienced frustration and even despair as they observe the numbers of confirmed youth who no longer participate in church life. Confirmation should mean a lot more to the confirmand than it generally does. There are many confirmands who slide through the academic work just to satisfy the requirements. Should they be confirmed? Shall we establish some bare minimum of indoctrination and settle for that? As one pastor commented after a discussion of what are the irreducible elements of Christianity, "How many parts of a sheep can you eliminate and still have a sheep?" That's a vital question.

Actually, confirmation has been changing all the time from the very early centuries in the history of the Christian church when it was separated from Baptism. So what we need to do before we tackle any of the questions that we have raised is to explore the history of confirmation. History enables us to climb a tower and look back over the way we have come. A sense of historical development of the church's sacramental system will also give us a balancing pole to help us cross the tightrope of decision.

3

A Checkered History

"History is bunk!" was Henry Ford's opinion. Perhaps it was for a man pioneering the development of a brand new technical gadget like the motor car. But even mechanical accomplishments pass into history and become part of the living heritage. Ford might be surprised to discover how many antique automobile museums have sprung up around the country, how many ancient-auto buffs care for their prized vehicles with fanatic zeal.

The present is always largely a product of the past. Wisdom distilled, customs encapsulated, traditions honed through countless generations—all shape us whether we realize it or not. We shake hands with one another in friendship, scarcely remembering that this brief encounter continues the practice of medieval knights who clasped each other's arms to prove that they were unarmed and trustworthy.

Often uncritically, we accept the practices that surround our festivals, sometimes even assuming that they have been part of the original celebrations from the beginning. Germans who settled in Pennsylvania brought with them a number of holiday customs that caught the fancies of all nationalities: Santa Claus and the Christmas tree at Christmas, Easter Bunny and the colored eggs at Easter. Each of us consciously and many times subconsciously reflect the inbred traditions of our own family history; this is how it is. A little girl who asks, "Grandma, why do you tie chicken's legs together like that when you roast it?" is apt to get the reply, "Goodness, child, I don't know. My grandmother always did it this way."

31

Most of us are smart enough to accept the fact that a lot of religious practices date back to the dim shades of yesteryear, but how and why they have come down to us we cannot explain. It is a healthy habit then, when responsible decisions are to be made, to examine history, probing meanings and importance. How did confirmation get started as a liturgical part of the church's ministry to its people? How did it change and develop through the centuries? As the commission's report bound in the back of this volume makes clear:

> *If the Lutheran church is seriously concerned with a reconstruction of confirmation, it must study its history in order to understand the rationale behind present day practices and be prepared to examine them in the light of its theology and current needs.*

There are a number of significant points that we should look at closely.

The New Testament Church

Let's start off with a categorical statement: The New Testament nowhere speaks of confirmation. There are no scriptural mandates for its inclusion in the rites of the church either from Jesus himself or from any of the leaders of the apostolic community. Yet the story of confirmation begins in the New Testament with the use of Baptism as the doorway into church fellowship.

As you read Luke's magnificent story of the primitive Christian church from the days of its beginnings, you will notice two important aspects about Baptism. First of all, it is the only way that persons outside the church are admitted to the inner core of the faithful. After Peter's stirring sermon at Pentecost, many who were moved by his impassioned words wanted to know what to do. Peter answered emphatically, "Repent, and be baptized every one of you in the name of Jesus Christ for the forgiveness of your sins; . . ." There it is: Baptism using water symbolizes the cleaning power of God in a person's life, an appropriate way to enter into the company of those who accept Jesus Christ as their Lord. But Peter went on ". . . and you shall receive the gift of the Holy Spirit" (Acts 2:38). This is the second predominant aspect of Baptism that runs like a thread through the New Testament and on into the decades to follow.

32

Keep these two aspects in mind, for here lie some of the difficulties Christians have had ever since those early days. Is Peter speaking of two acts in Baptism, one involving water, the "washing of regeneration," and the other bringing the power and strength of God the Holy Spirit into the newly forgiven person's life? In other words, is each act only half a sacrament? Or are these two spiritual phenomena simply two phases of the same baptismal act as essential as two sides of a coin?

On that particular day, Peter, like the other disciples, had come directly from a highly personal encounter with God. From an intense spiritual experience in that Jerusalem Upper Room, he went outside to address the gathered crowds. The twelve (Matthias having been elected by lot to take Judas Iscariot's place) had just experienced the coming of God the Holy Spirit into their midst like a rushing wind, like tongues of fire. Therefore, Peter was convinced that the sharing of the Spirit was the strengthening power people needed to link themselves with the newly formed fellowship of the faithful. He and the other disciples likewise believed that Baptism was the demonstrable, visible event that made this clear. According to Matthew, Jesus had instructed his closest followers to practice it:

> *All authority in heaven and on earth has been given to me. Go therefore and make disciples of all nations, baptizing them in the name of the Father and of the Son and of the Holy Spirit, teaching them to observe all that I have commanded you; and lo, I am with you always, to the close of the age.* (Matthew 28:18-20)

Whether this quotation is genuinely a part of Matthew's Gospel or whether, as some biblical scholars claim, it was added later is really immaterial. Because the disciples did baptize—and from the very beginning of the organized church. The Book of Acts presents scene after scene of the church's growth through this means. Here is Philip baptizing an Ethiopian official at a wasteland brook; here is Peter baptizing a Roman military officer in his own home; here is Paul baptizing the jailer at his cell in Philippi. Baptism was standard practice. However, the way Baptism was conducted was not so standard.

Many of the baptismal practices reported in Acts appear to be somewhat accidental. You really search in vain for consistency.

This is not so strange when you realize that the fledgling church was in the process of finding its dimensions. It had no book of committee-agreed-on rites, no listing of standard operating procedures. For instance, Luke described Philip's missionary trip to Samaria and how he baptized both men and women who believed the good news that he had preached about Jesus Christ. Shortly thereafter, Peter and John going through the same territory met these baptized Christians and laid their hands on them praying that they might receive the Holy Spirit. "For it had not yet fallen on any of them," Luke comments, "but they had only been baptized in the name of the Lord Jesus" (Acts 8:16). In another instance, the procedure was reversed. Peter felt that the Holy Spirit had really come into the midst of the Roman centurion, Cornelius, and his friends. The big fisherman rejoiced, "Can any one forbid water for baptizing these people who have received the Holy Spirit just as we have?" (Acts 10:47). The Baptism of this group of obvious Gentiles took place immediately. You can easily see that arguing which should come first, the water of Baptism or the presence of the Spirit, can degenerate into a kind of circular chicken-egg discussion.

From the scanty evidence we have of the New Testament church which corresponds roughly with the first century of the Christian era, the act of Baptism was one act implying a severance of the past, a virtual new birth. The church believed Jesus' pointed remark to the Pharisee Nicodemus: "Unless one is born of water and the Spirit, he cannot enter the kingdom of God" (John 3:5). Make no mistake about it: Baptism was a serious step for the converts to Christianity. They were no cardboard, bathrobe-wearing actors in some Hollywood extravaganza; they were flesh-and-blood people involved in the critical choices of everyday living. Their choice of Christianity made them pagan-world dropouts. They refused to worship the emperor of Rome as some kind of deity; there was only one God whom they could worship. They were the society-upsetters, preaching love in place of war, forgiveness in place of retribution, faith in place of doubt and insecurity. A heterogeneous mixture of farmers and city-dwellers, soldiers and merchants, poverty-stricken beggars and wealthy businessmen, the Christian communities beginning to sprout in the fertile soil around the Mediterranean world were conscious that their voluntary separation from the pagan climate in which they lived could mean trouble.

And trouble came; persecution and martyrdom became a hideous reality. Yet, as one of the early church leaders commented, "The blood of the martyrs is the seed of the church." For every Christian killed in the arena by wild animals or burned alive at the stake, it seemed that there were several other questing persons eager to fill his vacant place. By Baptism they were added to the congregations and by frequent observance of the Lord's Supper they were both forgiven for their sins and strengthened for day-to-day Christian living. They were a people set apart by God to be the salt and the light and the leaven of the world. They knew this and acted accordingly as the consciences of their society. They held to the promise of eternal life with Christ that Baptism offered and Holy Communion underscored, recklessly determined to live by the Lord's "law of love" under the ominous shadow of a threatening sword's edge.

Spreading Faith

In the second and third centuries, Christianity moved out from its humble beginnings to become eventually the official religion of the Roman Empire under Constantine. A lot of things happened to the church during that time. Not only did the Christians have to endure punitive acts of frequently hostile governments, but they were constantly tempted to water down their faith by fusing their convictions with popular fads of other religions of their day. Eastern religions offered exotic festivals and sexual binges to promote fertility of man and land. Grecian philosophy suggested categorizing mysteries of faith into logical, systematic terms that man's mind could grasp. Each new area into which the church moved, to Gaul (today's France), to North Africa, throughout Asia Minor, brought new challenges to the purity of the faith.

This is the period of creed-builders, those who tried to summarize the church's teachings in a form easily remembered. This is the time of forming what would be called the New Testament as church leaders weighed each bit of Christian literature on the scales of the core of Christian beliefs. The twenty-seven selections eventually chosen represented in the church's best judgment what people ought to know about Jesus Christ and his legacy to the faithful. In a sense, you could say that both creeds and the New Testament Scriptures were thought of as teaching tools guiding Christians to a clear-cut understanding of their unique relationship with God through Christ. A number of

35

prominent Christian leaders, in addition, were continuing to write to church members defending Christianity against intellectual attacks or dealing with ethical issues or describing suggested ways of celebrating rites.

Baptism in this period was becoming more and more complicated. It was now performed "In the name of the Father and of the Son and of the Holy Spirit" reflecting the ending of Matthew's Gospel (Matthew 28:19) instead of simply "in the name of Jesus." Adults being baptized were asked to affirm their faith with more lengthy creeds than the concise "Jesus is Lord" of biblical days. The rite itself now involved the use of oil as well as water. We do not know when the practice of anointing began.

Anointing

Oil was used in Old Testament days to anoint prophets, priests, and kings to set them apart symbolically for specific tasks in the family of God's people. For instance, the prophet Samuel poured oil over the head of Saul chosen to be the first king of the Israelites (1 Samuel 10:1). Isaiah, a later prophet, spoke more mystically, describing how the Spirit of the Lord had come upon him, "because the Lord has anointed me to bring good tidings to the afflicted;" (Isaiah 61:1). A similar sort of mysticism shows up in the writings of John in the New Testament. To the recipients of his letter encouraging their loving faithfulness, he says, "But you have been anointed by the Holy One and you all know" (1 John 2:20).

Somehow in the first couple of Christian centuries, there was a seven-league stride from figures of speech, such as John used, to the practice of pouring oil on the newly baptized to symbolize the entry of God the Holy Spirit into their lives. In some instances, the anointing took place before the actual Baptism with the bishop laying his hand on the head of the person, saying "Receive the Holy Spirit." This was true in the earliest Syrian rites, where those to be baptized were anointed on the forehead, the breast, and then on the body prior to their being led to the water for Baptism. Then they were dressed in white robes and admitted to Holy Communion. In other instances, the use of the so-called holy oil followed Baptism itself.

Around the end of the second century in Carthage in North Africa, a converted lawyer named Tertullian became quite influential in the Western church. Impassioned, witty, a prodigious

36

writer, Tertullian wrote stimulating tracts alternately defending and explaining aspects of his adopted Christianity. He, incidentally, coined the word "Trinity" to refer to the three ways that we know God and contributed many theological insights that helped shape the formulation of Christian doctrines. In his tract *On the Resurrection of the Body,* Tertullian explains the significance of each part of the then current Christian initiation ceremony.

> *The flesh is washed that the soul may be made stainless. The flesh is anointed that the soul may be consecrated. The flesh is sealed* [referring to the sign of the cross on the forehead] *that the soul may be fortified The flesh is overshadowed by the imposition of hands that the soul may be illuminated by the Spirit. The soul is fed by the Body and Blood of Christ that the soul may be fattened by God.*

Notice Tertullian's order: baptizing, anointing, sealing, the laying on of hands, admission to the Lord's Supper. Also notice that this is really one long ceremony with each event flowing into the next. Tertullian has nothing to say about any separation of these events by more than a few hours. The two great sacraments of the church, Baptism and Holy Communion, were inseparably linked both here in North Africa and in Syria.

The "Apostolic Tradition"

One of the fullest of the early orders of Christian initiation comes from the first part of the third century in Alexandria, several hundred miles east of Tertullian's Carthage. The "Apostolic Tradition" attributed to Hippolytus represents the standard Roman practices of the time.

Here is a basic outline of the whole instructional-sacramental process:

1. Those who were to be baptized were daily instructed and purified for a period of time that roughly coincides with our Lenten season.

2. They were examined by the bishop and if they were found worthy they were directed to bathe, to be exorcised (to drive out demons that might be plaguing them) on Thursday of Holy Week, and also to repeat the text of the Creed given them the previous Sunday.

3. They fasted on Good Friday and Saturday of Holy Week. The bishop exorcised them again and read to them many inspirational works.

4. The Easter vigil began at cock's crow on Easter Eve when the water was blessed. Two vials of oil were also blessed by the bishop.

5. The candidates for Baptism then undressed, formally renounced Satan, and were anointed with the oil of exorcism.

6. A deacon led each person in turn down into the baptismal water. There, a presbyter immersed him after he answered affirmatively to each of the three sections of the creed.

7. Then the baptized were anointed by the presbyter with the oil of blessing. They were dried and instructed to put on white robes.

8. The bishop anointed them again with the oil of blessing, made the sign of the cross on the forehead of each person, and gave each person the kiss of peace.

9. The service concluded with the admission of the newly baptized to the Lord's Supper.

As you look over the steps of this rather involved procedure, you will notice some changes taking place in what were once rather simple acts. For one thing, instruction is becoming more important and being formalized. People can no longer be taken into the church on the basis of their willingness to become disciples of Christ. Mostly former pagans, they have to undergo a trial period followed by examination. Another feature is the growing expansion of the various rites surrounding the actual Baptism by water. Actually, at this point it is still one sacramental act, but one with many parts.

Still another change involves the developing hierarchy among the clergy. Local congregational leaders such as presbyters (roughly corresponding to modern pastors) and deacons (the church councilmen of the day) are assigned specific operations. The bishop (or overseer of the congregations in a certain area) performs the final anointing and sealing.

All of these changes are important to our story of confirmation because soon they will become determining factors in the division of what will be called "confirmation" from Baptism. One sacrament will eventually become two in the thinking of both theologians and church leaders.

An Ending World

Underlying these changes were some vital sociological conditions that we ought to know about. Remember that the New Testament church under the leadership of men like Paul and John believed firmly that the world would soon come to an end. Christ would return to gather the faithful into his kingdom. Therefore, congregations lived on the brink of eternity. Life was fairly well oriented toward the unknown but glorious tomorrow. Paul frequently spoke of Baptism as the believer's participation in the life, death, and resurrection of Christ. To the church members at Rome, he wrote, "We were buried therefore with him by baptism into death, so that as Christ was raised from the dead by the glory of the Father, we too might walk in the newness of life" (Romans 6:4). He went on to point out in that letter that this Baptism unto death meant that our old sinful selves were crucified and that we were no longer slaves to sin: "So you also must consider yourselves dead to sin and alive to God in Christ Jesus" (Romans 6:11).

Now what happened is easy to chart. The world didn't end as anticipated. Christian congregations multiplied rapidly under a dynamic missionary outreach sponsored by the mother church at Jerusalem. As time passed, those who had known Jesus intimately while he was here on earth gradually died until only their treasured words remained as guidepoints for their believing brethren.

More and more converts came from the vast Gentile world, fewer from Jewish traditions. Baptism loomed even more significantly as a decisive break with one's past life; one now entered a select community dedicated to holiness. Therefore more emphasis in the actual washing with water was placed on washing out the evils, the demons, even old Satan himself, that had infested the pagan life. In short, the emphasis in Baptism became negative.

To stress the positive side and to remind the convert of what was happening to him as he came up out of the water into the new communal relationships with Christ in the people of God, various other devices were used. This is where the practice of the oil anointment, making the sign of the cross, and laying hands on the believer's head gradually moved into the picture. Those who followed these practices felt that they were signifying that God the Holy Spirit would thus be *with* his people, uniting them in a common cause, and *in* his people, strengthening them for any and all eventualities.

39

Divided Christianity

Somewhere in the third and fourth centuries, we don't know how or where exactly, the Sacrament of Baptism became two distinct parts. It was like a river dividing into two channels that run parallel and close together for awhile and then become more divergent. Also, about the same time, the one church disrupted by a number of issues divided into East and West. The Eastern church centered around Constantinople, the city of Constantine the Great. The Western church sought its hub at Rome. The attitudes towards Baptism-confirmation in these two halves of the Christian church became quite different.

The Eastern Orthodox church, as we now know the church of the East, for the most part kept both the negative and the positive elements in Baptism closely intertwined. If babies were baptized, they were considered full members of the body of Christ and given the sacrament of Holy Communion with a spoon. The church in the West, which we now call the Roman Catholic church, also baptized babies but added a period of instruction and postponed admission to Communion and confirmation to later childhood.

The East tended to stress the incarnation and crucifixion of Christ as the most important parts of Christianity and therefore saw the whole act of dying with Christ in Baptism as the key to the sacrament. The West on the other hand, put more emphasis on Christ's resurrection and moved in the direction of making confirmation the sacrament of newness of life. In fact, it was just a short jump in the West for some prominent theologians to speak of confirmation as completing Baptism, of adding the additional power of the Holy Spirit that the individual needed to live as a Christian in his society.

It is rather interesting that in confirmation practices, the Eastern churches stressed anointing while the Western church gradually dropped the use of holy oil, emphasizing instead the laying on of hands. Incidentally, the East was more concerned in honoring the baptismal day of Jesus than his birth.

Inconclusive investigations failed to establish when Jesus was born. The Western church was not satisfied to leave the matter dangling. Finally, December 25, an old pagan festival celebrating the birthday of the sun, was chosen as the birth date for Jesus. This holiday was used as a missionary witness to the pagan community. Christmas, as this date came to be called, suggested that

40

this significant day was still the birthday of the son, but he was the Son of God. It was only later that the Eastern church finally decided to honor Jesus' birth on January 6, the same day that they celebrated his Baptism. January 6 was appropriate in their thinking because this was Epiphany, the manifestation of Christ's glory, a glory that men could share as they share his death.

Fighting Heresy

Telescoping the years as we are now doing may give the false impression that changes took place rapidly. In most instances, to the contrary, they were slow and almost imperceptible. Generally, the church, both East and West, adjusted its practices to the demands of the times. The rise of false doctrines and popular heresies challenged the church to protect its people; education or, to use a more precise word, indoctrination became a necessity.

For some time, not all children were baptized. In some sections of the church, those who came from Christian families, were considered Christians because they were born into Christianity. The Christian faith was the normal atmosphere of their homes. They were naturally accepted as part of the church community. However, problems arose when these children grew to adulthood. Should they all be baptized like any adult who came from the pagan world? After all, Baptism of adults was mandatory as far as the church was concerned. And besides, some argued, why should children be restricted from participating in the gifts that Baptism confers? So infants were brought for Baptism and baptismal fonts soon became customary pieces of church furniture. (You can't really hold a newborn baby under a fountain or in the running waters of a stream.)

The local priest could perform Baptisms all right; he was the shepherd of his flock. But when the baptized child had been instructed in the faith and was ready for the gift of the Holy Spirit, the local bishop had better come around to the parish. It was the bishop's wisdom that evaluated the child's knowledge and loyalty as preparation for completing Baptism with confirmation. The bishop had to be sure that each confirmed child was ready to take his place with his elders in the fight against erroneous teachings always threatening the church's integrity. As a matter of fact, in those days there were so many twisted notions of Christianity circulating among the Roman provinces that you could almost set up a heresy-of-the-month club. Besides all this, suppose the priest who had baptized the child was a heretic himself? No one felt that Baptism as a Christ-directed act was repeatable. The only way this could be straightened out was to make sure that the bishop set everything right with the holy oil and the blessing of confirmation.

Consolidation in the Middle Ages

Mercifully, let's skip over the so-called dark ages when the Roman Empire came apart at the seams under ravaging attacks of barbarian hordes. Luxurious living and degenerate social customs ill-prepared the imperial citizens to withstand the onslaught. Moral decay coupled with savage warfare reduced the proud civilization of the Roman world to smoking ruins. The church was one of the few among the established institutions of society that managed to survive. This it did by conquering the conquerors with love.

Missionary work among the peoples from the northern forests, the eastern steppes, and from the southern deserts increased in intensity. A number of prominent invasion leaders were converted. The church became the cement that helped put the walls of order back up again. But in so doing, there were many expediencies. The sacraments were often used as acts of magic, of great power. So Charlemagne could order a whole field full of his troops to be baptized by spraying them with a hose. Later they could be instructed and confirmed, but now they had to realize that God controlled them through the Christian emperor and the leader of the church, the pope.

Holy Communion became a disciplinary tool which the church could wield to enforce its moral codes and the civil laws which it supported. Whoever failed to abide by the church's standards would be excommunicated, a fearful punishment. This meant that the person thus restricted was thrown outside the Christian community where there was no hope for eternal salvation.

As the church in the Middle Ages consolidated its gains, both the church and the newly developing countries took on a similar sort of structure. It was a pyramid of human authority with the common people forming the broad base. Power and decision-making were the prerogatives of the successively narrowing layers as you moved toward the top. At the apex stood the king or the emperor for society, the pope for the church. Their word was law and the nobles or archbishops were charged with seeing that

42

the word was carried out. It is not surprising that the game of chess became very popular; here were knights and bishops, kings and queens jockeying for control, while the pawns were more or less expendable.

Doctrines of Confirmation

The great flowering of Christian doctrine grew out of the seed-bed of consolidation. There was now time to explain all the mysteries, to fill in the missing pieces. Schools and universities were established to wrestle with the weighty problems of scriptural interpretation. All the vague occasional church practices came under careful scrutiny. Many were shaped to fit in an appropriate place in the jigsaw puzzle of the church's teachings. This is what happened to confirmation.

Although the Council of Orange in 441 had used the term confirmation for the first time, nothing official had been done about it for almost a thousand years. Prominent theologians now began giving it their close attention. Peter Lombard, author of an influential theological work *The Sentences,* called confirmation "the perfection of Baptism." Near the end of his life Peter became archbishop of Paris. Around 1150, he wrote that Baptism gave grace for forgiveness but that confirmation through the bishop gave strengthening and perfection for the Christian life. Confirmation was moving up the status ladder.

A hundred years later, a Dominican friar, large in girth as well as in mind, nailed down the doctrine of confirmation in a monumental series of volumes. The man was called Thomas Aquinas, a gifted intellectual; the volumes were called the *Summa Theologica,* which can be roughly translated in the light of subsequent influence "The Last Word in Theology." According to St. Thomas, confirmation gives the Christian the fullness of the Holy Spirit, which increases his indelible reservoir of grace and enables him to face the challenges to his spiritual life. By means of this sacrament (confirmation now being considered one of the seven sacraments), the Christian was given perfection and virtue. This to Aquinas was almost more important than faith because the follower of Christ had to achieve a Christian victory in his own spiritual growth as well as be a witness to the world. For Thomas, faith was an intellectual acceptance of doctrine and therefore needed supplementation with other "virtues" in the achievement of spiritual perfection.

Decisions by Councils

In 1439, the church held the Council of Florence, Italy and formally identified the seven sacraments—Baptism, confirmation, ordination, marriage, penance, Holy Communion, and extreme unction—and defined them in its canons. Actually, the council codified only what had already been accepted in practice since the time of Thomas Aquinas.

Following Thomas Aquinas' lead, many clergy and common people felt that confirmation was a more important sacrament than Baptism. Wasn't it true that a bishop had a more dignified station than a priest? Any priest could baptize but only a bishop could confirm and bestow the greater gift of the Holy Spirit. Their view was by no means unanimous. Various groups within the church and without attacked the Florence council's sacramental theology. Generally these dissident critics were suppressed or punished.

More threatening attacks came in the next century when Martin Luther and the other Reformers sought to purify the church of its shaky doctrines. Instead of accomplishing his task, Luther was excommunicated. The church fighting back sponsored the Counter-Reformation through an eighteen-years-long series of meetings at Trent, again in Italy. The Council of Trent in the years from 1545 to 1563 underscored the sacramental decisions made by the Council of Florence and thereby rigidly encapsulated confirmation in a pattern that has been part of the Roman Catholic church ever since. Not until the probing days of Vatican Council II has confirmation in its present form in the Roman Catholic tradition been seriously questioned by responsible church leaders.

Our giant strides through church history scarcely allow us time to do full justice to the story of confirmation. However, we are enabled to look more carefully at Lutheran confirmation practices in the light of what we have learned. We can spot some of the elements that have been carried over into Protestant traditions. We can, perhaps, see why the church made some of the modifications in Baptism and confirmation that it did. More important, we can evaluate these elements, these modifications in terms of how we understand the church's responsibility to its people today. Before we turn to a close examination of the opinions of Luther and subsequent leaders in the Lutheran churches, we should briefly note the status of confirmation in twentieth-century Greek Catholic (Eastern Orthodox) and Roman Catholic churches. Actually, this chapter quite properly ends in their present-day practices.

Greek Catholic Practices

Essentially, Greek Catholics follow the practices of the ancient churches of the East. There has been little change. Holy oil is used at the time of Baptism to signify the coming of the Holy Spirit. This is called chrismation and follows Baptism by water. Infants are given chrismation immediately after they are baptized and are permitted to receive Holy Communion. Their parents have the responsibility to bring them to the Lord's Table and to care for their spiritual welfare as they grow to adulthood.

Adults wishing to become members of the church are given chrismation if they have already been baptized in the name of the triune God. This follows a brief period of instruction. Otherwise, they are given Baptism and chrismation at the same time. The sacrament of chrismation in Greek Catholic thinking is a form of lay ordination, enabling the baptized members to participate in other sacraments and to contribute to the life of the Christian community. Without the seal of the Spirit, as chrismation is sometimes called, the baptized person, it is felt, will have a hard time achieving virtuous Christian living or achieving moral perfection. This is an extra power each Christian needs.

Roman Catholic Practices

While we are noting Roman Catholic practices in North America in general, we should be aware that these are not necessarily followed everywhere. For instance, in some parts of Mexico and Latin America, children and even infants are confirmed immediately after Baptism and admitted to Holy Communion. However, this is not the norm. Usually the baptized child is admitted to the Lord's Table around the "age of reason" which is accepted as about his seventh year. He then receives catechetical instruction for one or more years and is confirmed at a time when the bishop can visit the parish. Sometimes catechetical instruction may be separated from admission to first Communion by as much as seven to ten years.

At confirmation the children renew the baptismal promises made in their stead by their sponsors at Baptism. The bishop lays his hands on their heads and makes the sign of the cross on their foreheads. The use of holy oils has disappeared entirely.

45

Adults do not join the church by confirmation. It they have been properly baptized, they are admitted by a profession of faith which they repeat. They also sign a copy of it. Then they are admitted to Holy Communion and accepted as members. However, they will be confirmed at the next visit of the bishop to the parish or at a specified annual time at the local cathedral.

Vatican Council II has spurred a number of critical scholars and educators within the Roman Catholic church to press for changes both in theology and practice. Some voices are suggesting a much later age for confirmation, following or as part of the junior high years. Others are insisting that Baptism and confirmation belong together as a "twin sacrament." *The Constitution on the Sacred Liturgy* from Vatican Council II calls for a revision of the rite of confirmation and a clarification of the whole Christian initiatory process. Further, it suggests that confirmands renew their baptismal promises just before they are confirmed. Ferment within the church may issue in some innovative practices. Already the use of the common language of the people is relaxing the official Latin of the confirmation rite in many parts of the church. Where the council's influence on church leaders to initiate reform and renewal will lead is anybody's guess.

Postscripts

The Anglican church of England, while not directly accepting seven sacraments, still for all practical purposes has kept confirmation in a special sacramental basket. It is to them a definite completion of Baptism. Recently though, a church-wide study of confirmation has opened the floodgates of reevaluation. Significantly, a study book coming from an Anglican study conference is entitled *Crisis in Confirmation*. The title speaks volumes and generally parallels the growing attitude among Lutherans that the time has come to stop playing around with confirmation. If it is as important as we think it is, then we ought to be able under the guidance of biblical scholars, educators, and church leaders to determine both its nature and its proper function in the church today. Having said that, let's now make a careful examination of how Luther and the various Lutheran traditions have contributed to the state of confirmation today.

4

Luther and Lutheranism

The hammer blows on the oaken door were scarcely heard by passersby. The young university professor was nailing up a list of theses, points for arguments, on the local church-door bulletin board. A conventional spot; an everyday happening. Yet the echoes of those sounds reverberated throughout Christendom. Within a few short years the church was divided again. Martin Luther brought together in his symbolic act the largely underground complaints and clamors for reform that had been plaguing the church for some time. His ninety-five theses focused attention on the impurities that had steadily crept into the church's teachings, corrupting its practices. More important, the theses publicized the necessity for a change. The date was October 31 in 1517.

Ripe for Reformation

Luther's choice of the last day of October for making public the problems with which he had been wrestling was no accident. November 1, All Saints' Day in the church's annual list of celebrations, was a day of holy obligation, when all of the faithful were obliged to attend mass. There would be a good audience for Luther's theses. All Saints' Day was also traditionally an occasion for discusson of pertinent ecclesiastical issues. Learned scholars would join together in delightful day-long sessions for friendly argument. But this year would bring few delights and much shattering of friendships. Luther was primarily interested in exploring the nature of God's gracious gifts to his people and how those gifts were administered by divine authority. He questioned the human authoritarian structures that got in the way. He could not foresee, on that particular autumn day, that his challenges would be interpreted as undermining the very foundations of the established church. Some of his critics still feel that he was burning down the barn in order to destroy a hornet's nest under the eaves.

It is perhaps symbolic that October 31 was also known among the peasants as Halloween, the hallowed eve before the celebration for all the saints of the church. A mixture of the ancient English Druid customs and Roman festivals of the harvest, Halloween suggested an annual last ditch attempt of the forces of evil to overcome the world. The dawn of All Saints' Day would send the ugly denizens of the night back into their secret recesses, beaten by the forces of holiness. In a certain sense Luther was calling attention to the spooks and goblins that had managed to sneak into the church, twisting and distorting its biblical foundations. But don't think that his memo on the church door was simply a trick-or-treak prank; Luther was deadly serious about probing the grace of God and how that grace comes to man.

The Reformation came at one of those momentous periods in history when everything seemed to be changing rapidly. Luther was a nine-year-old schoolboy when Columbus first dropped anchor in the West Indies; he was in his teens when artists such as Leonardo da Vinci and Michelangelo were exploring new avenues of art. He watched the neatly established social and political orders of the Middle Ages being altered. Feudalism was dying; the rise of towns brought in the development of a new middle class. Merchants, craftsmen, innkeepers, artisans, bankers —the variety of job opportunities expanded rapidly. France had just become a nation under Louis XI; the end of the War of the Roses in England brought the age of knighthood to a close; Ivan the Great as the first national sovereign of Russia took the title of Tsar; in Spain, the united houses of Aragon and Castille were fighting against the Moors; in what would one day be Italy the Venetians were struggling against Turkish invasions; Russia and Lithuania ended their conflict at the peace table. In a time of transition there is a time of questioning: Who is God? What is man? How are the two related? These were the questions Luther asked. He was no longer satisfied with the typical answers the church gave.

Erasmus and Confirmation

Before we consider Luther's attitude toward confirmation, we need to pause long enough to get acquainted with Erasmus of Rotterdam. Desiderius Erasmus was one of the leading scholars and thinkers of his day, a philosopher who in his quiet way also suggested reforms for the church. He went at this task from his own particular point of view. Like many other prominent educators he was caught up in the glories of the Renaissance which swept up from Italy, calling attention to the magnificent achievements of mankind. Like many other Renaissance thinkers, Erasmus was a humanist, that is, he put man and his interests at the center of the stage. Therefore when Erasmus probed the nature of the church's sacraments, he was more apt to ask, "What should man do?" than he was to inquire, "What has God done?" And he was sure the answer involved human learning.

This becomes clear when you examine Erasmus' proposals for reshaping confirmation. While he was willing to accept the practice of infant baptism, he felt that somehow the child needed consciously and publicly to take for himself the obligations of discipleship. Erasmus consequently encouraged the church to concentrate on education, to prepare the children for this act of allegiance to Christ and the church by thoroughly grounding them in the catechism. In short, Erasmus tried to shift the emphasis in the prevailing doctrine of confirmation from God's gifts to man's obligations to appropriate those gifts, from liturgical rites to catechetical processes. The confirmand was in the spotlight and his confirmation was a subjective, freewill acceptance of his status as a baptized Christian.

The rite of confirmation following a catechetical period, according to Erasmus, would highlight the young person's confession of his faith and his taking the vow of loyalty. In this fashion, the "Sage of Rotterdam" hoped to help the church once again be a confessing church with its consecrated people fanning throughout society as living witnesses to the gospel. They would know what they were confessing and they would confess their faith in what they knew to be true. One recent estimate of Erasmus quite frankly labels him "the founder of catechetical confirmation." The sage would probably be pleased.

Erasmus is important to our study because he influenced both positively and negatively the attitudes of the Protestant Reformers. You can't keep him out of the picture.

49

Luther's Opinions

Those who feel that the way to solve theological and practical problems in the contemporary church is to see what Luther had to say about them are going to be frustrated when they inquire about confirmation. Luther had little to say. And what he did say is a minute part of his voluminous writings.

Like a number of church Reformers before him, the Bohemian Jan Hus, the Englishman John Wycliffe, and others, Luther rejected confirmation as a sacrament. As far as he could see, you would read the four Gospels in vain to find support for saying that Christ authorized any such act as confirmation in the way he initiated Baptism and Holy Communion. Confirmation for Luther, therefore, was a dead issue. He wanted nothing to do with any church-developed rite that openly proclaimed it was completing a sacrament that Christ did establish. How preposterous to think confirmation could add something to Baptism that Baptism lacked!

As far as Luther was concerned, Baptism was God's great act of incorporating the individual into the church. Through the use of water God announced that this person belonged to him, that his sins were forgiven, and that all of God's gracious gifts were to be his. It was God's act; it required no corresponding action on the individual's part. When God gave himself to someone, Luther felt sure, he gave all of himself; he didn't parcel himself out in dribs or drabs over a period of time. Nor did he make his gifts contingent on some kind of bargain-counter haggling. Therefore, to think of confirmation as adding more of God the Holy Spirit than Baptism did was intolerable to Luther. Bluntly, in one of his sermons, he called confirmation "monkey business."

In a famous tract he wrote in 1520, *The Babylonian Captivity of the Church,* Luther plunged headlong into a vigorous examination of the church's sacramental system. Here he points out that the laying on of hands as an act cannot be considered a sacrament on biblical grounds. Although there are many instances where the procedure was used, there is no scriptural evidence that Christ commanded it to be followed—especially to give believers a greater portion of the Spirit. The apostles laid their hands on the bread at mealtime and blessed it. Is bread a sacrament? They put their hands on the ill and healed them. Is healing a sacrament? "It is amazing," Luther comments, "that it should have entered the minds of these men to make a sacrament of confirmation out of the laying on of hands." Therefore he made no attempt to reform confirmation. Yet, he didn't mind its use in the new Protestant congregations as long as it was interpreted properly. As he pointed out, "It is sufficient to regard confirmation as a certain churchly rite or sacramental ceremony, similar to other ceremonies." In other words, confirmation could have a place as one of the church's homemade worship practices.

There was another aspect of treating confirmation as a sacrament that bothered Luther. For him, a sacrament imparted the fullness of God in his grace. "The sacrament is the gospel," he said simply. In his opinion, confirmation did not fulfill this expectation. The full power of the total gospel was as much his measuring rod in assessing church dogma as it was in determining the church's primary mission to the world.

Luther's critics suggested that he was not interested in confirmation at all. This is not quite true. He was deeply interested in the process that led to traditional confirmation but not in the rite itself. His was an educational bias: He was concerned about what happened to the growing child between his Baptism and the time he was admitted to the Lord's Table.

One of the basic ministries of the church, Luther felt, was to bring the Christian into the presence of the living Christ. Consequently, he emphasized the importance of repentence and absolution. In his liturgical writings, such as the *Formula Missae,* he talks about an examination for those who would come to Holy Communion and especially for those children who are coming for the first time. If this experience is to be meaningful for the child, then he has to be properly prepared. Here Luther's greatest contribution was made: He stressed the importance of catechetical education to link the two sacraments effectively.

The Catechisms

It is almost impossible for a Lutheran to talk about confirmation without at the same time talking about Luther's *Small Catechism*. In the minds of many pastors their task is to get the children of their parish through *The Small Catechism* somehow in order to confirm them. This has led to at least two misunderstandings of Luther's intent.

The first misunderstanding is involved with this notion that Christian education is only a springboard to something else. Luther wanted an informed church membership so that people could live with their Lord intelligently. He wanted people to

51

know why they made certain decisions in their daily living. Faith for him is a dynamic relationship with God through Christ; it is by no means a static cookbook with recipes for every eventuality. Therefore education takes time, time for growing persons to ask questions pertinent to them where they are in their daily situations. As they mature and change, they have new questions to ask and new insights to garner.

The second misunderstanding is closely related to the first: This is the idea that *The Small Catechism* represents the irreducible minimum of what a church member ought to know, the smallest amount of Christian content that he ought to master. You can readily see where this idea leads: Give each child the catechism like a hypodermic and he is automatically prepared for a participation in the church as a mature member.

At a recent conference on catechetical instruction, a Canadian pastor put his finger on the critical issue: "We have been using *The Small Catechism,* like some kind of vaccination." He went on: "Doctors use vaccination to protect people against disease. They inject a small amount of disease germs into the person's bloodstream so that his body can build up resistance; then he doesn't get the real thing. That's what we have been doing with The *Small Catechism,* cramming it into the kids when they are young. Maybe we are helping them build up a resistance to Christianity so that they won't get the real thing either!"

This wry comment is surprisingly close to the convictions of the youth psychologist, Horrocks. He points out in his study *The Psychology of Adolescence* that "a child who has been thoroughly indoctrinated faces even more serious adjustment difficulties if he finds his attitudes toward religion changing."

How Luther Developed His Catechisms

You can get a fairly clear picture of Luther's attitude toward what we have been calling the catechetical-confirmation process if you note how he developed his educational program. The program was always flexible, geared to the needs of the people.

Actually, the catechisms that he prepared grew directly out of his ministry. Appalled at the abysmal ignorance of both laymen and clergy in spiritual matters, he began to preach and teach the basic doctrines of the Christian faith quite early in his career. He used the catechetical idea that really had been a part of the church's heritage for a long time. There were in existence such "catechisms" or "primers" which included the Creed, the Lord's Prayer, the Ten Commandments, and often the *Ave Maria* and other material to be learned by heart as early as the days of the twelfth century. As we have noted, Erasmus, over in what would one day be Holland, was also pushing catechetical instruction as a means of rejuvenating the church. As early as 1516, Luther was preaching a series of sermons on the Ten Commandments.

For the next thirteen years, he seldom missed an opportunity to spend part of each year discussing the Decalogue (Christian life), The Lord's Prayer (Christian prayer), and the Apostles' Creed (Christian faith) in the pulpit and the classroom. He still was dissatisfied with his efforts. He wanted to find some way of encouraging people to probe the teachings of the church on their own and to apply the insights gained to their own lives— and situations.

Along with his teaching and preaching Luther published his catechetical sermons as a guide for fellow clergymen. To help laymen, he came up with the idea of using posters. The newly invented printing presses offered some imaginative prospects. So in the eye-catching broadsides in concise, easily remembered form, Luther tried to capture the essence of Christian beliefs. The first of these posters dealing with the Ten Commandments appeared in 1518. Using the techniques of modern advertising, Luther chose pithy, sharply pointed words. His grasp of basic Christian teachings was nothing short of phenomenal. Without space for involved theological explanations, he sought to get his message across forcefully and directly. At the low price of a penny apiece the posters sold rapidly; people clamored for more. Many pasted the posters on the walls of their rooms so that they could refer to the words easily. Other posters dealing with the creed and the Lord's Prayer soon followed.

In 1519, the first two series of sermons Luther preached on the catechism were published. By the end of the next decade these and similar sermon collections became the basis for his *German Catechism* (nicknamed *The Large Catechism*). The posters were collected and issued in book form as *The Small Catechism*. Here Luther added two sections on the sacraments to the traditional three parts; he considered Baptism and the Sacrament of the Altar as two other cornerstones of Christian faith and life.

The word "small" in the title referred to the size of the book and not to physical stature of its target audience. The fact of

53

the matter is that Luther addressed *The Small Catechism* to the landed farmer, the steady city burgher, to all heads of households whom he held responsible for educating their children and their servants. Luther wanted them to have a guide for home devotions, a starting point for family discussions. He also had the book in mind as a tool for the "lower clergy," generally assistant pastors or pastors of small village congregations who had little education. By working through leaders of home and church, Luther sought to reach all the people of his area.

Using the Catechisms

Luther worked out three ways to use his catechisms:

1. As an aid to memorization (the poster idea).
2. As a guide to understanding the basic parts of the Christian faith in terms of life experiences. Luther kept his explanations general enough to apply to virtually every person's situation, yet sharp enough to avoid misunderstandings.
3. As an outline for exploring the relevancy of Christian teachings to every area of life. Luther felt that interpretations of doctrine as well as its applications to life must be broadened and deepened. Here is where *The Large Catechism* came in handy with its suggestions for catechetical sermons.

Above all, Luther wanted pastors, as well as heads of households, to be sensitive to the needs of their people and to develop their own catechetical sermons to meet those needs.

Contrary to the way *The Small Catechism* is often used today (like a computer mechanically punching out sterile bits of information), Luther wanted it used as an opportunity for dialogue, exploring the meanings and the ramifications of Christian teachings for each person in his own situation. Further, Luther planned his catechisms for use by the whole Christian community, not only children but older youth and adults. You have only to read his letters counseling those who sought his help or eavesdrop at the discussions he had with his friends around the dinner table to see how he practiced what he preached. In addition, some years he preached as many as four different series of sermons on the elements of the catechism. Personally, he noted, part of his daily devotions was to meditate on portions of the catechism.

You see, Luther felt strongly that no one ever outgrew the need for studying the perennial challenge of the whole Christian gospel to his life. Therefore, it would be a mistake to ever think of the content of catechetics as primarily a train of boxcars, carrying discrete and isolated globs of facts, which must be sent highballing through the child's mind. Rather, think of the components of *The Small Catechism*, the Ten Commandments, the Apostles' Creed, the Lord's Prayer, Baptism, and Holy Communion, as spokes of a wheel. The hub represents Christ, the center of the Christian's faith. As the wheel turns in the simple process of living with Christ, the spokes blur and become part of the whole. Luther wanted to guide people in becoming whole persons. This involves blending emotions, understandings, actions, and the human will into a totality. While the catechisms treat various aspects of the Christian faith in a series of emphases, this does not mean that as each section is studied it is automatically mastered or blended with the others.

If there is a special use for the catechism in preparing the child for his first Communion (and Luther felt there was), it should also be used for the rest of that child's life, guiding him in his growth toward Christian maturity. Thus while the process of education linked the two sacraments, Baptism and Holy Communion, in the individual's experience, it also continued to prepare him to participate meaningfully in each of the celebrations of the Sacrament of the Altar to come.

Many Varieties of Confirmation

While Luther himself did not practice the rite of confirmation, he did not discourage those friends who tried to reform the rite in the light of Protestant standards. Just as he encouraged every literate pastor he knew to prepare catechisms of his own, so he supported, although lukewarmly at times we must admit, the efforts of those who were exploring new ways of guiding youth through the critical periods of their adolescence. Consequently, during the latter years of Luther's life some attempts were made to develop an evangelical rite. Other experiments followed. Soon there were so many varieties of confirmation being offered in Protestant circles that it was almost impossible to keep a box score. It was like the pickle manufacturer's fifty-seven varieties.

For three centuries, Luther's followers experimented. Each dukedom and principality in the then fragmented Germany tried to build practical church orders of confirmation of their own. Attempting to differentiate among the many suggestions offered

55

is like trying to separate strands of various hues from Joseph's coat of many colors. However, this is a job we somehow must do. The tangled roots of modern confirmation practices, particularly in North America, lie buried in this particular period of church history.

You will notice as you read the appropriate section of the commission's report (pp. 188-90) that, for convenience's sake ,six principle forms of confirmation are labelled; catechetical, traditional, hierarchical, sacramental, pietistic, and rationalistic. As we discuss these forms, please realize that our analysis is probably oversimplified. There was much overlapping among the influences and counter-influences that swept back and forth across Europe. Actually, it would be more proper to speak of the six major emphases rather than six forms or types. It is hard to find specific examples of any of the forms followed in complete isolation from the others. Few congregations used any particular form in a completely pure state. However, there seems to be no more practical way of going about our task. Let there be no overtones of condemnation if we find in some of these emphases elements that seem incompatible with our awareness of biblical and theological implications. Generally, in each period of its history, the church of the Reformation was trying to make confirmation a useful tool for the guidance of its parishioners. Decisions were made in terms of a sense of responsibility and genuine concern for the needs of the developing Christian.

CATECHETICAL EMPHASIS

Let's start with the catechetical type of confirmation which, strictly speaking, is not confirmation at all. That is, it is not a process culminating with a church rite, yet it had perhaps the most influence on subsequent practices of all our so-called types. The catechetical emphasis stemmed from Luther's program of education for receiving the sacrament of Holy Communion and for making a good confession, which, for Luther, was the prelude to receiving the sacrament. Under this emphasis pastors were encouraged to preach an annual series of sermons on the catechism for the entire congregation and to hold special classes for children and servants. The young attended catechetical instruction until their early twenties or until they were married. Older people, especially the unlearned, were also expected to attend these classes.

Luther saw this program as an integral part of the church's pastoral and educational ministry to its people. It is interesting that children, after they were admitted to the Lord's Supper, were still expected to continue in their catechetical studies; Luther's idea of the lifelong educative process was taking hold. There never was a graduation ceremony short of eternity.

Spreading Influence

From Germany, the catechetical type spread to Scandinavia. Johannes Bugenhagen, one of Luther's closest friends and his "father-confessor," left his Wittenberg parish to accept a call in Denmark. His assignment: to establish the Reformation there. This he did with dispatch and in the process introduced many of Luther's ideas such as the catechetical procedures. Lutheran reformers in Sweden were soon able to dispense with long-practiced confirmation rites that were considered sacramental and in their place substituted catechetical instruction.

Many who followed Luther's practices caught his vision of educational growth. They veered away from defining a set body of knowledge as the prerequisite for communing; they encouraged children to probe the meanings of their faith and to look forward with joyful anticipation to communing with their Lord. Pastors tended to personalize their instruction. They also examined the candidates for Communion privately. When they felt a child (or an adult for that matter) was ready to come to the altar rail, he was invited to participate in the sacrament.

Characteristics

In many areas of the Lutheran church that followed the catechetical emphasis, there were no associated formal rites for a long time. It really wasn't until the nineteenth century that children were examined publicly and were received at the Lord's Table as a group. Church leaders were reluctant for various reasons to adopt any public ceremony other than offering congregational prayers for the spiritual well-being of the confirmands.

For quick reference, let's underscore three major elements in the catechetical emphasis: instruction, confession of faith (acceptance of Christian teachings in the examination), and the prayers of the congregation. From here we can see how bridges were built to include other elements and develop new emphases in confirmation practices.

HIERARCHICAL EMPHASIS

The second emphasis in Lutheran confirmation practices that is important to our study is what we call the hierarchical or the "church discipline" type. The term "hierarchical" refers to the governing of a local congregation by its parish clergy and not to the Roman Catholic administrative structure. This accentuated emphasis on disciplinary control came largely through the efforts of Martin Bucer of Heidelberg.

Martin Bucer

Bucer's name looms large whenever Protestant confirmation practices are discussed. As a young pastor he became enthusiastic about Luther's stance in defying the church of Rome. Swiftly, he plunged headlong into the Reformation fray. Luther was quite proud of Bucer's accomplishments as a pastor. But the young scholar was not content with mundane pastoral duties. He wanted to contribute to the process of reforming the church, so he turned his attention to the ancient rites and wrote particularly about the rite of confirmation.

Bucer felt a certain kinship with Luther's staunch co-worker, Philipp Melanchthon. He appreciated Melanchthon's willingness to compromise if necessary in order to heal the breaches that were dividing Christendom. Not only did Bucer become something of a compromiser himself, he also excelled in amalgamating diverse ideas into a more unified whole. He thought he could please everyone. He didn't always succeed, but he kept trying.

More than any of his contemporaries, Martin Bucer put an indelible mark on confirmation. A lot of what we call Lutheran in present-day confirmation practices can be traced directly back to Bucer's desk. This is truer, however, in North America than it is in the European lands of the Reformation. Very few sections of Germany, for instance, were willing to adopt Bucer's selections in toto. Yet, because of his broad-based Christian concerns, he managed to have some influence on John Calvin and a great deal of effect on the Anglican development of confirmation

Bucer traveled around Europe a great deal—to France, different parts of Germany, and England. In Germany the Halle church orders came from his pen. In later years he moved to England permanently. He took a post as royal lecturer at Cambridge University and worked closely with the Anglican reformers who were shaping the Church of England.

Two years after Bucer's death, the vengeful "Bloody Queen" Mary came to the English throne. Her father, Henry VIII, had broken with Rome over the matter of divorcing her mother. Mary was determined to restore the Roman Catholic church to its rightful place as the church of the realm. She also intended to punish those who had corrupted the church even further by introducing Protestant notions. As one of her many acts of retribution, she ordered Bucer's bones dug up from their grave and burned in public.

Discipline

The hierarchical type of confirmation which Bucer recommended received its name because of his insistence that the individual should vow his allegiance to Christ through the church. Besides the Word of God and the Sacraments, Bucer felt that one of the key marks of the true church was discipline. "Where there is no discipline," he wrote, "there is no congregation." The person being confirmed should be asked to testify publicly that he was surrendering himself to Christ, that he was likewise willing to submit himself to the church's rule for his life. In this way, he would be consciously acknowledging his obligations.

Over Bucer's conclusions hung the shadow of Erasmus; Bucer was quite taken with that humanistic philosopher's emphasis on church loyalty through discipline. He also liked the way Erasmus worked for the oneness of the church. If he could only bring Luther and Erasmus together! This he tried to do in the church orders he helped establish for Hesse, particularly in the rite of confirmation he developed for use in that territory.

Motivations

Bucer had a number of strong motives. He believed that both Erasmus and Luther had ideas worth preserving. Further, he was confident that with a little careful planning, some widely separated branches of Protestantism could be brought together. When he was a young pastor, Bucer served in Strassburg, France. There he came in conflict with some newly organized Christian sects, especially the Anabaptists. They were proponents of immersion baptism of adults following their confession of loyal faith in Christ. In addition they thought of the church as a fellowship of the perfect, which those baptized could enter.

Bucer couldn't buy the idea of the church as a holiness community. He had very strong Lutheran convictions that the church, quite the contrary, was made up of ordinary people who were simultaneously both sinners and saints. However, the Anabaptist attack on his practice of baptizing infants was unsettling. Maybe they had a point. They maintained that infants could not consciously express their loyalty to Christ and his church. Every Christian needs to confess his own faith and accept his place in the congregation.

Bucer thought of a way to meet this need. He began to conceive of confirmation as a fine opportunity to supply this lack. When the baptized child had come to the age of discretion and was capable of thinking for himself, he then could be asked whether he would willingly place himself under church discipline. This would be a good time too for these children, according to Erasmus' suggestion, to confess for themselves the vows their sponsors made for them at Baptism.

Remembering Luther's stress on preparation for Holy Communion, Bucer went a step further. He wrote into his rite of confirmation a formal admission to the Lord's Supper. This was the first time that the rites of confirmation and first Communion were actually merged into one ball of wax.

The Father of Luthern Confirmation

You can see Bucer's rather skillful fusing of the views of Luther and Erasmus when you examine his order for confirmation:

1. Renewal of the baptismal vow (Erasmus), following instruction and examination (both Luther and Erasmus).
2. Intercessory prayers and blessings of the congregation calling attention to the mighty acts of God (Luther).
3. Laying on of hands as an act of the church's blessing (a traditional practice but not to be understood sacramentally).
4. Admission to Holy Communion (Bucer).
5. Acceptance of the discipline of the congregation (Erasmus).

Because of the way Bucer's contributions show up so frequently in the typical American confirmation patterns, you could call him, as Arthur Repp does, "the father of Lutheran confirmation." At the same time, he complicated the procedure for admitting children to first Communion. He made both confirmation and first Communion the twin goals of catechetical instruction. In so doing, he went far beyond Luther's understanding that these are but way stations in a lifelong catechumenate.

Our estimate of Bucer would be somewhat distorted if we thought of him only as a manipulator of church orders, attempting to patch up differences among Christians. He did have a deep pastoral feeling for the needs of children and youth; passionately, he wanted them to feel that they were really a part of the church. Basically all he was doing was trying to plug up the chinks in fortress walls where he felt the Lutheran church might be vulnerable. He wanted to defend the church he loved from attacks by the Anabaptists or for that matter by anyone else.

SACRAMENTAL EMPHASIS

When Bucer emphasized the laying on of hands in his rite of confirmation as a means of blessing, he had no intention of restoring the Roman Catholic sacramental meanings. He stoutly maintained that Baptism was effective and needed no completion. However, there were other Lutherans who followed Bucer's recommended order and fell into the trap. They began to treat confirmation sacramentally.

The prayer of blessing began to include such phrases as "Receive ye the Holy Spirit." The implications were evident. Confirmation added things that Baptism could not: the fuller presence of the Holy Spirit, fuller church membership for the candidate..

It should be pointed out immediately that the sacramental emphasis in Lutheran confirmation never existed as an independent type. It was generally hitched on to one or another of the other forms. Many who slammed the front door shut against any interpretation of confirmation as a sacrament went around and opened the back door to allow sacramental notions in. Why? Perhaps they felt that confirmands ought to know that something fine, something exciting was happening to them at confirmation: they were receiving more of the Holy Spirit's power! Perhaps church leaders thought that this was one way of granting the adolescent more status in the church; he had arrived at a new and higher plateau where he could share more privileges of membership.

There are doubtless many reasons why the sacramental ideas were appealing. In a number of areas of the church they became thoroughly entrenched.

Influence Today

You can see the influence of the sacramental ideas quite clearly today in the practices of both The American Lutheran Church and the Lutheran Church in America. Look at the Order for Confirmation in the *Service Book and Hymnal* (pp. 245-247).

Let's highlight a few significant phrases. First in the prayer of blessing where the pastor lays his hands on the head of the kneeling confirmands and says:

> *The father in Heaven, for Jesus' sake, <u>renew and increase in thee</u> the gift of the Holy Ghost, to thy strengthening in faith, to thy growth in grace, to thy patience in suffering, and to the blessed hope of everlasting life.* [Underline added.]

Then after the candidates rise, the pastor addresses them:

> *Forasmuch as you have made confession of your faith and have received Holy Baptism, I do now in the Name of the Lord Jesus Christ, the great King and Head of the Church, <u>admit you</u> to the fellowship of the Lord's Table, and to participation in <u>all the spiritual privileges of the Church.</u>* [Underline added.]

In *The Lutheran Agenda* (pp. 25-26) The Lutheran Church—Missouri Synod's rite of confirmation is not quite so specific but the overtones of the sacramental emphasis are still there. Note the underlined words in the pastor's blessing as he lays his hand upon each of the confirmands individually and says:

> *God the Father of our Lord Jesus Christ, <u>give</u> thee His Holy Spirit, the Spirit of wisdom and knowledge, of grace and prayer, of power and strength, of sanctification and the fear of God.* [Underline added.]

Then the pastor says:

> *Upon this your voluntary profession and promise, I, in the name of the Church of Christ, <u>invite and welcome you,</u> as a member of the Evangelical Lutheran Church and of this congregation, <u>to participate with us in all the rights and privileges</u> of the Evangelical Lutheran Church.* [Underline added.]

Problems

We need to ask ourselves some searching questions, such as: What is this gift or increase in the gift of the Holy Spirit; wasn't each confirmand given the full presence of the Spirit at his Baptism? Similarly, what are these "rights" and "privileges" to which he is now being admitted? They cannot refer to receiving the Lord's Supper; that's mentioned separately. You really cannot blame the confirmand if he is confused. In his catechetical classes he learned that it was in Holy Baptism that he was received by our Lord Jesus Christ and made a member of his holy church. Is the baptized person only a sort of church member, junior grade until confirmation promotes him?

One of the biggest problems with the sacramental type of confirmation is the confusion it brings to theology. Both the doctrine of Baptism and the doctrine of the church are almost hopelessly scrambled. You can have the situation, and unfortunately it occurs only too often, where catechetical textbooks and the rite of confirmation cancel each other out.

TRADITIONAL EMPHASIS

The fourth major emphasis in Lutheran confirmation has been labeled traditional for want of a better name. This was simply an attempt in various ways to retain the time-honored elements of the church's confirmation practices without echoing the sacramental overtones. Of course, developing a Protestant confirmation rite along these lines seemed like common sense to those who felt obligated to reform every part of the traditional church. The church in the German city of Brandenburg, for instance, authorized the production of a Lutheran rite of confirmation "which they wished to have observed according to tradition." They felt this could include an evangelical understanding of the laying on of hands and the bishop's participation in the ceremony.

Melanchthon

Although it is hard to pinpoint Philipp Melanchthon's stance (as he changed his mind a number of times), the shape he gave to confirmation in his master work *Loci Communes* (1543 edition) put him in the traditional camp. Here he suggested three parts to the rite: examination in the catechism, public confession of faith, and an intercessory consecration of the confirmands accompanied by the laying on of hands. The latter element was not considered sacramentally. The final form of Melanchthon's confirmation order is found in the Wittenberg church orders of 1545. However, the outline is substantially identical. This 1545 order, incidentally, had Luther's approval.

Admission to Holy Communion was definitely not a part of the rite as far as Melanchthon was concerned. Apparently, he shared a feeling with a number of his fellow theologians that children who have been instructed in the catechism could be brought by their parents to confession and Holy Communion before they were confirmed. This was one of the opinions arrived at in a convention of church leaders who discussed confirmation in 1548 in the city of Celle. The reason given for this view they simply summed up by quoting Jesus, "Let the children come to me, for such belong to the kingdom of God." At the same convention the theologians recommended somewhere between the ages of twelve to fifteen for confirmation "at an age of discretion when the children better understand their faith and their affirmation."

We must remember when we speak of these matters that the theologians involved were not engaged in detached and leisurely discourse. They were facing critical attacks by Roman Catholic leaders in their territories; they were looking for ways that would enable congregations in the Protestant and Roman Catholic warring camps to live at peace with each other. If there had to be a compromise in minor matters, many Lutheran leaders felt this was a small price to pay for establishing harmony. For example, they saw no difficulty in retaining the sign of the cross in the rite because this gesture could suggest the central meaning of Christianity. However, they were not about to concede their dearly won gains. No "peace at any price" for them. This brought an urgency to their conventions, a desire to find the best ways of guiding their people in the true spirit of evangelical witness while doing all they could to keep their suggestions inoffensive.

Martin Chemnitz

Martin Chemnitz is another shadowy figure from the past whom we ought to know better. The principle coauthor of the *Formula of Concord,* Chemnitz did his level best to ease tensions between Protestant and Roman Catholic groups. He also had the formidable task of healing a breach that had occurred in Lutheranism. Shortly after Luther's death in 1546, there was the prospect of the two parties. Some people were claiming that they were followers of Luther; others that they preferred to follow Philipp Melanchthon. "Master Philipp" had a way of shifting and changing his theology to fit the circumstances. No one really knew exactly where he stood at any one time. Those who called themselves "Lutherans" were therefore a little leery of Melanchthon. They thought he was always just one step away from throwing out the baby with the bath water.

While he found himself more closely linked with Melanchthon, Martin Chemnitz also appreciated the stature of Luther's thought. As a student and later a professor at the University of Wittenberg, Chemnitz came to know both reformers well. Through his strenuous efforts he managed for the most part to bring their two sets of followers together. His reputation grew and soon he was asked to take on the reorganization of the church in Prussia.

Chemnitz felt that confirmation should not exist in a vacuum; it should reflect links with the apostolic church. Therefore, when he had an opportunity to work on the rite, he tried to include elements that stressed Baptism (Luther's emphasis) and that also included the laying on of hands in a Protestant sense of blessing only (Melanchthon's emphasis).

A New Rite

When he completed his task, Chemnitz had successfully developed the most complete confirmation rite that has come down to us from the sixteenth century. Chemnitz's rite included:

1. Remembrance of Baptism (God's action in the baptismal convenant).
2. Personal confession of faith.
3. Examination in the catechism.
4. Admonition to remain faithful.
5. Admonition to remain true to the baptismal covenant.
6. Public prayer of intercession with the laying on of hands (nonsacramental).

While seemingly Chemnitz added nothing really new to the rite, his stress on a "personal" confession of faith and on the "admonitions" would within a short period of time be picked up and exploited by the Pietists.

As the sixteenth century drew to a close then, the four major emphases in confirmation we have considered thus far were in full use in one form or another. Little did people realize that the picture would get even more complicated. Within the next two centuries, two additional confirmation emphases would be stressed. Each would present a new problem to the theological foundations of confirmation.

PIETISTIC EMPHASIS

What a difference a hundred years can make! The seventeenth century was a violent time with most of the European nations struggling for supremacy. England and Spain fought viciously for control of the seas and more importantly for the virgin lands of the New World. France emerged as the dominant nation on the continent through a series of battles with her neighbors, only to receive a temporary setback when those neighbors formed an uneasy alliance and fought back. The Turkish hordes were thrown back from the gates of Vienna and Muslim inroads into Europe were halted.

Religious Ways

Peace of a sort came to Europe but soon religious wars broke out. The most terrible conflict destroyed much of the feudal principalities of Germany, leaving the countryside in smoking ruins. This was the Thirty Years War that pitted Catholic nations against Protestant countries. Soldiers were asked to fight not only for their homelands but also for their religious convictions. Sad to say, this often divided a country. Protestants were persecuted in France; religious dissenters were driven out of England.

Against this background, the young Protestant churches tried to establish a firm foothold on the slippery rocks of social and political change. It was touch and go. Lutheran, Anglican, Reformed groups struggled to consolidate their teachings and their ceremonies into watertight compartments that would keep them floating. Orthodoxy, church control, and discipline, and even some thought control became characteristic.

Reactions

Naturally, reactions soon set in. The churches that insisted on rigid, mechanical administration of their ministries were challenged by those who felt that individuality was being destroyed. Further, those church members who played the establishment's game were accused of "walking through their faith," of obeying all the church's rules but failing to live Christian lives.

Critics of the organized churches demanded that religion be personalized, that the congregation be an assembly of those who have genuinely felt the Spirit of God in their hearts and who were willing to set themselves apart from the world in a holy fellowship. In England, these were the days of the Pilgrims and the Puritans, sects that grew up within the Anglican church. Failing to purify the church's practices, they became separated from it, sometimes voluntarily, sometimes by force.

On the European continent, many groups emerged within the churches seeking a similar purification of ironclad formalities. These groups tended to cut across denominational lines. They were more interested in pious living than they were in playing denominational politics. For their pains, sneering church officials tarred them with the title "Pietists." A dirty name! But a name the purists bore with pride.

The Pietistic Thrust

Pietism came surging into the Lutheran churches in Germany and throughout Scandinavia. It gave tremendous impulse to missionary outreach. One of the patriarchs of Lutheranism in North America, Henry Melchior Muhlenberg, was sent to minister to the Lutherans in the American colonies by the dynamic Pietist center at Halle.

Philip Spener and other prominent Pietist leaders saw their task of inspiring people with a sense of true Christianity in two ways. First of all, the church should educate the children for committed spiritual living. Second, the church should provide a significant public ceremony where these children could express their personal willingness to believe in Christian teachings and to live a holy life. The catechetical-confirmation process was made to order. Picking up the suggestions of Martin Chemnitz particularly, the Pietists made a few adjustments in what had become the orthodox procedures and introduced a new kind of confirmation. The new ideas quickly became "the thing to do."

The Pietists considered confirmation as an "act of renewal." Children were instructed not so much in the objective facts of the faith as they were in their subjective acceptance of Christ as their personal Lord. This suggested some real changes in procedure. Catechetical training was redesigned to prepare the young person for a momentous conversion experience. At confirmation the young person would publicly declare his surrender to Christ. In addition, he would renew the baptismal covenant by vowing to keep his part of the covenant with God, as long as he lived. Memory verses were often introduced into the rite. Each confirmand would recite his own choice of a scriptural prescription for Christian living.

Contributions and Distortions

Lurking behind the scenes of this new confirmation rite was the Pietist feeling that Baptism was not completed until the confirmand himself accepted his role as a child of God. The completion of Baptism in the thinking of Pietists, however, didn't hinge on adding more of God the Holy Spirit as it did for those who were sacramentally inclined. Baptism was made full, complete, effective in the vow of the young confirmand willingly acknowledging his personal faith.

Pietism did make a number of healthy contributions to the church's educational program. Stressing personal Bible reading and prayer helped people balance the formalities of liturgical worship with private devotions. Pietists also upset the sterile question-and-answer, sheer memorization of doctrines that catechetics had become. In its place they suggested exploration of the significance of Christianity to life situations through free discussion. Further, they recommended that the length of time devoted to the catechetical program be increased so that pastors would have a longer period of counseling and guiding their young people. All commendable practices.

But some distortions crept in. If the Pietists' avowed purpose was to enlighten the confirmand's understanding, it was also to "sanctify his will." In their instruction they guided him through "order of sanctification," a carefully detailed road map of how he was to conduct himself as a Christian as he moved through life. How can anyone master ways of being holy for the rest of his life? How indeed can anyone, no matter how sincere he is, really promise to do so?

Abiding Concerns

Two parts of the Pietists' emphasis have caused the church headaches ever since. One was the notion of confirmation as a personalized conversion experience. This easily led to vigorous and often morbid self-examination on the part of the young people. Some youth learned to practice self-deception; others worried needlessly about their worthiness to receive Holy Communion.

The other burr under the church's blanket today is directly related: the idea of confirmation and admission to Holy Communion as end products of education. Up until this time, admission to the Lord's Supper was largely the congregation's concern;

now people were asked to come to the altar only after they felt worthy to accept the sacrament. This could only be after their public announcement at confirmtion that they were Christians and that they would participate in the sacrament faithfully.

As these and other pietistic ideas took hold within the church, Baptism became less and less important to the Christian. The time at which his Christian life and indeed his full membership in the congregation really began was when he was confirmed.

RATIONALISTIC EMPHASIS

Underneath the political and social upheavals of the seventeenth and eighteenth centuries, modern science was being born. Tremendous advances were made in chemistry and biology and physics; people were hungry for knowledge. How, they asked, and why, and where? Philosophers glorifying the potentialities of the human mind tried to answer. God was pushed back to the wings of the stage as the author of the play; man, the principal actor—could carry the drama from now on.

The Age of Reason came roaring into human history seeking explanations, logical and plausible, for all the facts of human existence. Old opinions would have to stand the test of thorough scrutiny. If they should be found wanting, do away with them. So the Age of Reason fathered the Age of Revolution. To honor man's mind, honor man himself. Down with the decadent monarchy—and the French revolution was born. Up with democracy —and the American colonies severed their ties with Great Britain.

The Rationalists believed that there wasn't anything that a man couldn't do if he put his mind to the task. Newspapers could hardly keep up with the reports of new inventions, of innovations in industry and transportation and the arts. Even more radical changes were coming. The thinking man had a tremendous task; he had to weigh in his mind the ideas, the new facts, the changes and determine which were worth accepting. Like a sonic boom, rationalism echoed loudly in the church; Christians are still vibrating from the blast.

Intellectual Acceptance

Rationalism affected confirmation in many peculiar ways, most of which as it turned out were detrimental. First, there was the matter of the confirmand's role in the rite. Since Pietism had introduced the subjective, personal-experience-centered approach, pastors of a rationalistic bent could carry the implications a step further. It became important that every young person about to be confirmed understand and be able to explain the church's teachings. He should be able to repeat arguments for the existence of God and tick off God's attributes. He ought to be able to defend his faith against attacks from the rising scientism.

Catechetical examinations soon became academic; confirmands crammed for their finals at church in the same way that they did in academic subjects at school. They were being trained as apologists for Christianity. Hopefully, they would move out to the front lines of a society rapidly turning secular to win converts by their superior arguments for serving Christ instead of mammon.

Graduation

Second, confirmation became a kind of graduation ceremony from the church's rigorous educational program. The newly confirmed were now considered adults in the minds of the congregation. Not only were they given new privileges and rights, but they were expected to accept new responsibilities in the mission of the church. It's not surprising that the time for confirmation in rationalistic-oriented congregations coincided with the time when the general schooling of their children ceased.

In a number of places in Europe, a young person of fourteen could join the work force and be treated as a citizen. Some congregations included the duties of citizenship in their catechetical programs. They even had courses on health to help those who were about to be married. It was not at all odd to have young ladies postponing their confirmation a year or two so that they could use the occasion as a kind of coming-out party to announce to the public that they were available for marriage.

By-Products

In the third place, rationalistic confirmation added some surprisingly sentimental by-products. Confirmands dressed in white robes; girls often carried flowers. At times, cool intellect merged with tear-jerking emotion. In some congregations, the confirmands left the altar during the rite to go to their parents' pew. There they confessed their sins against mother and father and asked their forgiveness. Not a dry eye in the congregation!

With this kind of family solidarity, confirmation grew into a real family festival. Family dinners and home celebrations abounded. With the gathering of the clan on such a joyous occasion, gifts were given to the newly confirmed, marking their passage into the adult world. Usually, youth were presented with articles of adult clothing. They now were allowed to dress in the fashions of their elders. Watches were a favorite gift—the young person could more wisely utilize his time as a Christian witness.

In those sections of Europe where the state officially adopted Lutheranism as the state church, confirmation was tailor-made for use as a means of keeping population records. The tax list and the voting list both came directly from the confirmation records. The right to hold public office was also dependent upon confirmation. This was the situation in Sweden, for instance, until quite recently. It wasn't long until the state had as much vested interest in confirmation as the church did. Here was a new club to hang over the head of youth: "If you want to amount to anything in this town, you jolly well better be confirmed."

Superior to Baptism

Finally, Rationalism severely wrenched the Lutheran teachings, particularly the doctrines of Baptism and the church. Many pastors frankly proclaimed that confirmation was superior to Baptism; some tried to do away with infant Baptism; others considered abolishing Baptism altogether. In any event, there was little doubt that confirmation was absolutely essential to complete Baptism.

As far as the doctrine of the church was concerned, Rationalism whittled it down from a broad theological concept of one universal fellowship in Christ to the denomination, and even further to the particular congregation on a particular corner in town. Why not! After all, a confirmand cannot take vows of loyalty or accept responsibilities in general. These procedures only make sense if he is swearing his support of old St. John's-by-the-River. So the reasoning went. If you belonged to a certain state church in a certain part of Germany, you might not therefore be able to commune in a congregation in another state church in another part— nor in any of the Lutheran churches in Scandinavia. Your loyalty belonged at home.

When you remember that it was from this kind of background that the great Lutheran immigrations came to North America, you have some idea why it has been a long slow process here in getting Lutherans together. We have come a long way from the spirit of Luther, not to mention the distance from the Upper Room.

Comparison of Six Lutheran Emphases in Confirmation

	16TH CENTURY					17TH - 18TH CENTURIES		NOW
	Catechetical	Hierarchical	Sacramental	Traditional		Pietistic	Rationalistic	Your congregation
Instruction	✓	✓	✓	✓		✓	✓	
Private examination	✓	✓	✓	✓		✓	✓	
Public examination	✓					✓		
Confession of church's faith		✓	✓	✓		✓	✓	
Confession of personal faith						✓	✓	
Prayer of the congregation	✓	✓	✓	✓		✓	✓	
Laying on of hands		✓	✓	✓		✓	✓	
Gift of the Holy Spirit			✓			✓	✓	
Baptism complete	✓	✓		✓				
Baptism incomplete			✓			✓	✓	
Remembrance of Baptism				✓				
Renewal of baptismal covenant							✓	
Renewal of baptismal vow						✓		
Conversion experience						✓		
Admission to Holy Communion as part of rite			✓			✓	✓	
Acceptance of church discipline		✓					✓	
New privileges in church membership			✓			✓	✓	
New responsibilities in church membership							✓	
Promise to live a holy life						✓	✓	
Promise loyalty to denomination or local church							✓	
Memory verses to live by						✓		
Lifelong catechumenate	✓	✓		✓				
Other:								

Comparisons

Imagine a lake fed by six streams. You can follow each of the streams clearly until they all mix together in the lake. The lake water is muddy and possibly polluted. How can we clear it up?

This simple allegory suggests the situation in Lutheran confirmation today. Six by no means straight flowing streams of confirmation traditions in both theology and practice have in general created the North American confirmation lake. And we haven't begun to examine peculiar regional influences that developed in so many sections of the United States and Canada. It's probably better that we don't. It's hard enough now to see the bottom of the lake, if indeed we do see it at all.

For convenience sake let's try to reduce our discussion of the six types of Lutheran confirmation to a simplified chart which appears on page 72.

Now look at the elements of confirmation that have come through the six major emphases. Where does your congregation, your synod, district, or conference fit in?

You may be interested in knowing the position of each of the three major Lutheran churches today. We can find out with some degree of accuracy by asking the pastors.

The 1960 survey made of 653 Lutheran pastors (206 TALC; 212 TLC—MS; 235 LCA) highlighted present practices and concepts of confirmation. This was a representative sample chosen at random from among all the pastors in these three churches. A sample like this gives us a general picture of the situation today even though not every pastor surveyed answered all the parts of each question. Among the questions asked about the rite of confirmation were: (1) Which procedures of those listed do you now use? (2) Which are the valid statements about the role of the confirmand? (3) Which are the valid statements about the role of the congregation? The replies deserve study.

The percentages shown on pages 74-75 represent those pastors who checked each of these items listed in the questionnaire.

Why not check those items that are a part of your current local practices? Use the blank lines to jot down items not mentioned. Here then is your congregation. But where do you go from here?

At this point we need to search for answers to these basic questions we have been raising about Baptism and Holy Communion and the church. What do we as Lutherans really believe about the Word of God. How do we conceive church membership?

Representative Survey Questions

1

Which procedures are now used in the rite of confirmation in your church?

	TALC	TLC—MS	LCA
Private examination prior to the rite	70%	40%	67%
Public examination prior to the rite	50	66	24
Public examination during the rite	3	10	2
Announcement by pastor that catechumens have been instructed and approved	63	33	67
Announcement by pastor of names of persons to be confirmed	78	57	82
Approach of catechumens to the altar	86	90	83
Catechumens' renunciation of the Devil	87	68	68
Confession of faith by the class as a body	72	98	82
Confession of faith individually	22	6	10
Recitation of vows by catechumens	55	73	62
Catechumens kneel for prayer of blessing	91	94	88
Laying on of hands	88	87	88
Intercessory prayer by the congregation	68	93	67
Authorization given by pastor to participate in the Lord's Supper	74	76	74
Handclasp or handshake used	66	88	56
Recitation by pastor of special verse of Scripture	36	92	27
Administration of the Lord's Supper to confirmands	47	58	50
Other	11	5	8

2

Which are the valid statements regarding the role of the confirmand in the rite of confirmation?

	TALC	TLC—MS	LCA
Renewing his baptismal covenant	60%	71%	86%
Recognizing his responsibilities as a Christian	87	79	85
Renouncing the Devil	74	59	51
Identifying with the mature congregation	67	59	69
Confessing his faith publicly	90	89	88
Becoming a member of the congregation	24	24	29
Promising a lifelong allegiance to Christ	76	74	74
Assuming the obligations of church membership	60	43	74
Demonstrating his understanding and knowledge of the church and its teachings	67	7	58
Other	3	8	4

3

Which are the valid statements regarding the role of the congregation in the rite of confirmation?

	TALC	TLC—MS	LCA
Offering intercessory prayer for the confirmands	96%	93%	91%
Making a pledge to nourish confirmands in their growth in faith	86	79	79
Accepting confirmands into its fellowship	63	40	62
Recognizing confirmands as having achieved full membership in the church	45	38	54
Acknowledging that confirmands have completed a period of study	55	60	54
Acknowledging the readiness of confirmands to accept some responsibilities in the congregation	77	63	79
Other	4	7	1

5

Word and Sacraments

In the sidewalk shops of Greenwich Village you can buy any kind of slogan button to suit your fancy. Pin one on your coat and tell the world how you feel. Some of the buttons offer cynical commentaries on today's problems: "Make love, not war." Some feature whimsy: "Snoopy for President," "Chicken Little was right!" Others offer caustic criticism: "Custer died for our sins." Still others add a fillip to current clichés: "God is alive—He just can't find a parking space." This last particular slogan is hard to ignore. Truth may lurk behind the wisecrack.

Is it possible that our affluent/poverty-stricken society has so clogged the parking spots that God is excluded? Sometimes you get the impression that God would not be admitted to some of our congregations unless he subscribed to all the bylaws of their constitutions. Can it be that we often so silverplate our liturgies, our rites, even our statistical reporting procedures that we are (with all good intentions, of course) working counter to his will? These are sobering thoughts. Glib, top-of-the-head answers won't do. Popular opinion polls only cloud the issues.

Our somewhat truncated historical study of confirmation has shown us that over the years the rite has developed almost as many arms as an octopus. Which arms should we lop off? Or should we attempt surgically to graft some arms together? We might end up with an even weirder specimen of committee-created animal. By now it should be clear that confirmation is a creation of the church, designed for specific spiritual purposes in a specific historical setting. To inquire how confirmation could be effective today, and in what form, suggests that we had better ask, first of all, how God can use this man-made rite to bless his children. Will we allow him to find a parking place?

Since the nature and practice of confirmation have been so bound up with the various understandings of the sacraments the church has had over the years, here is where our inquiry should begin. Lutherans, as a rule, talk about the supremacy of the Word of God and the Sacraments. What exactly does this mean? As we explore the implications, we may get some clues to the role confirmation can play in the church's ministry to today's world.

THE WORD OF GOD

Central to all Lutheran theology is the doctrine of the Word of God. It is the magnifying glass under which all our doctrines are scrutinized. Luther under attack by both church authorities and state officials could only humbly defend himself by saying, "My conscience is captive to the Word of God." Here he stood; here the church that bears his name also stands. The way we organize our churches, develop codes of ethics, publish our Christian education courses, in short, everything we do depends on how we understand the word.

The term, of course, causes some difficulty because we in the Western world particularly have a mental image of words as rather useless things. "Talk is cheap," we say. Or "Put your money where your mouth is." Shakespeare has Hamlet express contempt for words. When the pompous Polonius asks the young Prince what he is reading, Hamlet replies, "Words, words, words." You can see the disdain in the children's jeering retort to those who have called them dirty names:

> Sticks and stones
> May break my bones,
> But words can never hurt me!

Words spoken, written, plastered on billboards, blared by TV and radio—articulate man is swamped with words. Small wonder they have little value.

The Living Word

The Hebrews, however ,thought of words quite differently. To them, a word had a reality, a life of its own. Thus when the aged, half-blind Isaac was tricked by his younger son Jacob into giving him the blessing rightfully belonging to his older son Esau, the old man could not take back his words. The blessing had to exist; it was created, it lived, it carried a legacy. All Isaac could do was to give Esau a second-class blessing, pale by comparison. A man's words were considered part of him. His whole personality was involved in what he spoke. That's why the commandment forbidding false witness was taken so literally and seriously. Lies not only harmed others, they twisted self.

Words, you see, for the Hebrews were more than conveyors of communication, they carried with them the impact of the person speaking. Therefore, when the Hebrews spoke of the Word of God, this meant more than God's orders for his people. He in this way was making himself known to them as a person. His word was active, powerful, decisive. From the first chapter of Genesis where the creation stories hinged on "And God said" to the prophets' thundering proclamations of "Hear the Word of the Lord," the Old Testament people thought of God's word dynamically confronting them, in his mighty acts, with himself.

This Hebrew concept of the living Word provided a natural avenue God chose to use to come directly to his people. He became man, Jesus Christ. Born to a human mother, Jesus grew to maturity in the world of men, living dramatically God's message of love for his people. John explained the miracle of the Incarnation simply: "In the beginning was the Word, and the Word was with God, and the Word was God. . . . And the Word became flesh and dwelt among us, . . ." (John 1:1,14).

All that God in Christ did for mankind through parables and miracles, through crucifixion and resurrection was designed to make his word effective, to link his people with himself. As Jesus expressed it, "If a man loves me, he will keep my word, and my Father will love him, and we will come to him and make our home with him" (John 14:23).

For Christians, then, the Word of God is seen, heard, and experienced fully in Jesus Christ. Put it another way: Jesus Christ *is* the Word of God, through whom God speaks and acts. Marshall McLuhan's catch phrase, "the medium is the message," is most appropriate in discussing the nature of Christ. In Christ we meet God himself, receive his gifts of love and forgiveness, find our true identity as members of his family and our true destiny to live in intimacy with him. This is the gospel, the good news the church proclaims.

On many occasions, Luther used terms such as the gospel, the Word of God, revelation (God's self-disclosure) interchangeably. He saw these verbal distinctions as facets of the same diamond dazzling men with its purity and value. The authority for all the church teaches and, as a matter of fact, for all that the church is comes from this dynamic way that God enters the world of men. "The Word of God is not based on and contained in the Christian faith," wrote Karl Barth, "but the Christian faith is based on and contained in the Word of God." This is the only sound foundation on which the house of Christian theology can be built . . . and endure.

We often refer to the Word and the Sacraments as the "means of grace," the way God shares his gifts with his people. The term "grace" is used to underscore God's compelling love for mankind that fosters his free-will giving. No strings are attached to God's grace. He asks only that his gifts be accepted. He is like the sower in Jesus' parable, scattering the seed on the ground in the springtime; men are the soils. They can prevent the seed from taking root or choke out the young plants of faith that start to grow, but they can't stop the seed from being sown. This God does because he loves. He is always offering his people forgiveness of sins, freedom from the tyranny of evil and the fear of death, the joyful capacity to live a love-filled life. His word is the way they come to know about these gifts and, in so doing, come to know him.

The Inspiring Word

But there is a further step that God takes. God the Holy Spirit comes to live with man, helping him to perceive truth, guiding his interpretation of the Word, strengthening him to accept God's gifts. Paul stresses the critical role of the Spirit in the Christian's life: ". . . No man can say 'Jesus is Lord' except by the Holy Spirit" (1 Corinthians 12:3).

The Holy Spirit, even faith itself, are also gifts of God enabling us to grasp God's saving Word and make it our own. Through the Spirit, God thus internalizes his Word in us, brings it to the very essence of our being. No matter how we may prize our intellectual capacities to launch rocketships for the exploration of outer space or to computerize income tax records, we are still dependent upon God. Only he can guide us in choosing the most important part of life, living with him as life's center. This he is willing to do by coming himself to dwell in our hearts, encouraging, inspiring, supporting us. Luther understood this fact. He echoed Paul; "For no one can understand God's Word save by the mediation of the Holy Spirit."

The Confronting Word

Now let's examine how we come in contact with the Word of God. The Word is always an "enfleshed Word," as it was in Jesus. Although other bearers of the Word cannot embody the Word as Jesus did, their conduct is important in witnessing to the Word's truth. Actually, any medium of witnessing is possible. We can hear the Word in sermons but also in the counsel of Christian friends. We can read the Word in the Bible but also in other books. We can be brought face-to-face with the Word in hymns, paintings, sculpture, poetry, by dramas, by films, by television programs. It all depends on how the Spirit helps us discern truth.

But one thing we must know: the Word of God is greater and more powerful than media limitations. It can survive human error. In one of the early English Bible translations, the "not" was omitted in the Sixth Commandment so that it read, "Thou shalt commit adultery." What a field day for biblical literalists who were reprobates on the side!

The Word does not depend on perfect people to be channels through which it operates. Even a renegade pastor, for instance, could minister to a bereaved family and the Word coming through him would still be effective. It may be that the church today should be developing new channels through which the Word can communicate with men. Our task as a mission-minded fellowship is always exciting. "God works in mysterious ways his wonders to perform" has perhaps been quoted too often as a way of avoiding wrestling with explanations, but it is still true.

A desperate young woman on the verge of suicide happened to turn on her car radio and caught the tail end of a religious broadcast. She heard the words, "God loves you." That was enough to save her life. An artist who confessed that he had no faith was given an assignment to paint a series of biblical portraits. He retired to an island hideaway to research his project by reading the Bible. Months later, he emerged with his finished artwork and another confession: slowly he found himself converted to Christianity. It was the church that sponsored that radio broadcast; it was the church that collected God-saturated writings of prophets and apostles and made them available in book form.

Luther was confident that the church came into being because of the Word of God and that it only fulfilled its mission as it truly became a Word-sharing fellowship. The church's function is to bring the gospel to people wherever they are. As the Spirit-filled community, the church seeks in whatever it does to introduce all peoples to the living Word, the living God who claims them as his own. That means that every church service, every course of study, every piece of promotional advertising should glow with God's warm presence.

The Word and the Church

The *Augsburg Confession* says you can describe the church by what it does. Article VII says that the church is "the congregation of believers among whom the gospel is rightly proclaimed and the sacraments are rightly administered in accordance with the gospel." The Word of God is the primary factor in every part of that crisp definition.

The Word calls people together as the church and empowers them to proclaim it in many effective ways. It is the same Word, though, whether it is heard through a sermon or the reading of the Scriptures, whether it is demonstrated in Christian acts of neighborly service, whether it is made explicit in the dramatic happenings of the sacraments.

The Word also provides the dynamic for congregational life. It offer a yeasty, lively, change-bringing, a "won't take 'no' for an answer" kind of impetus to the Christian sense of mission.

Whatever else confirmation may be, first and foremost it must be a clear channel for the Word of God. However we adapt and shape the catechetical-confirmation process to serve the needs of growing children in the household of faith, we must remember that they need to bask in 'the unconditional, consistent love of God to whom they belong. Somehow the process should help the catechumen bring into perspective his unique relationship with God through Jesus Christ. This involves his personal confrontation with the Word as it comes to him through the sacraments. It is at this point that Lutherans seem to have the most difficulty with confirmation.

THE SACRAMENTS

Bill Cosby in one of his comedy routines portrays Noah getting directions from God for building the Ark. God tells Noah how to build it from gopher wood, so many cubits in height and width. Cosby's Noah grins broadly and says, "Right." Then after a long pause, he asks, "But what's a cubit?" After we talk so glibly about the church as the custodian of the Word and the Sacraments, we too get puzzled when we stop and think: "But what is a sacrament?"

Definitions

You cannot find the word "sacrament" in the New Testament. Therefore, there are no clear-cut operational definitions. Actually, sacrament is from the Latin legal term *sacramentum*. This term usually designated the sum of money which the litigants in a lawsuit had to deposit as a pledge that they would tell the truth. Here we have the "visible pledge" that a promise will be kept. Translators of the Latin Bible used *sacramentum* to convey the idea of the Greek word *mysterion*. The Greeks expressed the process whereby the Word of God becomes active in the world of men as a *mysterion*, a mystery.

Something should be said for the value of the word mystery. In the biblical usage mystery is not a complex puzzle that is fully explained in the last chapter, as in a whodunit; it refers to God's revelation of himself. The more one is grasped by the mystery, the more mysterious it becomes. As Paul wrote to Timothy, "Great indeed, we confess, is the mystery of our religion; . . ." (1 Timothy 3:16).

The Greek Orthodox church still prefers *mysterion* to sacrament; and they also are less precise than Protestants and Roman Catholics in their definition. It is sufficient for them that God uses visible means to dramatize his gifts. However, they still are in accord with the Roman Catholic church in designating seven sacraments. At the other end of the scale are the Quakers who prefer to do without the outward physical elements and actions associated with sacraments. They maintain that these external procedures only get in the way of man's close association with God. Everything God gives sacramentally man needs to receive inwardly. There is no need for formal rites.

Lutherans, and other Protestants in general, have tried to be specific about the sacraments. Gustaf Aulen's definition of sacraments as "the self-impartation of divine love in the form of action" is helpful, provided you add the idea of using earthly elements. Certain clear-cut criteria need to be established to differentiate the sacraments from the Word of God. A sacrament is usually explained, therefore, as that act of the church commanded by Christ to convey the promises of God through the use of earthly elements. Only two acts meet these standards, Baptism and Holy Communion. We should note that Luther talked about confession and absolution as a third sacrament in the early days of his ministry. He later abandoned the idea because no earthly elements, such as water or bread and wine, were used. Further, forgiveness was implicit in both Baptism and the Lord's Supper.

Essentially, all Christians cherish these two sacraments, Baptism and Holy Communion as direct links with Christ—the one an act of initiation into his church, the other an experience of his sustaining presence. You would assume that these acts unite Christians in a common cause. Not so! Instead, the sacraments have been a source of contention and division. No need to recite here the long and dreary record of twisted theological writings carefully prepared to support this position or to attack that one. All the argumentative books and tracts laid end to end would probably provide a jet runway from coast to coast.

To the shame of the church over the years, violent suppression and even fearful atrocities were often unleashed in the name of the sacraments. No punishment was too extreme to enforce acceptance for a particular point of view. "If the Anabaptists want immersion baptism so much, let's drown them and see how they like it. They can get to glory a little quicker that way." Name calling, the least detrimental form of attack, became customary: "Anyone who drinks wine at Holy Communion instead of grape juice is a drunkard."

Controversy often degenerated into pettiness. Some German immigrants refused to have their children baptized by Lutheran pastors in the territory to which they came because they conducted the service in English! To misquote Abraham Lincoln: "The Lord must have loved thickheaded people; he sure made a lot of them."

What Do You Think?

Instead of getting tangled up in peripheral matters of methodology, let's get right to the heart of sacramental theology. After all, what does it matter how much water is used in Baptism or whether you have cross-impressed wafers or freshly baked bread at Communion? The basic point is that in the sacraments the Word of God come to people in a unique way. This is the same Word of God that is read in the Bible or heard through a sermon; this is the same God-present-in-his-Word confronting men. And the Word always offers God's forgiveness and his strengthening presence. All this he does from his own will. He doesn't demand that people be worthy; he only asks that they accept what he has to give.

Why must we insist on complicating God's simple gifts of himself? The old gag, "A camel is a horse built by a committee," is applicable. A whole zoo full of camels has been created in sacramental theology over the years. Let's get rid of them.

Turn to the commission's report and read the section on Baptism and Holy Communion (pp. 193-95). Then, on the lines below, express in your own words what these sacraments mean to you, what they mean to the life of your congregation. What should they mean in the lives of your confirmands?

_____

_____

_____

_____

_____

BAPTISM

If Lutherans have difficulty developing a solid theology of confirmation, they can only blame themselves. Usually it is because their doctrine of Baptism has become fuzzy. Confirmation has come to speak so loudly that what Baptism says can't be heard clearly. Trying to find out what some of the Lutheran theologians of the past several centuries really believed about Baptism is like trying to determine what the condition of an antique chair is like under several coats of modern paint. In most instances, they successfully built up layers of explanations that often obscured Luther's clear thinking.

"Baptism is a living, saving water," Luther wrote in *The Large Catechism*. "The power, effect, benefit, fruit, and purpose of Baptism is to save." To be saved, he continued, is "to be delivered from sin, death and the devil and to enter into the kingdom of Christ and live with him forever." Baptism is therefore both personal and social; through it God forgives me, makes me his child, and incorporates me into his kingdom, the fellowship of those who call Christ Lord.

The personal and social aspects of Baptism are held in delicate balance. Both aspects are essential. Neither can be neglected without destroying the other.

The Personal Side

Let's look at the personal side of Baptism. Some of the current criticisms of the contemporary church "zero in" on its complacent impersonalism. Justifiably so. Far too many visitors to church services have received cold-shoulder treatment. But impersonalism can be far more serious than the carping about the way we greet newcomers would indicate. One perceptive church councilman commented recently, "My congregation on Sunday morning reminds me of a lot of mechanical men all wound up to go through certain routines without warmth and without vitality." Sometimes congregations unwittingly let all their programs become mechanical and people are processed through the standardized procedures. The individual either fits into the acceptable pattern or he can go find some other congregational home.

One of each person's basic needs is to accept himself, to develop healthy self-respect. The slogan on a popular lapel button these days proclaims, "I am a human being; do not fold, spindle, or mutilate." You recognize that slogan as the language of the IBM card. It is a protest against society's growing more impersonal every day. People are beginning to resent being reduced to numbers in a file: social security numbers, military serial numbers, zip codes, area telephone codes, numbers piled on numbers until something snaps. And someone cries out, "Hey! I am a human being. 'I'm me! Don't bend me, twist me, shape me to suit your fancy."

The church must be on the side of the individual. This was the way Jesus dealt with people. He called them by name, Peter and Andrew and James and John. He asked them to serve him as themselves. They in turn baptized others in his name. So the church grew one by one. It's similar to cowboys rounding up the newly-born dogies on the springtime range. Each "little critter" is branded with the mark of his owners. So Baptism brands each person with the mark of God signifying that we belong to him.

Baptism does come to the person, calling him by name. He is now John Jones, Christian! He belongs to God and God to him.

Whatever race or nationality he is, whatever occupation he follows, whatever political party or baseball team he supports, he is called by God to live as a Christian. When he faces temptation, his strength comes from remembering who he is: a baptized son of God. In fact, Luther's prescription for times of troubles, moments of decision, all critical crossroads, was simply to say to ourselves triumphantly, "I am baptized!"

The Social Side

Here is where the church can make wise use of its pastoral and educational ministry in helping people be themselves. The catechetical-confirmation program should nourish in each child his particular gifts so that he can grow in his relationship with God to the fullness of his potential.

But the individual does not live in isolation. He is always in some form of community, in some kind of interrelationship with parents and relatives, friends and teachers and employers. The social side of life is not a kind of "plus factor" to facilitate personal development; it is absolutely essential to fostering individuality. As Paul Tillich pointed out, individualization and participation are two of the polarities of all of life.

The newly born comes squalling into this world asserting his own individuality. No one else has the same whorls on his fingertips or identically shaped ear lobes. Yet he is helpless apart from others who would care for him and surround him with some kind of family arrangement. Similarly, the newly baptized becomes a part of the family of the people of God. Still keeping his uniqueness as a person, the baptized individual belongs to the church.

Paul explains this social relationship of the church by using the human body as an analogy: "For just as the body is one and has many members, and all the members of the body, though many, are one body, so it is with Christ. For by one Spirit we were all baptized into one body—Jews or Greeks, slaves or free—and all were made to drink of one Spirit" (1 Corinthians 12:12-13).

For a child, being a member of the Christian church means very little to him. It is only as he matures and seeks his identity as a person that the groups to which he belongs become important. In the church he discovers that he is a son of God, a fellow member of God's family. Through the church's guidance in his growing years, he can come to the place where he feels that he genuinely is an integral part of the people of God.

As far as Luther was concerned, no man-made acts could take the place of Baptism which he called, "the sacrament by which we are first received into the Christian Church." This special personal relationship with Christ in the fellowship of fellow Christians was the greatest experience of life. In one of his open letters he wrote, "Dear friend, in your Baptism you entered into a fraternity with Christ, all the angels, saints and Christians on earth. Hold to this fraternity and live up to its demands and you have fraternities enough."

Baptism Complete

The Lutheran confessional statements and the New Testament agree that Baptism is a once-and-for-all-time event. Like human birth, Baptism is the doorway into new dimensions of relationship and experience. Further, like birth, Baptism is complete. A child is not more born when he is six-months old or on his tenth birthday; nor can he be more baptized. Baptism, therefore, can never be considered, as some do, a half-finished sacrament in search of completion.

When God gives the presence of himself, he gives all of himself; he doesn't pass out bits and pieces like chapters in a magazine serial. This means that the strengthening power of the Holy Spirit in its fullest intensity is given to each person. None is withheld until he reaches certain maturation levels or fulfills some ecclesiastical requirements. As the commission points out, "To assert or even to imply that the saving power of Baptism is in any way contingent on any subsequent event is to deny its status."

Confirmation can perform a real service in the life of the growing child if, among other things, it serves as a reminder of Baptism. Confirmation can stress the fact that by Baptism you are made a member of Christ's church, that God in his love has reached out and called the individual to live with him. Luther would be in hearty agreement with this point of view. "No greater jewel," he commented, "can adorn our body and soul than Baptism, for through it we obtain perfect holiness and salvation, which no other kind of life and no work on earth can acquire."

Some of the Lutheran forms of confirmation, you will remember, did emphasize the remembrance of Baptism. This is fine. Other forms went further and spoke of the confirmand's renewing his baptismal covenant. Here is where we can get into theological hot water.

A Covenant

It is proper to speak of Baptism as a covenant, for God indeed promises to accept the baptized person as his child and heir to all the benefits of the kingdom. However, we generally think of a covenant as a bargain or an agreement reached between two equal parties. Each promises to do something for the other; each expects certain promises in return. A peace treaty is a covenant between nations, a wage contract "package" is a covenant between management and labor. Even marriage is a covenant with mutual promises of "love, comfort, and honor." The old cliché, "Marriage is a fifty-fifty proposition," proves it. However, married people who attempt to live by the cliché are in for serious difficulties. Who draws the fifty-fifty line?

The New Testament notion of covenant is not a bilateral covenant at all. It isn't dependent on two parties agreeing to do something for each other. It is unilateral; it is onesided; it refers to God's free gifts of grace. These he gives without demanding that his people be worthy of receiving them. No man is in a position to strike a bargain with God; he can only accept God's gifts. What is more, God never breaks his covenant. Though a person may proclaim that "God is dead," that God has no claim on him, yet simply by his coming to his senses and repenting, God accepts him back. Wasn't this the thrust of Jesus's parable of the prodigal son? God's covenant, his promise, stands as a reality. Therefore, it cannot be broken nor does it need to be renewed. Anyone can deny his mother and his father. He can leave home and vow never to return. Yet, as long as he lives biologically, he is linked to that human family. Perhaps, all human parents might not be godlike in receiving a wayward child back unconditionally. Yet, nevertheless, he is undeniably their child, bone of their bone.

A Baptismal Way of Life

To have confirmands renew the baptismal covenant as a part of a confirmation rite is to lead them astray from their evangelical faith. They need to know of God's constancy, of his continuous willingness to forgive, of his permanent partnership. All they have to do with the Holy Spirit's help is to take him at his word and accept his gifts. Baptized children, who grow up in the household of faith, really have no conversion experiences as a pagan would who consciously leaves his old ways when he becomes a Christian.

There is no good point being served in letting children feel that they are outside the inner core of the church where the action is, and that only on the strength of their promises and vows can they become a full member of God's family. Besides, let's be honest. No one can keep a promise or make a vow for a lifetime. He needs to renew his promises and vows daily. This is true in marriage, in loyalties to employers, in patriotism. It is basically true in our relationship with God. Every day we need to remind ourselves who we are—God's people—and confess our willing acceptance of him as our God. Without this daily saying "I love you" to God, faith withers into a museum piece.

Confirmation, to be effective, should help the child recall what God's promises first given in Baptism mean to him both now in his adolescent years and through all the years to come. This implies a careful program of education.

Eugene Ormandy, conductor of the Philadelphia orchestra, participated recently in a radio program with youths who planned to devote their lives to music. He talked to these young people seriously about their need for lifelong study of music manuscripts. He went on to say that he has never taken a day off, that he always feels compelled to probe those familiar works by Brahms and Beethoven and Tchaikovsky he has conducted so frequently. "You always find something new;" said Ormandy, "you always discover some exciting ideas that you have overlooked before." If this is true in music, it is also true in our faith relationship with God.

Baptism marks the beginning of the Christian life. The church therefore has the responsibility to educate its children and youth so that at every stage of their maturation they understand what Baptism means to them and how they can make full use of its power. Confirmation can add nothing to Baptism; it can, however, help make Baptism important. At the same time, the church needs to minister to its adult members, reminding them of their Baptism and encouraging them to make their baptismal relationship with God a way of daily coping with the challenges of living. "In Baptism," Luther noted, "every Christian has enough to study and practice all his life."

HOLY COMMUNION

The second sacrament of the church, Holy Communion, is equally important with Baptism in the life of the Christian. If

89

Baptism initiates the person into the people of God, Communion sustains and strengthens him in that fellowship.

Analogies are imperfect mirrors of reality. Yet analogies can illuminate facets of truth. Compare these sacraments with some basic facts of life. Baptism is like birth, a once-and-for-all event, a transition from one form of existence to another. Communion, then, is like our daily meals; we need food to keep life going and growing. In the sacraments you can see the real, life-giving dimensions of the means of grace. Baptism and the Lord's Supper are just that—means of grace, ways God uses to reach his people in their needs. Just as he provides a visible, dynamic act of symbolic washing to tell us that we are born into his family, so he also comes in another visible, dynamic way to remind us of his covenant with us.

Here at the altar, as we eat a bit of bread and drink a cup of wine, we come face to face with the gospel. God loves us; he gave himself for us; he unites himself with us and with the company of our fellow believers. You can see why Luther persisted in referring to the Sacrament of Holy Communion as a brief summary of the gospel. It is. And where the gospel is preached, there the Word of God confronts us with all its life-giving power.

What happens in Holy Communion? The truth of the matter is that nothing happens here that doesn't happen whenever and wherever the Word of God comes to man. Through the bread and the wine, God comes to us with the "old, old story of Jesus and his love." Here he again offers us forgiveness of sins, life, and salvation.

A Reminder

The uniqueness of the Lord's Supper lies in its homely, tangible reminder of what happened to Christ a long time ago. It is definitely a memorial: "This do in remembrance of me," Jesus said. But it is more than a memory-jogger about historical fact. We are not spectators watching a drama being acted on a distant stage; we are participants in the drama itself.

The table in the Upper Room extends through barriers of time and space. Salvador Dali's painting of the Last Supper in the National Museum of Art in Washington offers a painter's feelings about this phenomenon. Gradually, as you stand in front of the canvas, you become aware that you are involved in the painting. The oval line which can be drawn through the bowed figures of the disciples extends logically out into the gallery to include you, the observer. In fact, the imaginary oval isn't a complete figure unless you are part of it as a member of the believing community.

The Real Presence

At the Lord's Table we, together with the believing community, take the bread; we receive the cup; we hear our commission to be disciples. Here Christ gives us the body broken on Calvary and the blood shed for our sins. And what is more important, in some marvelous way Christ comes to each of us as we eat the bread and drink the wine, telling us anew that he is willing to live our lives with us. His strength can bolster our flagging ability to resist temptation; his love can inspire our capacity to love.

Lutherans have explained this Communion-happening with the doctrine of the real presence: Christ is really there at the altar rail with each of us, but how? Who can say? It is a mystery. If our logically trained minds are troubled, perhaps it is wise to remind ourselves that God is God. Isaiah the prophet reported how God said: ". . . so are my ways higher than your ways, and my thoughts than your thoughts" (Isaiah 55:9). We really can't spell out how God performs his miracle of coming to us; we can only experience the joy of having him with us.

Joy is of the essence of Holy Communion. God is with us, a time of great rejoicing! This essential element of gladness protects the sacrament from becoming a morbid exercise in sin-cataloging. Instead it permeates the sacrament with a sense of balance between confession and absolution, between sorrow for sin and God's forgiveness. Here is where barriers between man and God as well as between man and his fellowmen are destroyed. All who commune are joined with Christ and through Christ with one another. This is a lot to be thankful for. Perhaps this is the reason one of the familiar terms in ecclesiastical parlance for Holy Communion is the Eucharist—the thanksgiving.

Determining Age for Participation

At what age then is a person capable of receiving the benefits of Holy Communion? When is he old enough to know what God is doing for him in this manner? These are proper questions for the church to decide.

Most of the churches of the Reformation tended to postpone first Communion until after instruction and confirmation. They took seriously Paul's one condition for participating in the sacrament of the altar: "Let a man examine himself, and so eat of the bread and drink of the cup" (1 Corinthians 11:28). The Reformers generally felt that the Orthodox practice of communing baptized infants and the Roman Catholic tradition of offering Communion to six- and seven-year-olds were too premature. Babies and young children are not capable of honest self-evaluation. How can they examine themselves, see their need for God's forgiving love and thus come to the Lord's Table properly prepared for his gifts?

With this kind of reaction, the age-level pendulum began swinging. Gradually, later and later ages for first Communion were recommended. The new emphasis upon education, so necessary for adequate self-examination in the Reformation, soon in the Age of Rationalism pushed the pendulum to the farthest reach of its arc. Facts began to overshadow feelings. There were those church leaders who equated the individual's capacity to participate intelligently in the sacrament with his intellectual ability to explain in theological detail the implications of what happened. Adult understandings in adult language and even adult attitudes were soon being demanded of children.

Like two horses pulling a wagon, the heavy pietistic emphasis on building a personal faith began running in tandem with the rationalistic notion of "trained brains." This pulled the church more and more in the direction of accentuating adult thought forms and verbalizations. The adult-standard syndrome is still very much a part of the mind-set of most Lutherans in North America today. Many of us sense this situation but we don't know why it developed—or what to do about it.

Developing Practices

Actually, the adult-standard syndrome became a part of the way Communion was understood in much the same manner that certain Communion practices developed. Some of these practices reflected peculiar theological emphases. For example, consider the procedure of putting the bread into the mouths of the communicants instead of placing it in their hands. This practice actually grew up in a medieval fear climate.

The Roman Catholic church's teaching at that time gave the common people, who were already superstition-ridden, the firm belief that the bread had magically become the body of Christ.

Some persons would only pretend to eat the bread, and tried to carry it away with them. They felt if they could take it home, they could set up their own altars or use it as a talisman to ward off evil. Church authorities wanted none of these shenanigans. Priests were instructed to make sure that each communicant ate the bread before he left the Communion table.

Then too, there was a matter of propriety. Since the bread was really Christ in their thinking, it wouldn't do to have people fumbling around with nervous hands; to drop Christ on the floor would show extreme disrespect. Putting bread directly into the communicant's mouths seemed to the medieval church to eliminate a lot of headaches.

Some practices, on the other hand, grew out of economic conditions. For instance, some congregations offered the bread and the wine together to the communicant by "intinction." This means dipping the bread in the wine before putting it in the believer's mouth. The Orthodox church follows this practice to this day. A small silver spoon is used for transmission.

One reason the intinction method achieved prominence was not due to any weighty theological arguments at all. It was simply because in certain areas of the church, wine was scarce. In England, for a time, mead made of honey and wheat, the common drink of the people, took the place of wine. But this practical solution of the wine-shortage problem didn't last long. There was too much popular sentiment in favor of duplicating the details of the celebration in the Upper Room. In other parts of Europe, rather than substitute some other common table beverage, some congregations used intinction to conserve their meager wine supplies and still retain a link with early church practices.

Other practices have developed because of special emphases. Lutherans had their Pietists; Americans had their Puritans. Put those two influences together and you understand why a wave of anti-alcohol sentiment challenged the use of wine in North America. This was particularly true with the rise of the Prohibition Movement in the United States in the late nineteenth century. Many congregations, feeling sinful in offering wine to their members, switched to grape juice. At church conventions, bitter battles often raged between the "wine bibbers" on one side and the "grape juicers" on the other.

Imagine the Sacrament of Communion, of brotherhood in the name of Christ, being the cause of dissention! But it does happen. Especially when secondary matters usurp the place of what is important. In any case, few congregations today mix their Communion wine with water in the proportions common in Jesus' time. The Palestinian table wine of the first century usually consisted of two parts wine to three parts water.

Love for People

Love for people always needs to temper institutional practices. Most sensitive congregations who still regularly offer wine make provisions for special human needs. For instance, Alcoholics Anonymous stresses the fact that a former alcoholic cannot take even a small amount of alcohol in any form. His pastor, therefore, may serve him grape juice to help him in his rehabilitation. Perhaps no one else at the Communion table is aware of this personal ministry. Is his communion with Christ in this situation any less effective than theirs?

How should our loving concern for the needs of our baptized children affect our current practices? Admission to Communion should be based on criteria that combine some capability in honest self-examination and some understanding of what the sacrament means. Look at the list of prerequisites for receiving the Lord's Supper which the confirmation commission drew up in their report (p. 194).

The prerequisites are sound theologically. But at what age can a person meet these minimum standards? When is the individual capable of saying, "I'm sorry," and meaning it? When does he know that God loves him and forgives him and that Jesus Christ is his friend and savior? We'll come back to these questions again in Chapter 7. But right now, think about them. Also go to the other end of the scale. When does an adult ever know all the answers? Luther felt that each Communion offered to a congregation was a unique event for which every Christian needed special preparation regardless of his age.

Should Children Receive Communion?

There is a growing movement in the Lutheran churches today to admit children to Communion at an earlier age than they are now permitted to do so. They feel strongly that the church has withheld the Sacrament of the Altar from children without real theological justification. By making confirmation itself a prerequisite to Holy Communion, many congregations are implying

94

and even boldly stating that we merit admission to the Lord's Table on the basis of our maturational and academic achievements. This in itself is a distortion of the sacrament.

The New Testament is quite clear that Jesus instituted the sacrament for his own, and the early church administered it to the believer freely. Every Christian young and old must cope with daily problems and needs the strengthening of God's presence in his life. Not that he only receives this by eating the bread and drinking the wine at the Lord's Table, but the dramatic, visible retelling of the Gospel story there at the Communion reinforces all that he has heard and read elsewhere.

Growing with the Sacrament

When children are capable of expressing what Christmas and Easter mean according to the basic teachings of the church, they are capable of understanding something of the meaning of the power of the sacrament in their lives. To continue with holiday references, sometimes children can highlight the truths of these holy days more precisely and intelligently than can many adults. With their inbred sense of wonder and joy, they capture the essential thrill of God's gift to mankind. Suppose they do use childish words. The number of syllables in theological terminology is certainly no index of sincere faith.

The basic question to be answered is this: Why should children who are genuinely members of Christ's church by Baptism be prevented from sharing in Christ's heavenly meal? If the church is serious in its desire to educate its people, then, it will guide its children to understand and participate in the sacrament according to their capacities. In addition, this will help them feel more a part of the church to which they belong through Baptism. But the educational process won't stop there. As the children become youths and then adults, the church continually will guide them in probing even deeper implications of the sacrament for their new life involvements. This makes sense.

Shaping Attitudes

It is an educational truism that while we are able to shape many human attitudes through classroom processes, a number of basic attitudes are relatively unaffected. Think of racial prejudices, political loyalties, recreational values, ethical standards. In these areas, most of us tend to reflect the attitudes of our parents or other adults for whom we have a deep respect. The most meaningful attitudinal education in preparing children for receiving the Lord's Supper may very well be allowing them to participate in the sacrament in the company of their families. If children lack supportive parents, other significant adults in their lives could serve as their church families. At the same time that children are exploring their intellectual understanding of the sacramental mystery in class on their own level, they can also be learning by doing.

Note how secular education uses a similar method to develop attitudes. The Civil War in the United States was a tragic testing of a young nation's ability to solve its critical problems. Early in their school careers, children hear about Grant and Lee, learn names like Shiloh, Antietam and Appomattox. They come in contact with Lincoln's stirring words at the dedication of a national cemetery in Gettysburg: "We cannot consecrate—we cannot hallow this ground. The brave men, living and dead, who struggled here, have consecrated it, far above our power to add or detract." Perhaps children do not comprehend all that Lincoln was saying, but they can develop a healthy respect for brave men who gave their lives for their country. As they grow older and read Lincoln's Gettysburg Address again and again, fresh nuances will become evident. The names of leaders, the battles, all become part of the larger picture of a nation's struggle to preserve its valued integrity.

Perhaps the day will come when "that we here highly resolve that these dead shall not have died in vain," for instance, becomes a real part of their attitudes toward patriotism and citizenship. Society establishes a legal voting age. Society also insists that children be educated as citizens and treated as citizens through their impressionable years in school. They then can pass through the arbitrary qualifying age of twenty-one without missing a single stride.

One thing is clear. If the church believes strongly that the Word of God and the Sacraments are God's actions on behalf of and among his people, then there is only one course of action. The church must do all it can to provide open channels for God's love to operate. If we are intensely interested in helping children and youth develop meaningful experiences in their church life, we cannot treat them as second-class citizens of the kingdom of God. Otherwise we are defeating our healthy purposes.

There is no particular value to be gained by our insisting that children must follow the patterns we did at their age. Besides, our memories are pretty bad. You know that the older a man gets, the longer becomes the distance he walked to school as a boy. Our twin concerns must be: to honor God's word and to guide children's reception of that Word so that they walk daily with Christ as dedicated members of his church. If this sounds idealistic, it is. It can also be practical. How else can we make the ministry of our congregations attractive to young people? As often happens, a complex problem may have a simple solution.

6

The Church and its Mission

> *Built on a rock the church doth stand,*
> *Even when steeples are falling; . . .*

So begins Nicolai Grundtvig's magnificent hymn about the church. Grundtvig, the "Happy Dane," was confident that God's church was something more than the buildings in which solemn assemblies were gathered. The church was people, the people of God. His third stanza sings:

> *We are God's house of living stones,*
> *Built for his own habitation; . . .*
>
> (SBH 151)

Church buildings like people come in all shapes and sizes. As Parisian fashions come and go so do architectural styles. Without driving too far from our homes, we can usually take a Cook's tour of local churches and find everything from Gothic cathedrals and Colonial chapels to buildings that look remarkably like factories or supermarkets or drive-in banks. Yet each of these edifices houses a cell-group of the people of God. God only rents the buildings for their use.

House of the Lord

If you trace our word "church" back through Middle English and Anglo-Saxon usage, you discover that it means "the house of the Lord." Wherever God is with his people there is the church. There are New Testament references to churches in private

98

houses. In addition, early Christians often met out in the open in a field, beside a lake, any place they could conveniently gather. In times of persecution they went to caves and even to burial places like the Roman catacombs for protection. They had no steeples or bells or stained glass windows; they had only the joyous good news of the gospel and the sacraments to share with each other. For a long time they lacked even written New Testament Scriptures. But those first Christians proclaimed the Word of God as it was passed on to them and ministered to each other as well as to their communities.

Take away bricks and steel, organs and altar hangings and you still have the church—if you have people bound to each other in a common faith in God. As the *Augsburg Confession* makes clear, the church is essentially the congregation of saints who rightly preach the gospel and administer the sacraments. Anything else you care to add to your definition of the church is valid only if it is built on this foundation.

The People of God

As you read the section of the commission's report dealing with the church (pp. 195-98), you have the feeling that you are stripping away the sometimes gaudy trappings that often obscured the real nature of the church. You are getting down to its core. To use the New Testament word, the church is the *ecclesia*, "those called out." God calls people together to form his community.

To label God's followers "saints" is not to assume that they have achieved any sort of perfection. A saint is one who is Spirit-saturated, God oriented. As William Lazareth pungently puts it, "A saint is a sinner who knows he is a sinner." The saintly person, therefore, is conscious of his sinfulness, his need of God. God the Holy Spirit, empowering the community of his people, also guides and strengthens each one of them.

This understanding of the church should lie behind our confession of faith in church in the words of the Nicene Creed: "I believe one Holy catholic and Apostolic Church." Here are four identifiable marks, four characteristics that deserve close scrutiny.

THE CHURCH IS ONE

The oneness of the church has long seemed more myth than reality. It has taken the harsh realities of the atomic age to crack denominational complacency.

There is an old story that a newspaperman who died and went to heaven was being shown around the premises by Peter. They walked through the realms of bliss noting how happy people were in this and that activity. Finally they came to a walled section that was set apart. From behind the walls the newsman could hear other happy voices. "How come you have some people cut off from the others?" he demanded.

"Shhh," said Peter, "Those are the Lutherans; they think they are the only ones here."

Moving Ahead

The aggressive and rigorous Vatican Council II demonstrated that monolithic patterns could be broken. Pope John XXIII wanted the Roman Catholic church to embrace the twentieth century. Many of Luther's suggestions for purifying the church are now being adopted. In fact, there is even a movement afoot to have the ban of excommunication against Luther removed. If the United States Senate could finally restore the citizenship of Confederate General Robert E. Lee a hundred years after the Civil War, anything is possible.

Protestants are working closer together than ever before exploring ways of combining efforts in missions and in social welfare. It is an exciting time to be a Christian. Bitter attacks on the institutional church, intellectual assaults on its teachings have not destroyed the church. The church has had to reevaluate its message.

In the face of critical social issues, there is no longer any leisure to have fun and games behind a facade of respectability. Only concerted resources are strong enough to combat white racism, to destroy poverty, to inspire responsible citizenship.

The whole "death of God" movement has had several salutary effects. It has made us probe the essence of our faith and struggle to find adequate contemporary language to express its truths. Then, too, it has made talking about God and his relations with men socially acceptable. No longer are people confining their "God talk" to church environments. You can overhear them discussing him at patio parties and at coffee breaks. God uses crises to help his people see the church in proper perspective.

What Can We Do?

Time magazine characterized a prominent church leader as a good shepherd; he knew when to lead the sheep and when to kick them in the rump. Maybe that's the way God deals with us. One thing is certain, fresh air is surging through the musty vaults. God's people now are no longer content to play footsie with denominational niceties. They are determined to make the church effective. They are asking not what they can do for the church but what they can do with it in serving the needs of people.

Of course, the church is to be used. It is the functional presence of Christ in his world. In his name we are called to be his body, to carry out his ministry. This is where the sense of oneness lies. This doesn't mean that we have to act alike, dress alike, think alike or even conduct all worship services the same way. This does mean that we measure our beliefs and our subsequent actions by Jesus Christ. So the writer of the letter to the Ephesians rhapsodizes:

> There is one body and one Spirit, just as you were called to the one hope that belongs to your call, one Lord, one faith, one baptism, one God and Father of us all, who is above all and through all and in all.
>
> (Ephesians 4:4-6)

Tensions

The concept of the church's oneness leaves us with some distinct tensions. On the one hand, we have no right to promote sectarian exclusiveness that haughtily judges other Christians and finds them inferior. On the other hand, we likewise have no right to compromise the gospel to please everyone whether we use democratic voting or by any other means. True ecumenicity is ont built on establishing some kind of a least common denominator by which you can add all fractional Christian groups together. Ecumenical power comes from common acceptance of our loyalty to Christ and a healthy respect for differences of opinion.

This leads to the second tension that exists: preserving a sense of community in the faith and at the same time allowing for individuality. We must allow people to be themselves. No, even more than that, we must allow people to become the kinds of persons they are capable of becoming. Paul was convinced that God through his grace assigned each person a unique role: "For as in one body we have many members, and all the members do not have the same function, so we, though many, are one body in Christ, and individually members one of another" (Romans

12:4-5). This suggests important implications for the church's catechetical-confirmation process. Our educational task is shaped by our responsibility to our young people to help them accept the one central Christian faith in terms of their own growing personalities. There experiences within the schools of the church should guide them in focusing more on what common beliefs unify Christians rather than on what issues divide them. It is easy to think of a catechetical course or a rite of confirmation as some gigantic full-color press, printing posters of ideal Christians that all look alike. It is far harder to help confirmands make their own unique God-giving contributions to the community of the saints on the basis of a common faith.

THE CHURCH IS HOLY

Of all the adjectives the average person might select to describe the church in a brainstorming session, holy would probably be far down the list, if indeed it made the list at all. In fact, some of the chief gripes leveled against the church have been related to its lack of holiness. Witness the well-worn limerick:

> God's plan made a hopeful beginning,
> But man spoiled his chances by sinning.
> We trust that the story
> Will end in God's glory,
> But, at present, the other side's winning.

To say that the church is holy is to remind ourselves that it was fashioned by God, that he commissioned it for mission. Luther commented, "Where there is God's Word, there is God's people, and where there is God's people, there is God's word."

Being Whole

It is interesting that the word "holy" and the word "whole" come from the same root. God's church is his way of bringing together his living message and those who are to be living responders to that message. Holiness is a mark of his action, not ours. His daily cleansing, through the miracle of forgiveness, maintains that wholeness. The holy works that a Christian performs, therefore, are really the manifestation of his well-integrated and dedicated personality interacting with others. In the power of the indwelling Spirit, the church is constantly in a state of renewal. Its holiness is its being set aside for his purposes—to make all men whole.

A youngster in an eighth-grade catechetical class once described the church as "the place where we get our spiritual batteries recharged." That's a pretty good understanding of the church's function. Here, indeed, God's people are "recharged" regularly for their task of doing holy works. Here, they come with regrets and failures to be renewed for Christian living.

A child of ten knows the needs of having his motivations straightened out as much as an adult of forty. Admittedly, he sees his environmental involvements differently. But he similarly needs the loving support of the Christian community to grapple with life.

THE CHURCH IS CATHOLIC

The third mark of the church, its catholicity, is hard to explain without getting tied up in denominational knots. Because of its obvious association with the Roman Catholic church, the word "catholic" has been discredited among Lutherans. Usually, the adjective, Christian, is substituted. But this misses the point! By playing semantic games, a word that describes the church with rich meaning is foolishly rejected.

Target Audience

When you say the church is catholic, you are not talking about any kind of man-built institution at all. Catholicity or—to use the best synonym—universality describes Christianity's appeal. Madison Avenue admen harp on the necessity of determining the "target audience" when they mount a new advertising campaign. It makes a big difference whether you are trying to reach teen-aged misses or middle-aged matrons with "new, improved Angel-skin." Manufacturers make expensive decisions (depending on the age group) about which TV shows should plug the products, which magazines should carry the double-spread, four-color ads.

Right in the Nicene Creed is a precise statement about the church's target audience. The church is catholic; it is for everyone. There is no distinction about race, sex, nationality, or age.

Both Specific and General

The church has sometimes tried to accommodate its message to all men and then succeeded in losing its identity. Then it is hard for people to understand and accept the church's mission; they have a difficult time identifying with a generality. We learn by moving from the specific to the general. The concept of mud doesn't mean anything until we have squished mud, preferably homemade, in our own fingers and felt its summertime warmth oozing between our bare toes. Then we can go on to talk about the mud along the Nile or the Mississippi and have mental images that are realistic. Certainly, our understanding of the church comes through our experiencing congregational life in old St. Matthew's on the corner. Here we learn to confess a particular faith. Here we understand that we belong to the people of God, that our congregation is related to other congregations in the area and in the country and in the world.

The ultimate learning does not stop at the denominational level, although this has happened where confirmation rites ask the confirmand to vow loyalty to the Lutheran church. The Creed expands our mental horizons and admits no human-decided cut-off points. The church is for all people. This is its catholicity. Though some reject the church's claim upon their lives completely, though others may accept substitute religions or philosophies in its place, though others may not have even heard of the church of Jesus Christ, still the church exists to minister to them as well as to its dedicated members.

An artist brought in a well-worked-out sketch for an illustration he had been assigned to do for a book on the church. The drawing was a mass of people of all descriptions. If you looked closely you could distinguish workmen and professional people, factory workers and office workers, the young and the aged, men and women. There were obviously blacks and whites, Orientals, and Latin American types in the mixture. As you stood back from the drawing and looked at the overall form instead of the details, you could see that this mass of humanity was held together in the vague outline of a church building. Intuitively the artist caught the essence of the church's catholicity: the people of God, diverse individuals linked to a oneness in Christ through their common acceptance of him as their Lord.

THE CHURCH IS APOSTOLIC

History is very much a part of the church and the church is a part of history. Though the physical aspects of the church change, there is a spiritual continuity that links the disciples of

Christ with our present Christian communities. Each of us is incorporated into this century-spanning fellowship. Here is how the author of Ephesians describes this exciting phenomenon:

> So then you are no longer strangers and sojourners, but you are fellow citizens with the saints and members of the household of God, built upon the foundation of the apostles and prophets, Christ Jesus himself being the chief cornerstone, in whom the whole structure is joined together and grows into a holy temple in the Lord; in whom you also are built into it for a dwelling place of God in the Spirit.   (Ephesians 2:19-22)

Every now and then you hear someone insisting that the only way the church can be effective in our century is by recapturing the sincere simplicity of the early church. Some Christian sects have followed this idea even to the point of going about in flowing robes and sandals. But the apostolic age cannot be relived. Only its consecrated influence can be part of our church life. This is what apostolic means anyway—that the witness of the apostles to the living God in Christ is our witness, that their sense of mission in carrying the gospel to "the uttermost parts of the world" inspires our sensitivity to the church's most important and most critical task.

Like an electrical impulse surging along from cable to cable, the aspostolic firsthand encounter with Jesus Christ has been transmitted through Word and Sacrament from church fellowship to church fellowship to us. In each generation there is always danger that the cable may be cut. The church has weathered many storms. Neither persecution nor indifference has successfully stopped the message of Jesus Christ.

Translations

True to its apostolic impulse, the church seeks to proclaim the gospel to people everywhere. But what do you do when those to whom you want to tell the good news do not speak the same language you do.

Language barriers are overcome with translations. Frank Lauback and his literacy campaign in Africa with its slogan, "Each one teach one," indicates how the church has often faced almost insurmountable tasks. If you find a people without a written language, you must first invent such a language, then teach them to read and write it. Then you can translate the Bible so that they can read the Word of God for themselves. But one translation is never enough.

As civilization moves forward, language itself changes. Old words change their meanings; new words are formulated. "The finest words in the world are only vain sounds," commented Anatole France, "if you cannot comprehend them." So the apostolic witness is constantly being poured into "new wine skins," new translations. The faith must be communicated in terms people understand if they are to accept it.

Relive Christ's Life

The apostles testified to the mortal life and death and the resurrected life of Jesus Christ. In his name they formed the church. As the historian-philosopher Christopher Dawson points out, Christianity—as the church—lives again the life of Christ.

In the church's story, the life of Christ has often been reflected. Dawson writes, "The Church has its period of obscurity and growth and its period of manifestation, and this is followed by the catastrophe of the cross and the new birth that springs from failure."

So the four marks of the church—one, holy, catholic, apostolic —become directional signals for action as well as measuring rods for evaluation. In short, the basic responsibility of the church is to *be* the Christian community in Lexington and Vancouver, in Washington and Ottawa, wherever God's people are gathered.

THE MISSION OF THE CHURCH

During a harsh midwinter gale, a Greek freighter piled up on rocks off the coast of Newfoundland. Even while rescue vessels were moving through the heavy seas to pick up survivors, human scavengers came out from shore to pillage the wrecked vessel. By the time the rescuers had finished their task, the Greek ship was only a floating hulk, stripped of everything anyone could pick up or pry loose. Even the ship's wheel was taken.

Collectors

Do you wonder what the person who took the wheel will do with it? Will he stand it by the fireplace in his living room or erect it in his backyard with pots of chrysanthemums hanging from its spokes? Who knows? People are funny that way. They collect many functional things and prize them as dust collectors.

The church has had its share of collectors. There was a time when churches were relic conscious. If you could only have on your altar some memento from a saint or something directly related to Christ or his disciples, then your congregation would be very popular. People would come from miles around to worship there. One church claimed to own a hair from Peter's beard, another a tear from the eye of the Virgin Mary. Luther cracked once that if all the pieces of wood claimed to be portions of Christ's cross were to be brought together in one place, there would be enough wood to build the ark.

The trouble with relic collections was that churches began to resemble museums. The emphasis was on bringing both things and people out of the world. The church's task is just the opposite: to send things and people into the world.

Functional Christians

Jesus told us that we are to function as "salt," as "light," as "leaven"; we are to "go the second mile." Add up these and other colorful expressions he used to describe what he expected of those who would follow him. The end product is completely functional: committed Christians who are prepared to live their faith in all the communities of which they are a part. So Jesus greeted his disciples in the Upper Room following the thrill of the resurrection: "Peace be with you. As the Father has sent me, even so I send you" (John 20:21). How did this work out?

Within a few short years, the disciples were doing such an effective job of witnessing to the gospel that they had run afoul of the local authorities. Peter and some of the other apostles were hauled before the Sanhedrin, beaten, and charged to cease their public proclamations. Luke sums up the disciples' reactions, "And every day in the temple and at home they did not cease teaching and preaching Jesus as the Christ" (Acts 5:42).

Inreach and Outreach

It is true as Paul Tillich says that the church is the "medium through which the Spiritual substance of our lives is preserved, protected and reborn." This is the church's inreach, its sustaining ministry to its members. So the church supplies rich resources in worship and fellowship and education; it cares for its own.

107

But the church cannot stop there. It also has an outreach, an obligation to move out into society, to be the redeeming fellowship in the slums and in the resort areas, in the picket lines and in the arbitration chambers, wherever people are in need. This was Luther's concept of a Christian: "A Christian lives not in himself but in Christ and in his neighbor. Otherwise he is not a Christian. He lives in Christ through faith, in his neighbor through love." That's a good motto to hang by your front door.

The church then always stands in mission. It should be ready to put its resources and its potential in the struggle for justice for all men whether they are Christians or not. Not long before his tragic assassination, Martin Luther King, Jr. pointed out that the real conflict in the United States was not between white and black but between injustice and justice. And when we achieve justice, he added, all men—black and white, Mexican, Indian, Oriental—profit. A sense of mission in the church without a corresponding sense of justice is an anachronism. Mission then becomes a hollow word without much substance.

Do you agree? If you do, then your realize the responsibility of adults in your congregation to set examples for youth. Through church school classes young people are being taught that the joyous, compulsive sense of mission is what gives the church its significance. If they fail to find this sense of mission reflected in adult members' actions in serving the needs of the community, one more credibility gap is formed. When the time comes for them to identify with the adult congregation, they may ask an embarrassing "Why?"

During World War II, there were very few Danish Jews sent off to the Nazi concentration camp gas chambers. When Hitler ordered all Danish Jews to wear yellow armbands, Danish Christians led by their king also donned the yellow armbands. The conquerors were then faced with the proposition of deporting an entire country.

Mission can be dangerous. But then fighting for justice and truth and rightness is always dangerous. The cross is a grim reminder. Yet the open doorway of a tomb in Joseph of Arimathea's garden is also part of the picture.

The church's mission is never limited to sending missionaries to some faraway places or, even more narrowly, to establishing new congregations in the suburban sprawl around metropolitan centers. Mission goes beyond the statistics of membership rolls to suggest a way of life. And the child as a baptized member of the church shares in this mission as much as do the adult members of his congregation. But what can an ordinary child do for Christ? We could fill the rest of this book with examples of what children have done. "God does not so much need extraordinary people," wrote William Barclay, "as he needs ordinary people whom he can fill with his power so that they can do extraordinary things."

Priesthood of Believers

Out of this idea of every Christian's participating in the church's mission comes Luther's emphasis on the "priesthood of all believers." While the organized church has an ordained clergy called to preach, administer the sacraments, and minister to people, there is by no means a gradation of holy orders involved. A clergyman by his ordination is not set higher in God's estimation than a lay member of his congregation. Ordination only concerns a specific responsibility in a specific situation. All Christians share the invitation to proclaim the gospel, all are called by God to minister to their neighbors.

Paul wrote to the Galatian congregations quite forcefully stressing the freedom of the Christian no longer obligated to live under the terror of the law. In Christ, the believer is freed through the gospel, forgiven of sin, set apart to walk with the Spirit. But in this freedom, the gospel compels him voluntarily to become a servant to his fellowman, "For the whole law is fulfilled in one word, 'You shall love your neighbor as yourself' " (Galatians 5:14). This has many practical implications. Later on in the same letter Paul wrote, "Bear one another's burdens and so fulfill the law of Christ" (Galatians 6:2).

The promotional publicity of Boy's Town, Nebraska, usually features a larger boy carrying a smaller one on his back, with the caption, "He is not heavy. He's my brother." This is the priesthood of all believers in operation. Children and youth can understand that kind of language. Would that adults were equally perceptive. Where they are not, Harold Letts points out, they are in trouble. Where a congregation thinks only in terms of its worship and meeting the spiritual cares of its own members, it is losing its sense of mission. As Letts writes, "It is frequently content to let its pastor carry out his special functions while the membership of the congregation thinks of itself not as sharing that ministry but rather as being the object of that ministry. This kind of church, in effect, has demitted its ministry." This is a serious charge. But then Jesus never invited us to become members of some kind of spiritual country club where we can retreat from life. He, quite the contrary, sent us out to be his ambassadors to life.

So the church comes into the world as Christ's body made up of his people. Empowered by the Holy Spirit, the church serves as hands and feet and compassionate heart of Christ, reaching out to people in their needs.

The Lifelong Catechumenate

To talk about the church as the people of God is to describe a dynamic ever-changing population. People, as well as the culture in which they live, change—sometimes slowly, sometimes rapidly—but they change. No new day is ever like the ones that have gone before . . . nor are the opportunities, challenges, and responsibilities identical. A modern altar-hanging echoes this thought with its embroidered words: "I love you today more than yesterday, and less than tomorrow."

To help Christians grow in their capacity to love, the church has the obligation to serve them regardless of their ages through continual, intensive, pastoral and educational ministries. Change requires adjustments of all of us. Adjustments we often have a hard time making by ourselves. And only a sound educational program fired by a deep concern for the needs of people can guide individual Christians in interpreting and applying the gospel to contemporary situations. This is the underlying conviction supporting the church's idea of a lifelong catechumenate, of an unending catechetical progress for everyone. Adults never outgrow their need to learn. Only in this way can they be alert to new, effective ways in which the church can carry out its mission of inreach and outreach in today's world. Only in this way are they capable of determining how to shape the rites of the church to minister to people where they are. Confirmation should mark a way station on the individual's educational journey through life. It should not be the end of the line.

THE ORGANIZATION OF THE CHURCH

Lutherans have always felt that the way a church is organized to undertake its task is purely optional. And rightly so. God did not tell how to do the job; he simply gave us the job to do. After all, organization is a human invention. Different historical contexts, different social customs can suggest various possibilities for gearing up for the responsibilities at hand. The church has perfect freedom to decide the best plan for itself.

In Sweden, Lutherans follow a form of episcopal government; in Germany, they tend to be more presbyterian; and in North America, the emphasis is heavily congregational. Does organization matter that much? Obviously not! The important thing, Lutherans sense, is to establish the most effective ways of proclaiming the Word of God and offering the Sacraments.

The critical point in any organizational plan comes when you ask some serious questions, such as: Is this plan pleasing to God? By this plan are we fulfilling the church's mission as effectively as possible? Does what we are doing cloud the real nature and mission of the church? Answers do not always come easily. Take the matter of keeping church records. How shall we count Christians—baptized members, confirmed members, contributing members, communing members? The three major Lutheran churches in North America have tried honestly to come up with meaningful statistical categories and consequently each use two or more of these labels. The LCA even invented a new category "confirmed members in good standing," whatever this means. What qualifying designation do you assign people who are giving some "contribution of note" to the work of the church and are in attendance at worship, however sporadically. Parenthetically, it is very difficult, as you can imagine, to decide where the boundary line comes between confirmed members who are in good standing and those who are not. No one knows for sure.

At times, the rationalizations some of us develop to support this way or that of recording church membership are downright funny. It reminds you of George Bernard Shaw's witticism, "My way of joking is to tell the truth. It's the funniest joke in the world." Maybe it is good for us once in awhile to laugh at ourselves and especially at some of the complicated confusions we compound for the express purpose of keeping our church organization running smoothly.

Organizational Imagery

What a good many people think of when you talk about Lutheran church organizational patterns is a series of concentric circles. The largest circle of the church they would call the baptized membership which includes children, youth, and adults. Within this is the smaller circle labeled confirmed members, those entitled by their confirmation to receive Holy Communion. The smallest inner circle, of course, is called "communing membership" which represents those who regularly respond to the invitation to come to the Lord's Table.

Some congregations are thoroughly legalistic about communion practices. If a member communes at least once a year, he belongs to this inner circle. This attitude, incidentally, is a throwback to medieval Christianity and the notion that anyone who didn't commune at least once annually and particularly at Easter was committing a mortal sin.

The concentric-circle imagery of congregational organization is suspect on several counts. It presents a somewhat twisted notion of who is the church. It gives the impression, especially to children, that one has to work his way through the separate circles until he finally arrives at the true church in the core. And it's a long way from the baptized circle to the communing circle. Small wonder that Baptism has fallen into some obscurity among us. Or that confirmation is considered by many to be a more decisive event in a Christian's life. They see confirmation as the significant watershed in church membership, separating the stately forest from the straggly bed of seedlings.

While the church naturally has the right to use confirmation any way it likes for its own purposes, can it really select a course of action that tends to downgrade the importance of Baptism? This is like trying to drive a tack with a sledgehammer and doing more damage than good. Similarly, must Holy Communion be dangled beyond confirmation like a carrot before the nose of a donkey to keep youth studying in their catechisms.

The Baptized Fellowship

Whatever the church does organizationally, it can never forget that Baptism is the entrance to the church. A number of congregations use architecture to symbolize this truth by having the baptistry in an alcove at the back of the nave. Here at the doorway to the sanctuary, those who are baptized enter into their church home.

As Paul said, "For as many of you as were baptized into Christ have put on Christ. There is neither Jew nor Greek, there is neither slave nor free, there is neither male nor female; for you are all one in Christ Jesus" (Galatians 3:27-28). If Paul were sitting down with us now and taking part in our discussions, he might add, "And yes there are neither infants or children or teen-agers or adults. You are all part of Christ's body." The baptized fellowship of the church is the only kind of organization that the New Testament knows. And it is this fellowship that gathers together for teaching and preaching, for worship and the sharing of the Lord's Supper.

Rightly, the church can determine when children are able to take part meaningfully in the Sacrament of Holy Communion. The church can prepare for this event through a careful program of education involving both theory and practical implications. The church can choose to have confirmation either precede or follow first admission to the Lord's Table. But serious difficulties occur if confirmation becomes more important than it was ever intended to be. For instance, confirmation can indeed note that the young person has become more mature and now is more capable of identifying with the adult congregation than he was when he was a child. Therefore he is ready to accept more responsibilities in the church's mission and he can exercise more privileges in the church's life. However, the congregation must be aware that there is always the risk of confusion both in their own minds and in that of the confirmand. This is especially true, if confirmation seems to impose responsibilities and grant privileges that Baptism alone confers.

The Time Problem

The problem really is a problem of time. When adults are baptized they are not confirmed. We feel that they are mature enough to become communing members and identify themselves with the other adult members in the congregation. This, of course, is as it should be. But it is a different matter when we baptize children. We recognize that time is very important. There must be time for growing and time for learning. We know that they are not ready for certain more mature Christian experiences. We don't want to waste educational time trying to answer questions that children are not ready to ask. On the other hand, we don't want to confuse readiness for participation in the church's sustaining sacrament of Christ's forgiving presence with readiness to identify with the adult congregation and its mission.

113

Readiness is a growth factor. There is a clear-cut distinction then between the time when a child can engage in self-examination and come to the altar to receive the bread and the wine knowing that God forgives him and showers upon him the rich gifts of Christ's ministry—and the time when the child becomes an older youth more capable of accepting voting membership or appointment as a sponsor or serving on a parish committee.

A Case in Point

The commission's report indicates how the simple matter of the handclasp in some of the rites of confirmation can confuse these matters of time and readiness. At a certain point in the rite the pastor shakes hands with each of the confirmands and tells them about the new rights and privileges they now have. Different people can see this action from quite different points of view.

A man went to the house of a friend one evening for a game of chess. As he entered a huge St. Bernard dog bounded in with him. During the evening while the men were playing, the dog made a shambles of the living room, knocking over furniture and rummaging through wastebaskets. When the man was leaving he said to his friend. "You really ought to do something about that dog of yours. He's made a mess of your house." Startled, his friend replied, "My dog. I thought he was your dog!" So we have been living with the handclasp in the rite; each person has understood it in his own way.

Some of us have been seeing the handclasp as a mark of the confirmand's maturing. Now he can take his place in congregational life on a more adult level, taking more organizational responsibility. Others see this handshake as an indication that the confirmand now is admitted to the real heart of the Christian faith. Now he can get his name moved up to the communing membership rolls.

Well, what do you think confirmation should be? Is it to continue as it is, suggesting a higher level of church membership than Baptism? Is it the only way children can meet the congregation's requirements for admission to the Lord's Supper? Or should we begin to explore a fresh and bold interpretation of confirmation as a means of ministering to developing children and youth? Our answers must ring true to our understanding of the nature of the church and its mission.

SUGGESTED CHANGES

The commission is suggesting to its constituent churches that the time has come to rebuild the structure of the congregation's ministry to its children and youth. Revision of present confirmation rites and catechetical programs is not enough. In the light of the theology of the Word and Sacraments, the doctrine of the church and the needs of growing persons, the commission recommends a radical change in current policy. The change has two stages.

An Earlier Admission to First Communion

First, admission to Holy Communion would come prior to confirmation. The commission feels strongly that the right to partake of the Lord's Supper is granted to every Christian at his Baptism. The congregation has the obligation to prepare young Christians for exercising this right. Growing concerns and pressures within the three Lutheran churches have given support for this recommendation.

It seems to the commission that the demands upon a Christian youth in a highly mechanized, pluralistic society make it clear that the church must help him utilize the full rich resources of his close relationship with God in the congregational fellowship. The strengthening, healing, inspiring presence of Christ highlighted in the Sacrament of the Altar should therefore be made available to responsible children.

A Later Confirmation

Second, confirmation would come later in the life of the growing youth than it now comes. This would allow the congregation to take more seriously its obligations to carry on a pastoral and educational ministry with young people to equip them for living as mature Christians, to help them identify with the life and mission of the adult Christian community. This does not mean that we would be simply shoving up the graduation day from one age to another. The whole notion of confirmation as any kind of graduation must be shot down. It has dominated and distorted church life for too long. Confirmation itself should be only one specific celebration in the person's lifelong development as a disciple of Jesus Christ involved in the mission of the church. There is no final achievement time for discipleship. Nor should a congregation's educational and pastoral responsibilities end when an individual attains a magic age level. In fact the commission hopes that we can stop talking about a three-year catechetical program and begin talking, as we should, about a lifelong catechumenate. This is more congruent with what we know about human growth and development.

But before we consider the implications for congregational life of the commission's suggested changes, we should add the personal element to our discussion. Perhaps we should pause and look closely at those children and youth we are serving. Who are they? What are their needs? First, let's ask these questions in terms of their admission to first Communion.

7

Admission to First Communion

William Golding's novel, *Lord of the Flies,* is a shocker. Whether you read the book or saw Peter Brook's sensitive film version, you faced some brutal facts about human existence. Golding's story concerns a group of well-behaved British schoolboys evacuated from London just before the outbreak of a new war. Their plane crashes on an uninhabited island. Miraculously, the boys survive the accident, but all the accompanying adults are killed. Now the boys are on their own, forced to fight for survival until help can arrive.

The thin veneer of civilization wears away swiftly and soon the boys become savages. The horror of their violence to each other destroys their former happy camaraderie. It is only after they are finally rescued that the remaining boys are restored to a normal childhood state again. You can think of Golding's story on many levels. It may be a parable of society in general. Or it may be exactly what the plot lines imply, that children are not far removed from savagery, that left on their own without adult assistance, animal passions can replace human control.

The Task of Education

Society has known all along that adults must care for their young. Various groups have suggested different ways. Generally, the home has the first responsibility. In our Western culture, the family has become part of a triad, school and church forming the other sides of a triangle. However, triangles, to follow the geometric allusion, come in many different shapes. As long as there

117

are three sides to the figure, there is no guarantee, perhaps no desirability, for the sides to be of equal lengths.

Once the family side was much longer than it is now. Over the past several hundred years there has been a steady increase in what the school and the church are expected to do for the child. Less and less has been required of the home. Some critics of parental weakness have suggested that the state should take over child rearing altogether and put it on a sound scientific basis. B.F. Skinner's *Walden Two* is one behavioral scientist's dream for a utopian society. Skinner suggests that in his ideal society all children should be raised by well-trained experts to insure their best development.

The Church's Role

Carl Rogers, the prominent psychotherapist, however disagrees. It is not the training of children to fit into community life that is important all by itself. Rogers believes that children need to be guided to make their own decisions. "Responsible personal choice, which is the most essential element in being a person," he contends in his book *On Becoming a Person*, "is a equally prominent fact in our lives. We will have to live with the realization that to deny the reality of the experiences of responsible personal choice is . . . stultifying." Many behavioral scientist today are following Rogers' lead.

When parents have been less able to provide adequate religious instruction for their children, the church has moved in to take more and more responsibility for the job. Luther designed *The Small Catechism,* you recall, primarily for use by heads of households. And when the church itself has not taken up the task sufficiently, other religious groups have moved in. The Sunday school movement founded by Robert Raikes in 1783 was just such an experiment in adding the needed dimension of careful and effective Christian education to the programs of the Protestant churches.

Now the church is involved in the educational process on a full-committment basis. In the light of the Lord's command to "go teach," the church has accepted education as one of its essential ministries. And the responsibility belongs to the whole community of the people of God. But the teaching ministry raises questions of what shall we teach and to whom. These are very real and vital concerns.

As far as the church is concerned, it isn't just a matter of keeping its baptized children from reverting to savagery. The church conceives its primary responsibility to the young in its care in personal terms. Its concern is to help each child according to the fullness of his potentialities, to guide his maturing partnership with God through Christ, to encourage him to keep this relationship at the center of his life. This concern is akin to Carl Rogers' conviction that we must relate to others in such a way that they become fully functioning persons.

The more the church can help the child feel his "belongingness" to the people of God, the more the church can assist him in accepting and using the spiritual gifts his congregational life can offer. One of these great gifts comes through participation in the Sacrament of Holy Communion.

Deciding on an Age Level

The commission's final decision to recommend early first Communion was not arrived at lightly. Paramount in reaching this decision was an extensive study that commission members made of childhood. They explored psychological growth processes of the child at each age level to determine the strategic time when the experience of first Communion could become a significant event in his life. This has been the missing dimension in most of the church's policy-making decisions of the past. Decisions about age level participation in the Lord's Supper were generally imposed from the top down, when the "powers-that-be" felt that children were intellectually capable of explaining the meaning of the sacrament in adult terminology. Seldom did anyone listen to children themselves or examine their growth patterns. Few churchmen accepted findings from the behavioral sciences or from students of human development as helpful clues for determining where the rites of the church and needs of the growing individual could effectively converge. The commission would like to put the child back in the picture. The age for first Communion, therefore, should be chosen on the basis of the children themselves, who being baptized into God's family need to live and grow there, making use of all resources God gives them.

From its intensive study, the commission came to the conclusion that the latter part of the fifth grade is the time when children are capable of participating in the Lord's Supper meaningfully. Fifth-graders, now ten or eleven years old, have clearly defined for themselves what it means to be a member of social groups, including the church. They have been testing the limits of their participation and behavior. They are ready for deeper experiences and intelligent guidance.

Given the advantages of continuing church-related experiences such as Christian home life and Christian education, they are ready for participation in the sacrament on their own age level. However, without these advantages fifth-graders may be somewhat slower in their development. In this case, the pastor, in consultation with parents and teachers may decide to delay their admission to first Communion for awhile.

The Profile of a Fifth-Grader

The more you examine the profile of a fifth-grader, the more you can see why the commission selected this age level. Let's take a look at the ten-year-old as he appears in the study report of Arnold Gesell, Frances Ilg, and Louise Ames at the Yale Clinic of Child Development. In their book, *Youth: The Years from Ten to Sixteen,* they report:

> *Year Ten holds an interesting and highly significant position in the scheme of human growth. It marks the culmination of a decade of fundamental development which began with the prenatal period. A decade of adolescent development looms in the vista ahead.*

They point out some factors that are important for our study:

> *Ten is a year of consummation as well as of transition —an amiable relatively relaxed interlude in which the organism assimilates, consolidates, and balances its attained resources. Accordingly, a classic 10-year-old embodies both the specific and the generic traits of childhood. Only mildly does he foreshadow the tensions of later youth. In a frank, unself-conscious manner he tends to accept life and the world as they are with free and easy give-and-take. It is a golden age of developmental equipoise.*

These comments reflect as well as any what fifth-graders are like. In one way or another most developmental psychologists strengthen this view as they stress the child's growing sense of independence, his tendency to depend more heavily on his peer group friends, and yet at the same time to identify strongly with his family. It is with a good deal of pride that the ten-year-old speaks of "my family," "my friends," "my school," "my church."

Dr. Vernon Anderson, Dean of the College of Education at the University of Maryland, thinks that characteristics of the fifth-grader offer some important implications for Christian education. In *Before You Teach Children* he writes:

> *This seems to be a most strategic time for Christian education to utilize the influence of the family and the active participation of the child in family life. He needs to see Christian faith and worship as a natural part of his family life.*
>
> *He is educationally amenable and responsive, hence this is an important age for dealing with basic facts about the Bible and for completing a general factual framework in understanding the Christian heritage.*

But before we categorically invite fifth-graders to come to the Lord's Supper, let's see what some other educators and psychologists have to say about this age group.

Age Group Characteristics

Let us briefly review some of the age group characteristics which the commission felt were particularly important. These characteristics are described on pages 203-04 of the report. Think of fifth-graders you know as you read.

"The average fifth-grader 'has reached the prime of childhood —a plateau of growth, an emotional balance, and the peak of childhood capacities. . . .' " He can accept new experiences without the bewilderment of the emotional upset of other age levels.

"The child at this age possesses an agreeable balance of his emotional self, is happy to be what he is . . . seems to have found himself as a child and is content." He no longer has to spend so much time 'proving' himself as a participant in his childish society nor is he yet involved in the adolescent confusion of establishing himself as an independent individual. Unless he is one of those rare fifth-graders who has not yet achieved this resting stage in his emotional balance, participation in Holy Communion will enable him to expand his wide, wonderful world.

Ethics, right, wrong, and fairness, are important to him. He is ready and usually eager for the help that preparation for first Communion will provide.

" 'He is particularly open to close family companionship.' " For the first time, he can really appreciate his parents as real persons who make mistakes. He can commune with them on a common ground. He is able to put more trust in his own abilities, having tested his limits a few years earlier. Hence, he feels less challenged or threatened by building close ties with those who excel in different abilities. Therefore he can build close rapport with his fellow Christians and most of all with Christ.

" 'He is increasingly able to make responsible contributions to group activities.' " An idealist, he may dream high visions of possibilities through his association with the best in Communion.

" 'He is educationally amenable and responsive . . .' " to new information. Whereas, according to the British educational psychologist Ronald Goldman in his book, *Religious Thinking from Childhood to Adolescence,* "he will accept these facts in the light of his childish outlook on the world and he is unlikely to generalize them, he is laying foundations for new understandings to develop during adolescence. He can develop a concept of God as an invisible Spirit, provided that he is achieving a new relationship with his parents and other adults to break free from modeling God after human heroes." Indeed this is the time in the fifth-grader's maturational journey when he should be introduced to new and deeper significant relationships with God through Christ.

Other educators and child psychologists have described characteristics of this age which support the commission's recommendation that this is the proper age for first Communion.

Developmental Tasks

In his influential book, *Human Development and Education,* Robert Havighurst describes what he calls the individual's developmental tasks. These are, says Havighurst, "those things that constitute healthy and satisfactory growth in our society. They are the things a person must learn if he is to be judged and to judge himself a reasonably happy and successful person." Some of these tasks are strictly biological, such as crawling and walking and running. Others are imposed by society, such as learning to read and to write.

Different tasks, of course, present themselves at different times in the individual's life. But according to Havighurst, the time that the tasks appear is critical. He notes, "If the task is not achieved at the proper time, it will not be achieved well, and failure in this task will cause partial or complete failure in the achievement of other tasks yet to come." That sounds like an overstated argument. Yet, think of the way children learn mathematics, for instance. First, they have to develop a concept of numbers and learn how to manipulate those numbers, adding them, subtracting them. Slowly, they are led through the mysteries of multiplication and long division. These tasks must be mastered before a person can move on to the more abstract and symbolic use of numbers in algebra and calculus.

If a child doesn't master the art of reading relatively early in his school life, every other subject he studies will suffer. Ours is still a print-oriented culture for the most part, despite television and other electronic communications wonders.

Specific Tasks

Some of the specific developmental tasks Havighurst assigns to middle childhood are these:

Building wholesome attitudes towards self as a growing
   organism;
Developing concepts necessary for everyday living;
Developing conscience, morality, and a set of values;
Developing attitudes toward social groups and institutions.

We have purposely avoided citing the entire list. While the skills in reading, writing, and calculating are important, they need not concern us here. Similarly, the child's need to develop ways of getting along with his family and agemates, to master physical skills for ordinary games, to build a conception of his appropriate sex role are all vital for the healthy growth of an integrated personality. However, we are primarily interested in those developmental tasks that have implications for the child's participation in Holy Communion.

Remember that Havighurst is writing from the standpoint of an educator. He is not talking about the child's involvement in the sacramental life of his church. Yet, the church too is interested in education and if it is serious about its responsibilities, then it must realize that one of the chief functions of education is to help the individual accomplish at least some of the developmental tasks that confront him.

Teachable Moment

One other concept that Havighurst emphasizes is worth noting here. This is the idea of the "teachable moment." Briefly, this means that when a certain individual biologically and psychologically is ready for a certain task, when society (the family, the school, or the church) feels that this task is a reasonable expectation, then the teachable moment has come. "Efforts at teaching, which would have been largely wasted if they had come earlier," writes Havighurst, "give gratifying results when they come at the teachable moment. . . ."

The commission feels that the fifth grade is the teachable moment for guiding the Christian child through his first experience of receiving the Lord's Supper. His active participation in family life and his closer identification with groups beyond the family readies him, the commission says, for participation in the Lord's Supper as a "natural part of his family's faith and worship."

Further, the fifth-grade child is conscious of his shortcomings. He is also increasingly aware of what is right and what is wrong. Havighurst's emphasis on the child's need to develop a sense of morality, his own conscience, and a set of values to live by fits quite naturally with the child's concern for guidance in making ethical decisions. This is where the sacrament of Christ's forgiving and guiding presence can offer the kind of spiritual help the child needs and wants.

Ronald Goldman feels that the fifth-grader is developing a new understanding of his relationship to the church. His insights underscore Havighurst's point about the teachable moment. Goldman writes about this grade level:

> . . . Ten to eleven years appears to be a crucial time when concepts of the church take on a new perspective. From this time on the spiritual purpose of the church is seen more clearly as distinct from its physical features, as the function of worship, although the child is still confused on many points. Duty and habit no longer account for adults going to church, and the child feels it must be because it helps them in some way, if

*only to learn more about God and Jesus. From nearly
eleven years onward, he sees that children can be helped
by churchgoing, not in trivial or extraneous matters, but
to be a better person morally and spiritually.*

Psychological Tensions

Let's explore the ethical dilemmas which a fifth-grader experiences from another direction. The psychoanalytic writings of
Erik H. Erikson offer some keen insights. In *Childhood and Society* Erikson, Professor of Human Development at Harvard, sees
human life as a series of stages in which the human being must
resolve a central problem which has become dominant.

By the time the child has reached the years of middle childhood, he is wallowing in new experiences. Like a puppy nosing
around an attic full of discards, the child happily explores his
world seeking his place in it. He is neither capable of nor invited
to take on an adult role. He looks ahead with eagerness toward
growing up but this doesn't faze his determination to enjoy what
he has. His boundless energies and keen interests lead him to try
to master all the living skills he finds so fascinating. In the words
of a popular song, "It's A Big Wide Wonderful World to Live In."

The fifth-grader is now moving out into a social world beyond
his family. He measures himself not only by his parents' expecta-
tions of him but also by the attitudes of his friends. Mom and
Dad are still O.K. as far as he is concerned. However, he is beginning to see them as representative of other communities in which
he must operate. Therefore, he looks to other adults, such as his
teachers, his scoutleaders, his coaches, his pastor, significant
adults and older youth in his neighborhood, to serve as models
for his behavior. Yet, he translates these models into comparative
terms that he can test out on the playground with his pals. He is
sensible enough to realize that the continuous association with
those of his own age is the best arena for evaluating his abilities
and his values as a person. But this isn't easy.

Erikson sees the tension in middle childhood as "acquiring a
sense of industry and fending off a sense of inferiority." Coupled
with the child's desire to master his environment, to control his
muscular and mental skills is his fear of failure. Now, he knows
that he is an incomplete person but his mind says he ought to be
able to play the infield like Jimmy next door or he should be as
smart as Marcia who sits in front of him at school and can work

fraction problems in her head. But he's not. Always he is torn between plodding ahead, practicing skills, seeking to raise his performance level, or dropping out of the competition altogether.

If the child's sense of inferiority overwhelms him, his efforts at improvement are blocked. He is, naturally, his own severest critic: "I'm no good. Who would want me?" Therefore, he is sharply aware of his faults, his weaknesses, his need for help. He knows full well when he lies or steals or hurts others. He really doesn't like himself at these times.

When you think of this situation in theological terminology, you can see that the fifth-grader has a built-in readiness to understand his need for repentence, confession, and forgiveness. Holy Communion, which emphasizes God's love for the person as he is and the fact that no one is inferior in God's sight, can be a vital, growing, buttressing support for the child in his moments of self-doubt and self-accusation.

Concepts of Sin

There is a side issue here related to the concept of sin that is worth examining. We are well aware that, for many adults, sin is tied up primarily with sexual problems. In fact, many equate sinning with stepping from standardized sex mores. Part of this consistent misinterpretation may come from the church's practice of admitting youth to the Sacrament of the Altar during the tumultuous adolescent years when sexual drives are the strongest.

The plateau of childhood may be a better time to help the child understand the true nature of sin as turning away from God's will for his life. The fifth-grader is searching for his sex role as a boy or a girl but he is not motivated by organic bodily changes. Sigmund Freud called this time the "latency period" when the powerful sexual drives lie dormant. Perhaps by helping these fifth-graders understand the real meanings of sin and their dependence upon forgiveness, it will be easier to guide them in developing a significant perspective of sex in God's world as they become teen-agers.

Social Groups

Erikson points out one other important aspect to the child's tension between industry and inferiority that merits our attention. At this time in his growth he is experiencing a broadening sensi-

tivity to his participation in community organizations. He is beginning to think of himself as a member of a team, a club, a school,
a church.

Part of his awareness of who he is and what he should and can
do comes directly from the influences not only of individuals but
of groups in which he has been accepted. Obviously, then, the
more the groups to which he belongs reach out and give him a
feeling of genuine belongingness, the more he is reinforced in his
dependence upon them for guidance. This suggests that the
church has a real opportunity through its educational program
and admission to Holy Communion to foster the child's feeling of
being at home within the Christian fellowship.

Intellectual Growth

When the child enters the intellectual world of the fifth-
grader, you are struck by his imaginative powers. His mind, no
longer bound in a time-space prison, can operate on many levels,
past, present, and future. While he is artistic, creative, and expressive of his own ideas, he is much less attracted to the fantasy
world and much more concerned about reality. He has discovered how he can control words and numbers, how he can perform simple scientific experiments, how he can go to library
resources and locate dependable facts. This gives him a new
sense of his own powers, faulty though they may be. Jean Piaget,
the Swiss genetic psychologist, calls this stage of middle childhood "the phase of concrete operations."

Piaget has devoted a great portion of his life to investigating
how children learn to think and especially to studying the gradual development of their mental powers. By determining where
a child is in his psychological growth, Piaget feels, parents and
schools will be more realistic in what they expect of a child at any
given age. This makes sense. The fifth-grader comes at the end of
Piaget's "phase of concrete operations." Let's see what this means
to us as far as equipping fifth-graders to participate in Holy
Communion is concerned.

First of all, the fifth-grader is now thinking in terms of wholes
instead of parts. He is trying to integrate bits and pieces of information into some kind of structure. He now accepts good old
Rover as a member of the animal kingdom, more specifically a
mammal, and even more specifically, a dog; he no longer thinks
of his pet as a member of his immediate family. He can put Eng-

land and France and Italy and Germany together and begin to think of Europe.

His sense of time is expanding. He now realizes that the cavemen came before the knights and that the knights preceded pioneer families. Many of his questions are in terms of belongingness and relatedness. How is a Ford like a Chevrolet? How is it different? He has what Piaget calls the power of "operational thought," that is, he can use his mental capacities to order and relate experiences.

Mental Integration

For Christian educators, fifth grade is a good time to help the child pull together all the bits and pieces he has heard about God into a more unified picture of who God is. Similarly it is a time to help the child see the continuity of the biblical witness to God across the centuries from the beginnings of the Old Testament to the ministry of Jesus Christ in the new.

Piaget makes it clear that, though the child can think abstractly in terms of time and space he still needs to have various elements linked logically. He needs to see how one part is connected with the next. His mental concepts could be diagrammed like a picket fence with each upright joined to the next by a crosspiece. Unattached fenceposts even though aligned are much less meaningful. Since he is very much a realist, he wants to know how and why B follows A and leads to C. He can understand therefore (as he is fully aware of his guilt) why his need for repentence should lead to confession and then to forgiveness. Perhaps, he is even more capable than many adults of understanding something of how the Sacrament of the Lord's Supper guides this process.

Equilibrium

Most of all, the fifth-grader wants a sense of equilibrium within himself. As he orders his experiences in a manageable relationship to each other, he is building an inner climate of certainty. This provides a structure on which each new experience can be added or evaluated. You can see the necessity for helping establish a strong foundation on which he can build his house of faith through the rest of his lifetime. This certainty, this constancy opens the doorway to new understandings.

Previously, if you showed him a tall, thin bottle of water and then poured that water into a short wide-mouthed glass, he would tell you that there was less water in the glass; the glass looked shorter to him. Now, he is well aware that the amount of water is the same. You can't fool him easily on sleight-of-hand tricks. He is too savvy. A traveling magician had better be on his toes if he is to entertain the fifth-grader; he has an uncanny knack of figuring out where the rabbits are that come out of the hats. This mental ability should demonstrate the fallacy of assuming that theological explanations pulled out of hats will satisfy his shrewd mind.

When he asks about his relationship to God or why he should pray or what Jesus' death on the cross should mean to him, he expects more profound explanations. He is past accepting the simple satisfying answers of earlier childhood. He has an internal cognitive framework that now tends to reject odd-sized pieces that seem to appear from nowhere. Everything he learns must help his inner world hang together. This is because, as Piaget indicates, his mind is shifting from inductive to deductive modes of thinking.

Forms of Thinking

Inductive thinking, which is the way most children learn best, proceeds from the simple to the complex, from the example to the rule. In other words, you learn that square pegs don't fit round holes by trying it out for yourself. You plant a seed, water the ground, and watch the unfolding plant to comprehend the mysteries of botanical growth.

With deductive thinking, the child can begin with general principles and then explore the implications. You can posit that fire is hot and can burn; you can accept the danger of the flame of an acetylene torch; you don't need to test it out. The swing to deductive reasoning allows the child to make applications beyond his immediate experience. He can now think more abstractly beyond that which he can taste and touch and see and feel. A cool glass of apple juice can symbolize the orchard, the apple pickers, and the ciderpress, provided the necessary associations among these elements are carefully established.

Several other unique features of children's thinking at the fifth-grade level according to Piaget include reversibility and capacity for considering several points of view simultaneously. Reversibility refers to the child's ability to pursue a line of thought to its logical conclusion, find the conclusion unsatisfactory, and then start in at the beginning again. It also indicates that he can reason from causes to effects or from effects back to causes. Younger children have the "one-track minds" but not the fifth-grader. He can operate on a number of levels. This gives him the capacity for considering several points of view simultaneously. It means that he is capable, for instance, of recognizing the way God comes to us through the Word, by sermon and conversation, by Bible reading and sacrament.

Ability to Verbalize

One thing should be clear about the child's responses to the questions adults may ask him about his thoughts. Piaget, as a result of his studies, suggests that the child's ability to verbalize, that is, to express himself with words, lags about a year behind this thinking capacity.

The fifth-grader can get emotionally and intellectually involved in significant experiences that are still hard for him to explain in the more limited vocabulary he has at his disposal. One of the reasons is, of course, that words come as vehicles for conveying understandings of experiences for the fifth-grader and not the other way around. Words are the vehicles he eventually learns to use to split up his involvements into small chunks so that others will know what he is experiencing.

Often, educational programs for children of this age get the proverbial cart before the equally proverbial horse. The church has often fallen into the trap of spending a lot of time and effort teaching words before providing experiences. Perhaps the fifth-grader needs the experience of the Lord's Supper in order to make the explanation of what happens in the sacrament something that is really meaningful to him.

What the Church Expects

Now that we have listened to men like Havighurst and Erikson and Piaget who write from the standpoints of education and psychology, how does the church's expectation of its fifth-graders compare? One way of checking is to look at the age group objectives for ages ten and eleven in *The Age Group Objectives of Christian Education* prepared by the Lutheran Boards of Parish Education. Fifth-graders generally include these two age levels. You will notice how many of these objectives reflect the insights of the child study experts concerning the fifth-grader's abilities.

We can sample some of these objectives under the appropriate headings of understandings, attitudes, and action patterns. Six objectives in each category should be sufficient.

UNDERSTANDINGS

To understand what God does through the means of grace

To understand that God speaks to us in many ways

To understand more fully the mission of Christ and our need of him as our Savior

To grow in understanding the meaning of the "Holy Christian Church, the communion of saints"

To become acquainted with the place of the sacraments in the life of the church

To understand the true meaning of forgiveness for himself and forgiveness toward others.

ATTITUDES

To be more aware of his need for repentence, confession and forgiveness in relation to his thoughts as well as his actions.

To desire to experience more fully the grace of God

To be aware of his personal need of a Savior

To begin to feel a kinship with the communion of saints

To have a growing desire to become a confirmed and communing member of the church

To desire to dedicate his entire life as a response to God's forgiving love

ACTION PATTERNS

To gain skill in expressing his faith in God in his own words

To worship in church with true Christian responsiveness and joy

To repent before God of wrong-doing

To find satisfaction in "righteous behavior"

To trust in Christ as his Savior and the Lord of his life

To seek the guidance of God before he makes important decisions

Direction for Curricula

As you read over these objectives, you should know that they are the building blocks of church school curricular materials. Authors, editors, and course designers use them in planning the kinds of study books, records, and filmstrips fifth-graders should use in a program of Christian education. These objectives also give direction to the classroom learning experiences which teachers conduct.

Look at the objectives a second time in the light of the prerequisites for participation in Holy Communion. Admittedly, these objectives are on an elementary level. Even so, how much more would you require of a teen-ager or an adult who was coming to the Lord's Supper for the first time? Here is guidance for the fifth-grader in self-examination as he prepares to receive God's forgiveness; here is emphasis upon God's forgiving love.

Outside of actual participation experiences, the age group objectives already favor the change of policy the commission recommends. The careful study of all the age level characteristics reinforces their opinion that the fifth-grader may be capable of participating in the Lord's Supper effectively, even though he is still unable to identify with the full life and mission of the adult Christian community.

Implications for Education

If fifth-graders are to be admitted to Holy Communion, some structural changes will be necessary in the overall design of the Christian education program for this age group. This will not require any wrenching of the age group objectives at all. As a matter of fact, only a few new objectives need to be added.

To understand the meaning of Holy Communion for his daily living

To desire to participate in Holy Communion when it is offered as a means of receiving God's forgiving presence in his life

To examine his need of God's forgiveness as a means of preparation for receiving Holy Communion

As far as instructional courses are concerned, though, education for first Communion should be more than simply adding a number of sessions or a new unit to existing courses. The whole educational scheme, which is designed to help the child function as a Christian, should provide the preparation for this momentous occasion.

Certainly, there should be some practical guidance in how to receive the sacrament at the altar rail. But general education in the meaning and implication of the sacrament should be embodied in the context of the whole gospel, not in an isolated segment of the curriculum. In other words, the church would see participation in Holy Communion as one of the "developmental tasks" of its baptized fifth-graders. Therefore, its educational curriculum would probably begin with preparing fourth-graders to anticipate the coming event. Then, in the fifth grade the focus would narrow a bit to concentrate on the pupil's involvement in the sacrament. Subsequent grades would revert to the broader view.

The commission has worked out a fairly complete description of objectives for the fifth-graders' educational program. Examine these objectives for yourself. Read pages 206-07 of the report.

It should be clear that at no time in the individual's life is he completely competent to receive the sacrament in a worthy manner. Every time Communion is offered, the individual finds himself changed; the sacrament comes as a new experience to him where he is.

In *Travels with Charley* John Steinbeck records the log of his journeys in a truck-camper through much of the United States with only Charley, his French poodle, as a companion. Steinbeck wanted to look at the countryside with fresh eyes and listen to what the people he met along the way had to say about their land. As he was glorying in the brilliant hues of New England's autumn mountain foliage, he met a New Hampshire woman who told him, "It's a glory and can't be remembered so that it always comes as a surprise." In a sense, each participation in Holy Communion brings a new sense of beauty in the sacrament, grasping the worshiper with regenerative vitality. He finds that he cannot hold all the significance of the sacrament in his mind. He approaches the Lord's Table each time as a new experience with his Lord. He receives the bread and wine with the wonder and the awe he feels before the scarlets and the yellows of the woodlands in the fall. Education for first Communion then is just one step in a staircase of needed preparation for the Christian's continual participation in the Lord's Supper throughout his lifetime. This fits in with the church's concept of the lifelong catechumenate. It also stresses the dynamics of communing.

Guidance for Parents

Another educational implication is the necessity of providing more adequate courses and educational material for parents. The fifth-grader coming to Holy Communion for the first time needs the warm support and sound guidance of those closest to him. He is still largely family oriented. Even though he enjoys being with his friends and doing the things that they want to do, his happiest moments (as he will gladly tell you) come when he and his family do things together.

Parents need to realize how important this family consciousness is to their fifth-grade children. Further, parents themselves need guidance in capitalizing on their children's loyalty and love to help them make easy transitions to those other groups beyond the family which the family considers important.

Sponsors for First Communion

Perhaps this is the place to suggest that the church should revitalize the role of sponsors for child members. For a long time it has been customary to have sponsors at a child's Baptism. In earlier days when life expectancy was much shorter than it is today, sponsors provided a needed safeguard for society in making sure that, should anything happen to the child's parents, there would be responsible adults ready to care for him. The church, of course, saw the matter from a slightly different point of view. Over and beyond the physical care of the child's well-being, sponsors could take the responsibility of seeing that the child was brought up within the atmosphere of the church life. They would supervise his Christian education, bring him to The Service and be available as his spiritual counselors.

Unfortunately, the practice of having baptismal sponsors has eroded over the years. In many cases, the parents themselves act as the child's sponsors at Baptism. If there are additional sponsors, they attend the Sacrament of Baptism and take the vows to care for the child with the parents. But their position is generally honorary. Very few take their roles seriously. Seldom do congregations provide education to help them.

Broadening the Concept

The idea of having sponsors who are willing to complement parents' guidance of their children is a good one. Perhaps, though, the concept of sponsorship could be broadened to link the child's involvement in the two sacraments. Sponsors therefore in carrying out their responsibilities could help prepare the baptized child for his first Communion. The commission feels strongly that this would contribute a great deal to the child's preparation. The commission report states:

> It is further recommended that each candidate [for admission to Holy Communion] have a sponsor or sponsors who are themselves communicant members of the church, and who shall, if possible, be present for the rite. In the event that the baptismal sponsors or the parents cannot assume this duty, another sponsor or sponsors may be appointed by the pastor in consultation with the candidate and his family.

The commission also feels that sponsors could continue their association with the child on through his confirmation. Thus sponsorship would be rescued from the dusty closet of disuse and would be restored as a viable way of offering the congregation's baptized children adequate adult concern and supervision. The sponsor would once again be a functional person. Then too, children without parents, those from broken homes, those without parental support would have adult friends who care enough about their spiritual growth to minister to them. Here is one way that the doctrine of the priesthood of all believers as translated from theology comes into action.

Implications for Congregational Practices

A change in the time of first Communion has more serious implications for present church organizational patterns. The notion of communing membership will have to be reconsidered. As the commission points out, "The statistics on the church register should, however, never be mistaken as the statistics of the true church that is always hidden." Perhaps, the church may be able to move away from its use of Holy Communion as a mechanical means of determining congregational loyalty or of measuring faithfulness to Christ.

One particular congregational practice comes under heavy fire from the commission. This is the Sunday morning scheduling pattern in some areas where Sunday church school classes are held at the same time as The Service. Even though there are earlier or later times in the morning when The Service is also conducted, there is a tendency for some people to assume that education is for children, worship is for adults. Others fall into the trap of allowing Christian education to take the place of The Service or conversely to argue that their participation in The Service precludes any involvement with Christian education.

Worship and education are not competitors for time and interest; they are two sides of the same coin. Church school teachers as well as the children they teach should be a part of The Service when the congregational family of God gathers for worship. This is basically how children grow into a natural association with an adult community. They observe their parents, teachers, and other adults whom they respect and try to imitate them. Learning begins with doing what others do.

If fifth-graders are to be admitted to Holy Communion, it is obvious that this special celebration in their lives should come as a result of continuing association with the worshiping community. Their experiences in Christian education should not be competing with their experiences at The Service. Why shouldn't they have both? This is the very least their congregation can do for them. And as for adults—the congregation is doing them a great disservice if it fails to motivate them to continue their participation in Christian educational courses as an essential part of their church life.

A Rite for Admission to First Communion

The commission has offered suggestions concerning appropriate elements that should be included in a rite. While the commission has not been charged with the task of developing a rite of admission to first Communion, it nevertheless feels that in keeping with the theology of the Word and the Sacraments certain features should be emphasized. Read this part of the report carefully (p. 209).

The insistence on the rite's language being contemporary and on the fifth-grade level makes good sense. The child needs to know that the church is talking to him directly and is concerned about his taking his rightful place at the Communion rail. Well-chosen contemporary words that the child can understand strengthen the effective communication and make the teaching-learning process more easily handled.

Then too, the rite, being an occasion for joy, as the commission suggests, "should communicate the note of celebration as well as responsibility."

Flexibility should characterize the rubrics for the rite. ("Rubrics" is a fancy word for stage directions.) This is important. There should be no attempt to build a rigorous ritual that misses the individual's needs and attempts to fit children into a system. What the church is concerned about is helping young persons feel at home at the Lord's Table.

A Sample Rite

It is not the responsibility of the commission to prepare and recommend a specific rite for admission to first Communion. Properly, this responsibility rests with those charged with developing the liturgical offices of the church. However, unofficially several liturgical scholars have prepared a sample rite to illustrate how the commission's convictions might be translated into practical terms.

ADMISSION TO FIRST COMMUNION

* Young people presented for this rite shall have first been instructed in the meaning of the sacrament and of confession and shall have been approved by the pastor and the church council.
* Each young person shall have a sponsor or sponsors who are themselves communicant members of the church, and who shall, if possible, be present for this rite. In the event that the baptismal sponsors or the parents cannot assume this duty, another sponsor or sponsors shall be appointed by the pastor in consultation with the young person and the family.
* This rite shall follow the Gospel for the Day in The Service, and there shall be Holy Communion.
* At the confession, the young people about to be admitted to the sacrament may receive absolution at the Communion rail, accompanied by the laying on of hands.

---

* A clerk (the secretary of the church council or other appointed layman) standing before the congregation, shall say:

The following young people have been instructed and approved by the pastor and the church council and are now presented for admission to Holy Communion.

* He (she) shall read the names of the young people and after each name the name(s) of the sponsor(s). As the names are read, the persons named (both young people and sponsors) shall rise. After all the names have been read, the minister shall say:

In Holy Baptism these young people were received into the family of the church and accepted by Christ as his own. As a gift of his love our Lord Jesus Christ gave his church his Holy Supper and invited his own to receive this sacrament in faith for the forgiveness of their sins, as he said: Do this in remembrance of me. Now these young people have learned what Christ has done for them and the gift that is being offered them. They know what it means that they are sinners and need forgiveness. They know the joy of being loved and accepted by him. They are eager to say thank you by sharing the love they have received. Therefore, as members of the family they are now ready to receive the Lord's Supper.

Let us all confess the faith of the church.

* Then shall all say the Nicene Creed.

* Then shall the minister ask the young people:

Do you believe that in Holy Baptism God accepted you as his child?

Answer: I believe.

Do you believe that you should share in the Lord's Supper with joy because in it Christ comes to you, forgives your sins, and strengthens you to trust him and to love one another?

Answer: I believe.

* Then shall the minister say to the young people:

You are about to be admitted to the Lord's Supper. The church invites and expects you to come regularly to the services of God's house to hear what he has to say to you and to thank him for everything. You will also have to continue to be taught so that you may better understand and live in the Christian faith. You will want to come to the Lord's Supper as often as you can. When you are old enough, you will be confirmed and take a more active part in the church and its work. All this will help you to live as God wants you to live as his own baptized child. So I ask you:

Do you promise to do this, knowing that God will help you?

Answer: I do, with the help of God.

* Then shall the minister say to the sponsors:

You have heard the confession of these young people and the obligations they have accepted. God's whole family shares the concern and responsibility for helping them to grow up in Christ. On behalf of the church and of the young persons whom you serve as sponsors, will you help them to fulfill their promise?

Answer: I will, with the help of God.

138

* Then shall the minister say:

By the authority of the church, I now invite you young people to the Lord's Table to receive with us his gracious presence in his sacrament.

* The congregation shall rise (or kneel) and the minister shall say:

Let us pray.

* There may follow a space for silent prayer by all present for those now admitted to the Lord's Table. The silence ended, the minister shall say:

O God, whose son Jesus Christ loved the young and called them to him: We ask you to bless these young people and to strengthen them in their faith through his gracious presence in the sacrament, so that as they grow physically and mentally they may also continue to grow spiritually, and so may bring blessing into the lives of others, and honor to your holy name. We ask it in Jesus' name. *Amen.*

The blessing of Almighty God, the Father, the Son and the Holy Spirit be with you always. *Amen.*

* The Service shall continue with the Hymn and the Sermon and the celebration of Holy Communion.

Strategy for Today

Despite the difficulties that arise when comfortable old practices are changed, the commission feels that it is serving its constituency best by recommending that Lutheran churches in North America inaugurate a new program of early admission to first Communion and that this be localized in "the latter part of the fifth grade." This policy change offers the church some fresh and creative ventures in its ministry to its baptized children.

The church has full freedom to make this change. It is not bound by any scripturally ordained patterns; it can choose what is best in the light of its understanding of the nature and mission as the people of God. Under the power of the Word of God, the church can be flexible in order to meet the needs of the people living in a changing society. A joint decision to adopt this recommendation would go a long way toward establishing uniformity of practice among Lutherans in North America. The time has come to make the change.

8

Building a Functional Definition

Mountain climbing is more than a sport; it is an adventure in perspective. As you wind your way up the trails from the valleyland, eventually you come to a place where you can look back over your route and see how the various parts of the landscape fit together. You can see the field, the road, that lake over there with the snake-like streams feeding it, the town in the distance. No longer do these exist by themselves as they did when you were passing by them. Now they are pieces in a panoramic jigsaw giving you a feeling of integral unity. From your rocky height you can see the world to which you belong with a new vision.

As you have read and studied the previous chapters of this book, you have been following the trail which members of the commission took as they explored the many aspects of confirmation and its related rite, admission to first Communion. Now you are in the same position they were when they made their final decisions. Looking back you can see how the various elements in the picture, history, theology, psychology, and social implications, fit together. The time has come to take the last step and define what confirmation should be for the Lutheran churches in North America at this particular point in time.

Fencing an Idea

Definitions, of course, are limiting word prisons. To define is to build a fence around an idea. Most dynamic ideas are broader than the areas described by their definitions. However, only by insisting on definitions can persons communicate with each other. If they are to understand each other, the word coins they spend must buy the idea they want to convey.

Those who want to define confirmation are at a distinct disadvantage. There is very little to go on. Confirmation simply has not been defined. Lutheran theologians, particularly, had a way of talking around the subject without coming to grips with it. Lacking a solid, workable definition, the church has suffered ever since. It is not surprising that apples and bananas and oranges got all mixed up, and confirmation became a kind of fruit basket.

The commission members, therefore, are pioneering. They suggest that a sound and practical definition of confirmation for our day can and must be developed. According to their best judgment the definition is:

> Confirmation is a pastoral and educational ministry of the church that is designed to help baptized children identify with the life and mission of the adult Christian community and that is celebrated in a public rite.

Confirmation on Its Own

By separating confirmation from admission to first Communion, the rite now has a chance to stand on its own feet. It now can become a particularly significant maturational experience in the youth's Christian consciousness of belonging to the people of God. The commission is frank to admit that there may be other public occasions where stages of Christian growth may be celebrated. However, confirmation is a special acknowledgment of advancing maturity. It is the church's way of recognizing that the youth has developed to the point where he is able to feel more at home with the adult members of the congregation. Consequently, he can move into more areas of sharing with them in the life and mission of the church.

At the beginning of this book, you had an opportunity to think about what confirmation could and should mean to the youth in your parish. If you wrote down what you thought about confirmation, reread your comments. Have you found your mind changing? This is what happened to many members on the commission. Although their statement of the definition of confirmation comes at the beginning of their report, in point of time it was one of the last things they did. The definition actually grew out of the studies they conducted. As the critical factors that shaped confirmation were examined one by one, the definition took shape. Finally, it emerged as a guideline for the church to consider. When you read the preamble to the definition (p. 185) and the commentary on pages 185 and 186, you are considering opinions distilled from three years of work. Let's examine some of the points they emphasized about the definition itself.

What Confirmation Is Not

Since so many distortions have occurred in the concept and practice of confirmation through the years, it is wise to list what confirmation is not. This is what the commission calls "definition by exclusion."

To summarize our consideration of theology and church history we must say that confirmation —

Is not a sacrament.

Does not in any sense complete Baptism.

Is not a ratification of the vows or promises made by sponsors at Baptism.

Does not add any special form of God's presence or gifts that the baptized person does not already enjoy.

Does not confer special privileges.

Is not a prerequisite to Holy Communion.

Is not essential to the Christian life.

When we have said all those negatives about confirmation, it may seem that there is absolutely nothing left. But this analysis only reflects what the Reformers wrote in the *Apology to the Augsburg Confession:* "Confirmation and extreme unction are rites received from the fathers, which however, the Church never requires as necessary to salvation, because they are not commanded by God."

If we can agree on what confirmation is not, freeing it from the misguided linkage to the two sacraments, then we are in a position to make of confirmation a very useful and important ministry of the church to its baptized youth. As the commission points out, confirmation "means a 'strengthening,' a work which God performs."

A Pastoral Ministry

The pastoral ministry expresses the loving concern of the parents, sponsors, and all the agencies of the church for the welfare of the child.

One of the key words in the definition is ministry. Ministry implies service, concern, helpfulness, consideration. To speak of it as a pastoral ministry is to stress the church's concern for its youth. This involves not only the pastor but everyone who is in a position to contribute to the youth's development, his parents, his sponsors, his relatives and older friends, his church school teachers, his youth-ministry advisers. In short, the pastoral ministry seeks to surround the youth with the climate of love and interest in his well-being.

Often, youth themselves have seen confirmation as one more hurdle they must get over somehow in order to please a legalistically minded adult Christian community. No wonder they sometimes feel they are not persons at all but simply globs of humanity on the conveyor belt of catechetical instruction being fed automatically through ecclesiastical machinery. The definition of confirmation seeks to restore the importance of "person" while strengthening the concept of "community."

Confirmation should be a way and a time to strengthen each person in the business of living as a Christian within the fellowship of his church home. His ideas, his worries, his hopes, and dreams are important. And, in addition, he can contribute from the uniqueness of his own personality to the effective work of the church.

The concept of a pastoral ministry is much broader than the current practice of more or less confining concern for confirmands to a formal educational program. It involves counseling and visiting and being a friend. This is where the confirmand comes to realize that he is being accepted as a person, that he is liked and wanted for who and what he is right now.

A strong pastoral ministry can build strong motivations on the part of youth to retain their membership in the society of the church. This is one answer to the dropout problem, certainly not the only answer, but one good attack on the roots of the dropout syndrome. People, any kind of people, tend to stay affiliated with groups that support them, that genuinely make them feel valuable, that show respect for their contributions to group life. When belongingness is interpreted in terms of "have to," there is usually some form of rebellion. We may grudgingly do what we are told we have to do in order to do something else, but our hearts may not be in the enterprise at all. We as human beings bitterly resent being made to jump through hoops.

More than one college fraternity has faced open rebellion from a pledge class that has gotten fed up with degrading hazing procedures. The only solution has been to turn "hell weeks" into "help weeks." Instead of spending time dreaming up devilish ways of humiliating the boys who are being considered as potential members of the fraternity, the upperclassmen worked with the pledges in some constructive community service. In an eastern metropolitan area, for instance, one fraternity uses this "help week" each year to work on a program of beautification for a slum neighborhood. Paddles are exchanged for paint brushes.

What has happened with the pledges has been that miraculously the distasteful "have to" has been replaced by a "want to." This is precisely the kind of motivational change that the congregation needs to encourage in its youth of confirmation age. A keen sense of pastoral ministry on the part of the congregation will issue in the kind of relationships with youth that foster this "want to" attitude. And confirmation becomes a vital part of the central mission of the congregation.

An Educational Ministry

The definition of confirmation also highlights the church's educational ministry to its youth:

> The educational ministry is that phase of a lifelong catechumenate which nourishes in a child his particular gifts so that he can know and confess as his own the Christian faith, live his role as a child and servant of God, and grow in the life of the Christian community.

Seen in the light of an all-embracing pastoral ministry, an educational ministry takes on new dimensions. The building blocks of this ministry still consist of courses and textbooks, films and records; the young person does need to know the content of his faith. But the ministry idea pushes further to focus on the purpose of curricular materials. It isn't the age-old misguided notion of unscrewing the top of the pupil's head, filling him up with information, screwing the top back on, and sending him on his way. The concept of education should have gone out of date along with antimacassars and highbutton shoes. But it didn't. It still hangs around like an Asian-flu virus waiting to infect new educational programs.

An educational ministry is committed to serving the individual far beyond providing him with necessary facts. The commission has described this ministry pointedly as "that phase of a lifelong catechumenate which nourishes in the child his particular gifts." Notice the twin emphases on individuality and lifelong learning. Both are essential psychological realities.

The emphasis on the person's particular gifts reminds us that learning is always highly personal. No one can learn for another; no one can perceive facts, think through their significance, and apply them for another either. Each thinking person brings his own genius (using "genius" in the right way) to the educational process, finding the fulfillment of his capacities and contributing his own insights. And the process never really ends. That is why the commission did not end their description of the church's educational ministry with a comment on personal learning. They went on to underscore a lifelong catechumenate. The hoary old saw that says, "You can't teach an old dog new tricks," is a lie. As a matter of fact you had better teach an old dog new tricks if you want him to get older. When we stop learning, we start dying. This is especially true of our mental processes.

As a person grows, his mind develops. New experiences force him to evaluate old thoughts and to think new ones. He is reshaping constantly the orderly patterns of his mental images to adjust to the world as he finds it. This is the only way he can live securely with himself in a continually changing environment. Education is as much guidance in handling new concepts as it is techniques for mastering old ones. Of course, a person needs a foundation or some sort of starting point.

There is a time and place for teaching children the basic construction of English sentences so that subjects agree with predicates, and adjectives and adverbs do the job they are supposed to do. First of all, the child must learn how to communicate with others to make himself clear and to avoid misunderstandings. But this is not the stopping place in general education. He is encouraged to read how others have used language, how they have spun words into a gossamer poem of great beauty or fashioned an engrossing story to capture interest.

The learner, too, must find the thrill of playing with words. So, he has opportunity to compose poems and write stories, in short to explore ways he can express his opinions and ideas forcefully. And all the way through grade school and high school and college, if he is in a sound language program, he will keep coming back to the basic rules of grammar. Sometimes he will simply be reinforcing his understanding of the rules and their usefulness. At other times he may be reinterpreting their values, even altering them to do the job he has to do.

Christian education is no different from any other kind of education in this respect. It constantly has the responsibility of helping the person live as a Christian on his age level in his particular corner of the world. You can only educate fifth-graders to be ten- and eleven-year-old Christians; you can't guarantee that they will eventually be adolescent Christians. You have to come to them through each grade level and help them be Christians where they are.

Similarly, you can't help adolescent Christians solve all the problems of adjustment that they will face when they become adults. You can only guide their functioning as teen-age Christians in the only realistic environment they know, that is, what they experience daily in the communities of which they are a part. This is why the idea of the church's educational program as a form of ministry is important; it focuses on the person and his pressing needs. It also provides the kind of climate that fosters effective learning.

The really creative educational atmosphere that is necessary if learning is to occur offers support for each individual in his own individual learning task. At different stages in his development, the tasks are different and the educational means and methods used vary accordingly. There is a time and place for highly concentrated courses taught over a period of weeks or months. There is also a time and place for other kinds of educational experiences such as weekend conferences and retreats, field trips, and even time-disregarding bull sessions. But no matter what the means of introducing subject matter, whether it be book or film, brainstorming or research, the atmosphere that surrounds education must encourage the person-pupil to interact in such a way that he grows in the process.

Identification

According to the commission's definition of confirmation, the purpose of the pastoral and educational ministry of the church is to help baptized children identify with the life and mission of the adult Christian community:

The ability to identify with "the adult Christian community" denotes a level of Christian maturity rather than an age reference. The initial boundary of such maturity cannot be defined precisely, for there are wide variations in personal growth, development, and achievement. Nevertheless, there is a point at which the adult community recognizes that the young person has developed elements of maturity, such as stability, independence, and self-confidence, that enable him to identify with and to accept a more responsible role in that community.

"Identify" is a big word. It implies sameness, unity, "withness". To identify with a person or a social group is to feel closely tied to his or their approach to life. In the process of identification you begin to change your self-image. You no longer think of yourself as an isolated person. Instead, you think of yourself as a supporter of a certain political party or a rooter for a specific college football team or a part of a neighborhood group.

In 1873 Father Damien, a Belgian priest, went to Molokai, one of the Hawaiian Islands, to minister to the unfortunate lepers confined there. At one particular Sunday service after he had worked with the sufferers for quite a while, he electrified his congregation by beginning his sermon, "We lepers." There's the shift in identification dramatically illustrated—the change from "you" or "they" to "we." Confirmation should mark the time in the life of a youth when he begins to say "we Christians" and includes himself with the adult congregation in his thinking.

Admittedly, confirmation will not and cannot imply that the process of identification is complete for the teen-ager. It marks the beginning of a process rather than the height of it. But it does suggest that, simultaneous with the adolescent's identification with the world of adult automobile drivers and adult jobholders (even though he may only be working at a store or in an orchard or at a factory part-time), the church can help him feel an integral part of his congregational community. In the eyes of the people of God, this youth is now one with them. He may still have some considerable maturing to do. Legally, he still may not be permitted to vote on money matters in some states. But they recognize that he is now developing more of an adult Christian point of view regarding the church's importance and mission.

In at least one state there has been a program involving senior high students in identifying themselves with the state government. Delegates from each of the state's senior high schools gather in some central location to learn the business of running the state for a day. They assume the roles of state officials, legislators, judges, the governor and his staff. As they practice moving legislation through the state senate or hold hearings on critical issues, they learn a great deal about state government. Adult advisors working with the program are impressed with the attitude of the students who have participated. These seniors return home to their local civics classes and begin talking about what "we do in our state government."

Using confirmation as a means of helping youth identify with the adult Christian congregation does not suggest that we immediately begin placing young people in various role-play situations. Role play is an extremely useful educational tool for assisting the learner to see the other fellow's point of view and responsibilities. Therefore, it is an important phase of the educational program. But real identification comes as we move beyond role play to reality.

Making Identification Meaningful

In many congregations confirmed youth have the privilege of stuffing envelopes and folding bulletins, both equally useful operations and helpful in the general running of the congregation but scarcely inspiring! Why shouldn't confirmed youth be permitted larger responsibilities? Some congregations are moving ahead in this area, recognizing that youth have many contributions to make to effective congregational life if anyone will take the time to listen to them or to utilize their abilities. A number of congregations therefore have put youth on congregational committees, such as music and worship, education, stewardship, evangelism. Why not?

How do we train our members to be church councilmen and other congregational leaders? Do we just take for granted that because a person has reached adulthood and is fairly successful in his line of work that automatically he can serve the church efficiently? How should he be educated for his task? New courses for potential church leaders are being prepared. But maybe we need to do more than offer educational classes to adults. There are a few congregations which have been experimenting in this area by admitting junior members to the church council. These are usually one or two confirmed youth elected by the congregation's youth group. In council discussions they are permitted voice but no vote. In a sense they are apprentice church leaders. And they should have carefully guided experiences in leadership while they are still primarily learners.

Identification is a continuous process. Confirmation acknowledges that fact but it also serves to point up its importance. Instead of representing graduation from childhood, confirmation can serve as one of the significant events in the youth's life to help him in his transition into adulthood.

The Life and Mission of the Adult Christian Community

As the commission points out, "The 'mission' of the adult Christian community with which the young person identified is as broad as the gospel and as specific as a cup of cold water given in Jesus' name." This has been the church's mission since the day of Pentecost. It always has had the mandate from Christ to encompass the whole world with its concerns for the welfare of people. Its gospel proclaims God's love for all people; its ministry is geared to provide truth and justice for everyone. This is a large order. It would seem presumptuous if it were not powered by God himself.

But the church in its mission recognizes that time does not screech to a halt to allow the church to order society. Life is constantly in the throes of change, new dimensions of living are either slowly or rapidly coming into being. Although the mission of the church remains the same, it must always be ready to translate its message into contemporary terms, to revise its structure and methodology to reach people where they are. As the commission phrases the church's obligations:

> The church must, therefore, equip the young person with the ability to recognize the need to adapt that mission to his own time and to accept his responsibility to it, using the resources which the church has received from the Holy Spirit.

Each oncoming generation has the responsibility in the church to carry its mission forward into the coming world climate of which they are a part. By helping youth identify with the life and mission of the adult Christian congregation, the church is

149

providing for the passage of the torch from one set of hands to another. It is senseless to promote the myth of the "generation gap" as an established fact when the possibility exists for bridging the gap through mutual acceptance by youth and adults of their joint responsibility.

Confirmation is a time to help youth develop the sensitive, feeling heart of a mature Christian who sees that the mission of the church extends far beyond its service to his needs to reach and minister to others and the congregation can profit from the vision of youth. Youth is a time of idealism, when the person is most conscious of the imperfections about him and eager to set things right. He can feel what it is like to live frustratedly without much hope in the dead-end ghetto; he can agonize with people whose land and culture is devastated by war's horror; he has empathy with other youth caught up in an agonizing despair and seeking escape through drugs and sex exploits. Here is where he can genuinely help his congregation become an agent of change, assisting those in distress with the healing power of the gospel.

How the church goes about its task of equipping its youth to adapt the mission of the church to their own time and to accept the responsibility for it cannot be spelled out in detail. There is no programmed-instruction device to do the job. God's people, adults and youth, simply have to worship and work together, making adaptations and even changes in the church's program as the resources of their faith lead them. But the church has within its educational ministry the opportunity to encourage people to grow cognizant of the human needs which the people of God must meet. Thus again there is the strong emphasis on the lifelong catechumenate in which confirmation marks a vital stage in the development of mature Christians.

Memories

Human memory is a tricky function of our brain cells. According to research neurologists, we store certain images and associations in brain cells for future use. Some event, like hearing a snatch of a popular song we once knew, can set these storage cells firing one another like a string of Chinese firecrackers to bring to our consciousness a host of memories. For most people looking back on their childhood and youth, the memories that are the easiest to retrieve are those associated with extraordinary events such as holidays, vacations, a death in the family, some great reward or punishment, a favorite person or pet. Why? Simply because the experiences stood out from the routine.

Memories are only made from significant things that a person for one reason or another feels are worth keeping. The dull, the humdrum, the unpleasant, the ugly are sloughed off along with discards of broken dreams and shattered hopes. A mother finds that, with the coming birth of a second child, she cannot remember much about the pains of childbirth associated with her firstborn. The joy of bringing a new life into the world pushed the discomforts aside and wouldn't let them make indelible marks in the memory library. By the same token, we remember the thrill of graduation and forget rather quickly the nerve-racking agony of final exams. We remember occasions when we are publicly recognized as significant people and tend to forget other instances when, hurt and despondent, we felt that we were disliked. A well-designed rite can build lasting memories.

Celebrated in a Public Rite

The commission feels that the celebration of confirmation according to the new definition deserves a significant and public rite:

> In the public rite the people of God recognize the confirmand as capable of identifying with the adult Christian community and its mission. They recall with him the event of Baptism, through which God, by grace, received them into his church, and they testify to the strengthening they receive through the Word and Holy Communion. The confirmand gives assurance that he believes the Word and promises of God and affirms his commitment to the Christian life. The people pray God to sustain the confirmand and to strengthen him further in Christian life. This prayer may be individualized by the laying on of hands.

The rite of confirmation has a useful part to play in the life of the developing youth. It is the unique occasion when the whole congregation celebrates the fact that he is regarded as a significant person in the eyes of the mature Christian community, when they feel that he is capable of identifying with them and their mutual involvement in the church's task. This is a splendid time to pull together other stages that the youth has gone through in his march to maturity.

Through the rite, the congregation can recall with him the fact that he became a member of Christ's church through Baptism, that through the years he was strengthened in his growing faith as he participated in worship and educational classes and in recent years as he received Holy Communion. The confirmand at the altar rail, feeling the pastor's hand on his head to individualize the prayers of the congregation on his behalf, senses that this is really a red-letter day in his life. He is valuable and wanted for himself. He is being invited to accept a role in an important undertaking and the congregation is expressing confidence that he is both capable and reliable. These are the experiences of which memories are made, memories that can come back again and again to buttress conviction, to offer power for right choices in moments of temptation, to give a renewed sense of belonging to God as one of his people.

Objectives for the Adult Christian Community

The commission's definition of confirmation is not oriented toward youth alone. It implies and in many cases makes specific a series of objectives for the adult in the Christian community. They are the ones charged with the responsibility for the ministry to their young people; they are the ones to prepare the celebration in the public rite.

Most adults are sensible enough to realize that they cannot command anyone, even their own children, to love them. They must be lovable to merit the love of another. In similar fashion, they cannot order respect and loyal allegiance to groups that they form in the name of Christ. They must prove that they who make up his fellowship live in such a manner that they are worthy of respect, that this community is richly worth the risk of a young person's identification. He may reject their way of life unless they demonstrate practical Christianity attractively.

As you read back over the words of the definition, you can pick out some straightforward objectives for adults in a congregation. Unless they willingly and gladly work toward the fulfillment of these objectives, changing the nature and practice of confirmation in their congregation will mean little in the lives of their young people.

Let's pull some of these objectives out for inspection. It is the commission's feeling that adults in the Christian community should be prepared to—

1. Share in the pastoral and educational ministry to youth.
2. Recognize the confirmand as capable of identifying with the adult Christian community and its mission.
3. Recall with him his Baptism.
4. Testify to the strengthening they receive through the Word and Holy Communion.
5. Pray God to sustain and to strengthen the confirmand.
6. Involve the confirmand in a lifelong concern for his own Christian education.

These objectives alert adults to the necessity of knowing the confirmands and of participating with them in the church's mission. This involves more than taking part in the rite. It suggests a feeling of companionship, a program of dialogue, an opportunity to deal with common concerns.

The Definition Is Critical

So the commission has produced a definition of confirmation which it believes will serve the church at this point in its history. Further, the commission believes that this definition well serves the needs of both the church's youth and its adults. The definition is critical in your estimation of the commission's report. When you accept the definition, you will find that the whole report falls into place, each section building a part of the church's program for tomorrow.

9

An Age for Confirmation

Bill: Well, I think we ought to do something about it!

Jennie: You mean set up a tutoring service?

Betsy: Why not? Those kids need help. I mean they haven't any place at home to study. It's too noisy with all those people running around. We could fix up a study hall here in the church basement and . . .

Bill: Exactly, and maybe we're not all super-A students but we could at least help the kids who are having trouble with math and English.

Nan: Yeah, but I bet the church council won't like the idea. They'll say that the kids will just hack around the church and break up things.

Todd: Oh, I don't know. Maybe they will take to the idea. You can't shoot a guy for trying. Maybe they just never thought about it before.

Bill: You know we could work out the idea a little more and then see what the pastor thinks of it.

Jennie: I could check it out with my folks too. They could think of things maybe that we've overlooked.

Nan: Well you do that. Mine wouldn't be interested.

Betsy: Well, mine would, I bet . . . and I bet a lot of people here would be if we could sell them on the idea.

You are eavesdropping on a group of tenth-graders. Whether the plans they are cooking up succeed depends upon a lot of x-factors. We'll never know how their project turned out, but by listening to them briefly we have learned to know something about them. Idealistic yet practical, they have lost much of their early adolescent shyness. They are no longer afraid to say what they think even if it means disagreeing with each other.

We want to know a lot more about this age group. This is the group level that the commission feels should mark the age of confirmation.

The Nature of Tenth-Graders

There are many good reasons for the commission's choice. Tenth-graders are moving to a new level of independence where they now can see more clearly the kind of adults they are becoming. It is a critical period for their self-evaluation as they honestly wrestle with ideals that can shape them into the kind of persons they want to become. Therefore, they are continually engaged in testing their newly defined sense of identity. They depend upon their close friends and adults whom they respect to serve as mirrors of a sort, reflecting the image they project. This gives them unique opportunities to work out personality difficulties and to pursue those activities that merit approval.

Tenth-graders are also making some critical decisions about the foundations on which they are building their lives. They have passed through the stress and strain of shifting from the model of themselves as dependent children to that of responsible adults. They are now recognizing their abilities to make personal choices and decisions. The youth psychologist Argyle calls adolescence "a time of religious choice." Dr. Raymond Kuhlen observes that middle adolescence is the last period during which a person may decide on his beliefs before he becomes "sot in his ways."

This decision-making process is not without its hazards. Based on hundreds of parents' reports, the religious-education psychologist Ernest Ligon points to parent-child conflict as characteristic of middle adolescence. This is quite natural. The fifteen-year-old is engaged in testing his skills to defend his points of view without risking defeat by matching them against the arguments of his more mature parents. Often, teens are in the position of rejecting the help they want the most. At times, too, they come to realize the inadequacies of their definitions of themselves to the point of feeling extreme humility. It is interesting that Psalm 8 is one of the favorites of this age group, particularly verses 3 and 4:

> When I look at thy heavens, the work of thy fingers,
>   the moon and the stars which thou hast established;

> *What is man that thou art mindful of him,*
> *and the son of man that thou dost care for him?*

It is the church's responsibility to help these "amateur adults," to use Ralph Loew's phrase, go beyond these verses to the rest of the psalm:

> *Yet thou hast made him a little less than God,*
> *and dost crown him with glory and honor.*
> *Thou hast given him dominion over the works of thy*
> *hands;*
> *thou has put all things under his feet, . . .*
> *O Lord, our Lord*
> *how majestic is thy name in all the earth!*
>
> (Psalm 8:5, 6, 9)

Freedom to Become

In spite of their conflicts and self-criticism, tenth-graders tend to be idealistic. At the same time they have a strong, practical streak. They are no longer too shy to say what they think, even if it means disagreeing with their friends or parents or teachers. Yet, unless they have been forced to be defensive, they know humility in a measure unknown at any other age. This is a healthy balance. If their parents permit them to do so, they can reach a new harmony of give-and-take with others while they are in the process of establishing a more adult-like independence. It is noteworthy that much of the fifteen-year-old's criticism of his parents is really a desire to demonstrate his pride in them, which he usually will not admit openly.

The tenth grade, therefore, is a time when most youth are moving into a broad plateau of equilibrium. They are successfully completing a great many of their tasks of adolescent adjustments. The inner drives and sense of need that impel them are tempered somewhat through their willingness to accept another's point of view. In fact, they are genuinely moving out into the world of others, expanding their circle of friends rapidly, eagerly forming deeper friendships with adults and youths older than themselves. They are achieving an emotional balance and a good sense of humor. They can even laugh at themselves as they are increasingly able to accept valid criticism in their march toward self-improvement. They ask only to be allowed to be themselves and to have the freedom to become what they can become.

156

Realize, of course, that any group of general characteristics describes the group as a whole. Individuals vary. Some fifteen-year-olds may seem by these measurements to be more mature than some sixteen-year-olds. Each person grows and develops according to his own personal maturational timetable. Glands that govern his body chemistry are strictly his own. Then too, along with individual physical development, experiences the person has in his society of home, school, and church have a lot to do with the way he matures. But when you add up all the tenth-graders you know, you will probably find that they, as a group, fairly well follow the age group characteristics the commission cited in their report (pp. 204-06). Let's examine some of the commission's descriptions in greater detail.

Patterns of Growth

By tenth grade most of the girls have reached their adult height. The boys are catching up rapidly and usually pass the girls at this time. Both girls and boys are becoming sexually mature. Almost all of the girls and about 85 percent of the boys have gone through the dramatic changes of puberty. They are now settling down emotionally and getting to know their changed selves. Many adolescents in their junior high days feel that every so often they are living with complete strangers in their inner selves. That's how radically they change from month to month. But by senior high days youth's physical growth slows down considerably. It will continue gradually, of course, until the person reaches his adult level.

Since they are learning to live with themselves, tenth-graders are quite concerned about the image they project to others. They are eager to demonstrate their abilities—athletic, artistic, or scholastic. They want to put their best foot forward, so they spend a great deal of time and money on their personal appearances. They want everyone to think well of them.

Because of physical maturation tenth-graders are more capable of handling their emotions than they have been for years. Pressured by strange drives that seemed so overpowering, they now are learning that they can master themselves and indeed, must do so if they are to get along with others in the societies they choose.

Self-confidence is increasing as the young person is compromising with his idealized concept of himself and is willing to accept himself with his potentialities and limitations. You can see that he is becoming more relaxed. This doesn't mean that his self-image is completely formed. His goals often are further out than his grasp and he is miserable in his failures. But he keeps experimenting with new experiences to find his capabilities, to test his talents and skills.

While he has mastered some of the fine art of self-discipline, he is by no means confident that he can always control himself. He wants adults to help him define a set of dependable and realistic boundaries. The emphasis is on the word "help." Boundaries are much more acceptable to him if he has some part in forming them than if they are established arbitrarily. What he wants most of all is respect for himself as a person and trust in his capacity to make good decisions. When adults make it clear that they do respect and trust him, he welcomes their suggestions for his life.

Intellectually, the tenth-grader has developed the ability to reason. This means that many of the former ideas he accepted unquestioningly are now subject to critical analysis. Some doubts and confusions are apt to come. He is achieving independent thought. Now when he accepts an idea as his own, he does so on a more rigorous basis than ever before. And when he has come through this intensive questioning process, he is likely to stick by the ideas he accepts. This particular factor has some rich implications for confirmation, which we shall consider later.

In their school studies tenth-graders are pursuing subjects at more adult levels. The new dimension, the future, has become part of their daily mental framework. They are looking ahead to possible vocational choices, to college and occupational experiences, to marriage. True, they may change their minds many times in the process. But the process of identification with the adult world is beginning to grow in intensity. They are not adults but they are trying to think like adults in order to find their eventual roles in an adult world.

The Teen-Ager's Developmental Tasks

Let's go back to Robert Havighurst's book *Human Development and Education* and his idea of developmental tasks. The tasks which the individual must learn are those things, Havighurst says, "that constitute healthy and satisfactory growth in our society." We have already looked at the tasks he suggested for middle childhood. Now we can examine some of his suggestions for adolescents:

Accepting one's physique and using the body effectively;

Achieving emotional independence of parents and other adults;

Selecting and preparing for an occupation;

Developing intellectual skills and concepts necessary for civic competence;

Desiring and achieving socially responsible behavior;

Acquiring a set of values and an ethical system as a guide to behavior

When you look at these tasks and others which we have not specifically cited relating to the individual's acceptance of his sexual role and his preparation for marriage and family life, you realize how rapidly the adolescent is moving toward the adult world. There isn't much time to help him equip himself for all the responsibilities that will soon be his.

If the church expects to be central in the life of the growing adolescent, then it must foster in him a sense of partnership, a feeling that in this particular congregational fellowship he is being helped to accomplish his tasks. This eases the process of identification and encourages him to throw his weight behind the church's mission. This sounds a bit like tit for tat. It isn't; it simply means that teen-agers like most people tend to link their interests and willingness to give of themselves to those organizations that offer them support.

Personality Integration

To return to Erik Erikson's provocative book and the chapter entitled "Eight Ages of Man," we find some keen insights embodied in his description of adolescence as a time of psychological tension between the search for identity and role confusion. That is to say that Erikson sees the adolescent struggling to find himself—his identity—in the midst of all the confusing optional roles open to him. He begins to see clearly some of the choices he has to make about his sex life, his social and economic life, his intellectual life, his spiritual life. Who is he? What role should he play that is really expressive of himself?

As the adolescent attempts to integrate his personality, his new sense of identity is more than simply the summation of all the identities he experiences through the stages of childhood. Now he must find himself as he pits his reasoning and emotional powers against every opportunity to be someone else.

Erikson suggests that much of a teen-ager's "falling in love" stems not so much from his maturing sexual drives as it does from his concern to see himself reflected by someone else who cares a little for him. That's why teen-age lovers probably spend more time talking with each other than anything else. They are trying out ideas, emotions, and plans and testing reactions. If I say that I will do this, will it change my image in her eyes? If he finds out that I really like this, will his opinion of me change? In other words puppy love can be a kind of laboratory school in identification, a chance to know something more about oneself through the eyes of another.

Testing Identity

The danger of role confusion is always present for the high-schooler. There are so many claims upon his time and energies, so many possibilities for what he can do with his life when he grows up. He looks to trusted adults and their meaningful groups for answers. Then he tests them, often by attacking them in one form or another, to see if the mature roles exemplified can be genuinely his.

In presidential election years you can often see this curious happening. At school the youth may play out the political-party roles his parents communicate at home. Among his friends he expresses his parents' viewpoints and opinions. But when he comes home, he can just as easily argue with his parents, deliberately baiting them by supporting an opposing candidate to their favorite. Between the two experiences, he is coming to find himself and where he thinks he should stand as a political animal.

Some of the same process is bound to happen in his church relationships. A similar sort of testing is going on all the time to put beliefs and doctrines and practices under the microscope. What often on the surface looks like a rank form of heathenism is just a good-natured trial of identity possibilities. The one thing that adolescents cannot accept is an adult who is inconsistent. Holden Caulfield, the badgered hero of J. D. Salinger's *Catcher in the Rye* spoke for all teen-agers when he said he couldn't stand "phoneys" no matter who they were.

Social Roles

Erikson's latest studies have all been generally in the area of identity crises that confront youth, particularly as they seek to relate to their world. His keen insights offer much that will be helpful as the church shapes its educational and counseling program for youth. Perhaps, though, the emphasis on youth's identity-seeking needs to be balanced with what the sociologists tell us about the person's need to accept his appropriate social roles. History has a way of changing them. Think of the way the roles of parents have changed in our society in our lifetime. Mother may now follow a career after her children are in school without social stigma. Father may help with household chores along with his regular masculine pursuits. Incidentally, some high schools are now offering cooking classes for boys—and boys are electing the courses!

The changing of social roles in a changing society is only one of the many problems that youth must deal with in their search for personal identity and in their selection of social organizations with which they can identify. These are two facets of the same adjustment. The church itself is changing as it grapples with the challenges of the contemporary world.

The roles of the laity and of the clergy are coming under close scrutiny. More role diffusion is taking place. Now we are beginning to expect our clergymen to be more associated with the worlds in which their parishioners live and operate. Pastors are beginning to go to the coffee houses and the bars, to the recreation areas, the ski resorts and the seashore, to the factories and the offices. Counseling and dialogue (and even worship) are no longer confined to a minimum number of "holy" hours scheduled only on Sunday mornings.

Similarly, laymen are expected to take on more and more of the duties that were once exclusively the pastors'. Laymen are charged with witnessing to the faith in the midst of their daily responsibilities, with ministering to their neighbors in their needs. The church is slowly coming around to Luther's notion that Christians should serve as "little Christs" to everyone they know, translating the gospel into living terms of human involvements in the business of living.

As we help tenth-graders identify with the adult Christian community, we must accept the fact that we cannot permit them to think of their roles in the stereotypes of even a generation ago. The identification has to take place on the growing edge of the new community of saints, which is always in the process of coming into being. And youth themselves will play a major part in defining these roles for the days ahead. The commission's definition of confirmation highlights their needed contribution.

Mental Operations

Let's return to the matter of the adolescent's mental development. Here we find the foundations for his newly functional abilities to identify with the church's life and mission on more of an adult level. According to Jean Piaget, the Swiss genetic psychologist whose work was cited earlier in the discussion of the age for first Communion, the adolescent is in the developmental stage Piaget calls the "stage of formal operations." By this label he is referring to the teen-ager's mental capacity to think more abstractly, more theoretically. Until now, the child dealt with reality solely in concrete terms; he could learn to master what his senses told him was true. He did some abstract thinking but it had to focus around his immediate needs. In adolescence, however, the continuous mental growth pattern erupts in a boundary-chasing adventure in thinking. Youth can think of the future as well as of the present and past in new ways.

Piaget's article, "The Mental Development of the Child," in his *Six Psychological Studies* describes how youth freed from childish limitations can construct theories and build concepts that outstrip the information of his senses. He can operate intelligently in an adult thought-world, dealing with idealistic schemes for change. In other words, youth have the capacity to work on all kinds of problems, scientific, social, aesthetic, economic, or religious, and come up with well-thought-out schemes for solution. In fact, they can get carried away with the soundness of their proposals and become quite impatient with adult dimness of vision in not putting these ideas into operation.

A Time of Testing

What youth lack most of all is personal experience, the fiery furnace for trying out their ideas in the harsh reality·of life as it is. When youth build their "castles in the air," adults are often tempted to let the young persons live alone in their ethereal real estate. What they should be doing is enabling these teen-agers to attach stout cables to their castles, pulling them down to solid rock where the structures can be tested.

As confirmed youth become more involved in the church's task, they can be guided through many opportunities to help the congregation plan for the future and also to experiment with these plans. When teen-agers feel they are free to contribute their ideas for improving the church's program and, what is more important, that adults are both willing to listen to them and to take seriously what they say, they are drawn into closer fellowship with those adults.

A Time of Integration

Piaget points out that it is not until adolescence that youth is really capable of integrating his religion with the system of life he is developing. Now he is becoming more of a whole person, in short, more of a personality so that he is not one individual here on the playground, another in the classroom, and still another at home. He is himself wherever he goes, whatever he does. He tries out through logical deductive thinking the possibilities for the occupational choices visible in his own future. Imagination and daydreaming play a considerable part in his thinking as he tries to visualize what it would be like to be an important person in this or that type of work. "We see, then, how the adolescent goes about injecting himself into adult society," Piaget writes. "He does so by means of projects, life plans, theoretical systems, and ideas of political or social reform."

The church's task is to help youth see their formative life systems bound up with others in the people of God. This can only be done effectively by allowing youth to try out their ideas and their abilities as an integral part of the adult community they are expected to accept. Failure by the church to do so just gives the impression that young people are only in the way until they have matured a great deal more. And youth seldom hang around groups that treat them like that.

To quote Piaget again, "True adaptation to society comes automatically when the adolescent reformer attempts to put his ideas to work." And let's not forget that the teen-ager is very much a reformer. What he doesn't like about his world, he is going to try to change. Good for him! Give him the chance. Piaget goes on, "Just as experience reconciles formal thought with the reality of things, so does effective and enduring work undertaken in concrete and well-defined situations, cure all dreams." Maybe that's a lot to take in. What Piaget is suggesting is that there is no substitute for involving the adolescent in the kind of life toward which he is moving.

163

When you consider the tenth-grader as a confirmand in the light of his mental growth, you can see many advantages. He is capable of integrating the faith of the church into his own life-view; he can explore the importance of his concepts of God in his life to guide the vital decisions he must make; he can recognize the many Christian learnings of his earlier years into a more unified whole. In brief, he is able to fulfill the details of the commission's definition of confirmation as he is accepted into the adult Christian fellowship.

Comparisons

Perhaps this is a point for a significant digression. In reviewing the characteristics of tenth-graders which the commission listed in their report (pp. 204-06), perhaps you began to notice certain striking similarities between the social-emotional situations of the fifth- and tenth-graders.

Both have passed through the emotional periods of establishing themselves in a new status, fifth-graders as group members, tenth-graders as individuals. Both are in a period of slow physical and mental growth. In a sense, both are in a period of consolidating gains before the next spurt of growth. Both have found new levels of becoming important, responsible beings. Both are characterized by better emotional balance, sense of humor, ability to accept criticism, and a need for adult guidance, although the tenth-grader is less able to accept it openly. Both are eager to get an honest picture of themselves and work out improvements.

It is interesting that at both age levels, youth are challenged by having their mental abilities stretched through discussion of important issues. Although the tenth-grader may seem to lack interest in learnings about the institutional church, he is eagerly seeking for the meaning of his own personal religion in association with other Christians. Confirmation with the preparatory education which precedes it becomes a vital step to link him with the people of God. Thus at both ages, new levels of religious participation are apparent.

Finally at both age levels, youth are seeking to understand right and wrong. The tenth-grader has gone beyond asking why God demands certain actions to a deeper understanding of Christian ethics based on a faith relationship. He is truly ready to understand the meaning of sin and redemption in ways that were not possible for him previously.

Implications for the Church's Educational Program

Suppose we do establish confirmation as a special ministry of the church that reaches its culmination in the latter part of the tenth grade. What does this do to Christian education programs?

Probably there will be some who will complain that the church is trying to add yet one more year of intensified catechetical instruction to the already overloaded schedules of high school youth. This would be neither necessary nor advisable.

The commission feels strongly that depth studies of Christian faith and life in the catechetical program should be continued on the junior high age level, grades seven, eight, and nine. These are foundation studies carefully integrated with the youth's public school curriculum, building on the Christian education he has received in other schools of the church. Preparation for confirmation would include this program but would go further, much further. It would offer the confirmand much more counseling and opportunities to try out his ideas about his faith in more informal educational situations.

For the churches the tenth grade should be a time of private and small group conferences with the pastor and other lay leaders. Here youth could critically examine their faith, raise their doubts and confusions, explore workable ways of reconciling their dreams with reality. Weekend conferences and retreats could play a larger part in the congregation's ministry to youth on this age level. This could and should be a time of consolidation, assisting the youth to take their places in the adult Christian community. Important groundwork should be laid so that youth realize that education is a part of their life in the church, continuing to serve them as they seek to adjust to the many demands being made on them during their maturing years.

Suggestions for the Future

Take time now to turn to pages 207 and 208 of the commisson's report. Here are suggested objectives for the church's confirmation program. Notice how the three major sections of those objectives dovetail to help the confirmand pull together the various aspects of his Christian faith in a new and vital way. There is no stress on any kind of mastery of a course of study for graduation from childhood. Instead, the objectives are written in terms of his apprentice adulthood.

When the change in the age for confirmation takes place, congregations will have to take objectives like these seriously. New educational programs geared more specifically to the needs of tenth-graders will have to be devised. There will be a necessary and exciting period of experimentation. Think of the opportunities to get youth and adults together in learning situations quite removed from the classroom atmosphere. It could be in the form of a wilderness canoe trip or a camping adventure. Some groups might like to spend some time working together in slum neighborhoods or planning new programs for the congregation's ministry to the community that surrounds the church building. This is the time for a lot of creative thinking about how the church can best serve its youth as it prepares them for their transition to a more adult point of view.

A Broad-Based Program

Another point to consider is that the church's pastoral and educational ministry to its youth may not take the same form for everyone. The individual's interests and concerns should be considered. As the pastor and other youth leaders come to know the confirmands well, they can help them tailor the kinds of programs that will meet most effectively their individual needs. Instead of a narrow base of required courses for tenth-graders, the church may broaden its educational offerings to allow a wide range of optional choices. Naturally, this will involve more congregational leaders. But such a development is good. Youth will be much better equipped to make up their own minds when they can hone their spiritual insights against the opinions of a variety of others.

Obviously, if the kind of broad-based youth program we are talking about here is to succeed, it must include the parents of the confirmands in some way. For instance, panel discussions involving parents and their youth can help focus on critical issues of concern. In addition, the church needs to develop a stronger program of parent education so that parents themselves can make full use of home opportunities to guide their tenth-graders in their gropings toward a mature Christian faith.

The Rite of Confirmation

Any rite which the church devises to serve its people should be consistent with its teachings and practices. A rite becomes a historical and an emotional focal point for significant personal experiences. Most of us can remember in great detail and clarity what happened when we were confirmed, if we think long and hard enough. It was an important day, capturing our feelings and our youthful sense of commitment. In a large measure those experiences tend to color our attitudes toward our role in the church. (And don't they also contribute to building up an emotional mind-set that resists suggested changes in the catechetical-confirmation process?) We might as well face this particular problem honestly. In building for the future of the church's ministry to its baptized youth, we need to sever ourselves from what can easily be the tyranny of the past in order to develop what can be more meaningful for youth today and for the lives of future groups of confirmands.

Suggested Elements in the Rite

The point in looking backward to the importance of the rite of confirmation in our lives is to stress the value of fashioning a new rite that will have equal significance in the lives of future groups of confirmands. The commission wants to make sure that this new rite reflects the convictions of the definition of confirmation. Read through the commission's comments on the rite, pages 209-11 of their report.

Here are the elements they want to emphasize in the rite as a result of their studies:

1. The remembrance of Baptism;
2. Acknowledgment of the word of God by which God creates faith;
3. The confirmand's affirmation of the faith of the church, his acceptance of God's grace in his life and his willingness to live according to this grace;
4. The blessing of the congregation, prayer on behalf of the confirmand for God's continual favor and strengthening;
5. The laying on of hands solely to personalize the prayers of the congregation.

On the other hand, the commission feels that the new rite should avoid:

1. Any kind of implication that confirmation completes the Sacrament of Baptism;

2. Statements that the confirmand is now a member of the church, or that he is being admitted into "full communion";
3. Ambiguous suggestions that the confirmand is receiving rights and privileges he already had received in his Baptism;
4. Formal vow of any sort. No person is capable of keeping a lifelong vow. Besides, the Christian stands in need of daily renewal of his faith relationship with God;
5. Emphasis on the confirmand's confirming what has been done for him. It should focus on God's confirming the unilateral covenant he makes with each person at the time of his Baptism.

A Sample Rite

By putting together these two lists, what a confirmation rite should contain and what it should not contain, it is possible to plan an evangelical rite that will be both inspirational and functional. Following these criteria, for example, is a rite developed by some liturgical scholars to illustrate the possibilities:

THE RITE OF CONFIRMATION

* Candidates for confirmation shall be instructed in the faith and life of the church as it finds expression in the Lutheran Confession, and shall be approved by the pastor and the church council in such manner as may be deemed satisfactory. The rite may be preceded by a public examination of the candidates, or by an occasion at which they give public expression to their faith and what the church means to them.

* Confirmation shall be administered at a public service of the congregation. Should this be impossible in an individual case, confirmation may be administered in the presence of members of the congregation privately. Such confirmation shall subsequently be announced publicly to the congregation.

* When confirmation is administered at The Service, this order shall follow the Gospel. If there be Holy Communion at the same service, this order shall follow the Sermon.

* Before the Epistle and Gospel for the Day, one or more of the following Lessons may be read: Ezekiel 36:26-28; John 14:15-17; John 15:1-16; Acts 8:14-17; Romans 8:12-17; Romans 10:8-11 (Begin: The word is near you . . .); Ephesians 2:13-22.

* Each candidate for confirmation shall be accompanied by a sponsor or sponsors.

* A prie-dieu or prayer desk may be placed before the altar for kneeling, with a space left clear for access to it.

---

* A clerk (the secretary of the church council or other appointed layman) standing before the congregation shall say:

The following, having been instructed in the Christian faith as witnessed to in the Lutheran Confession, and approved by the chuch, are now presented for the rite of confirmation.

> *He shall read the names of the candidates and after each name the name(s) of the sponsor(s). As the names are read, each person named (both candidates and sponsors) shall rise. After all the names have been read, the candidates shall come to the altar. If space permits, the sponsors may also come to the altar and stand to the rear of the candidates. Where space does not permit, the sponsors shall sit after the candidates have reached the altar. (Pastor and local congregation should feel free to adapt the procedures here given to their peculiar circumstances.)

> * The minister shall say:

In Holy Baptism you were received by our Lord Jesus Christ and made members of his holy church. Later, after instruction in the meaning of the sacrament of Holy Communion, you were admitted to the fellowship of the Lord's Table. Today, after further instruction in the Christian faith and life, and having attained greater maturity in your relationship to your Lord, his church, and his world, you have been approved as prepared for the rite of confirmation. I therefore ask you:

Do you believe in one God, the Father, the Son, and the Holy Spirit?

Answer: I believe.

Do you accept Jesus Christ as your Lord and the Savior of the world?

Answer: I do.

Let us all confess the faith of the church into which we have been baptized.

> * Then shall all present say the Apostles' Creed.

> * Then shall the minister say:

Do you intend to remain in this faith and in the covenant God made with you in Baptism, and toward that end to continue to study God's Word, to be regular in attendance at worship and in prayer?

Answer: Yes, with the help of God.

169

Do you intend to live your life in harmony with the gospel of Christ as revealed in Holy Scripture, and to accept as your own the mission of Christ's church in the world?

Answer: Yes, with the help of God.

* **Then shall the minister say:**

Let us pray.

* **The congregation shall rise, or kneel, and there shall follow a space for silent prayer by all present for those about to be confirmed. The silence ended, the minister shall say:**

Almighty God, heavenly Father: we thank you that in Baptism these your children have been born to a new life and relationship with you through the forgiveness of their sins. Strengthen them now, we pray, with the Holy Spirit and increase in them daily the gifts of your grace, that they may know you and understand your will for them, that they may thank, praise, and love you, and that they may receive the strength to live as your servants in the world: through Jesus Christ, your Son, our Lord. *Amen.*

* **Then the candidates shall kneel. The clerk may read the name of each candidate and the minister shall lay his hand on the head of each in turn and say the prayer of blessing. The clerk and/or sponsor(s) may also lay his (their) hand(s) on the head of each as the prayer of blessing is said. Where a prie-dieu is being used, each candidate shall, in turn come to the prie-dieu and kneel there for the laying on of hands. The minister shall say:**

The Father in heaven, for Jesus' sake, renew and increase in you the gift of the Holy Spirit, that you may be strengthened in faith, grow in grace, have patience sufficient for every trial, and confidently live in the assurance of everlasting life.

* **Here may follow the prayers of blessing customarily used in the participating church bodies.**

* **Each candidate shall respond: Amen.**

* **All having received the prayer of blessing, the minister shall say to the newly confirmed:**

Confirmation is an important stage, but only one of the many stages in a lifetime of learning at the feet of our Lord and of service to your fellowmen. The church expects you to continue to learn and to assume always greater responsibilities as members of the family of God, and as ambassadors of Christ in the world.

> * Then the parents and teachers shall rise, and if the sponsors have not come to the altar, they too shall rise. The minister shall address them substantially as follows:

When these young people were admitted to the fellowship of the Lord's Table, parents and sponsors promised that they would be further instructed and one day be brought to the altar for the rite of confirmation. Their presence here today is evidence that you, the parents, sponsors, and teachers have been faithful in your obligations. The church, the family of God, on whose behalf you have acted now thanks you and expresses the hope that you will be forever rewarded in the lives of those whom you have brought to this day.

> * The congregation shall rise, or kneel, and the minister shall say:

Let us pray.

Almighty God, heavenly Father, confirm the work you have begun in these young people. Grant that they may remain in the fellowship of your church and in the faith of your gospel. Keep them so that no false teaching, no selfish desires, and no idolatrous worship of this world may lead them away from you and the truth they have confessed. Give them joy in obeying your Word. Grant that they may always know you more intimately, love you more fervently, and serve you more faithfully in word or deed, for the welfare of their fellowmen, for the upbuilding of your people and the glory of your name; through Jesus Christ our Lord. *Amen.*

> * The minister may then add one or more of the following prayers:

Lord God, our loving Father, from whom come all the good things in our lives: for these young people and all of us this is a happy day and we are grateful. Grant, we pray, that this same gladness in your presence and the fellowship of your people may remain with them in all the days ahead. Whatever problems and temptations may confront them, may the leading and power of the Spirit keep them from losing their way. In the midst of confusion, may they remember what they really want out of life, so they may always know the highest joy of serving you; through Jesus Christ our Lord. *Amen.*

Father in heaven, your glory is hidden in all the wonder, beauty, and good things of this life, in parents, teachers, and all who labor for the benefit of mankind, wherever your will is done and there is love and truth and justice. We pray that we may all find meaning and joy and peace in doing your will in the world; through Jesus Christ our Lord. *Amen.*

Heavenly Father, you alone can make us will and do what is good and true and altogether lovely. Bless these children of yours, watch over them as only you, their heavenly Father can. Give them your creative Spirit, let them know you and understand what you have to say to them, so that they may always be yours now and forever in the life you have promised to those that love you; through Jesus Christ our Lord. *Amen.*

O God, who made man in your own image and whose love extends to all you have made: Make us know the oneness of your family and the breadth of your love. By the example of your Son, Jesus Christ our Savior, enable us, while loving and serving our own, to enter into the fellowship of the whole human family; and forbid that from pride or lack of concern we should despise any for whom he died, or harm any in whom he lives; through the same Jesus Christ our Lord. *Amen.*

O God, who through the gift of the Holy Spirit confirms us and strengthens us for our daily round of life: Grant us such knowledge of your will and trust in your grace that we may truly show forth the life we profess, and by our good works and loving concern bring all men to you, the only God; through Jesus Christ our Lord. *Amen.*

* **Then shall the minister dismiss them, saying:**

The blessing of Almighty God, the Father, the Son and the Holy Spirit, be with you always. *Amen.*

* **Then shall those confirmed (and the sponsors, if they have been at the altar) return to their places, and The Service shall continue.**

Sponsors

The suggestion by the commission of having sponsors for the confirmands is a practical way of strengthening the emphasis in the definition of confirmation on the youth's identification with the adult Christian community. Hopefully, the sponsors could be the same persons who served each confirmand in that capacity at the time of his admission to the first Communion. This would promote adult concern and counseling during his formative years.

Sponsors would play a much more active part in the church's ministry to its youth than ever before. If the former sponsors were not available, the congregation would appoint new ones some time before the rite of confirmation is to be celebrated to allow a maximum amount of time for their building friendships with the confirmands. This is also a way for the congregation to provide additional guidance to youth who come to the congregation without parental support or adequate home concern.

All attempts should be made to involve the sponsors actively in the confirmation process. This means that they should have a significant part in the rite itself. This also suggests that the church should develop a practical educational program for those adults who will serve as sponsors. They can be a vital link in the church's pastoral and educational ministry, personalizing the church's concern and being available to youth as a strong Christian friend in time of need. Only persons can really minister to persons. And those who seek to minister must be educated for this ministry.

Responsible Persons

By suggesting the latter part of the tenth grade as the time for confirmation, the commission is not advocating a new form of legalism to replace current practice. Generally, young baptized church members coming through the schools of the church will be ready for the kind of confirmation the commission envisions. However, this by no means is saying that we are now to process all young persons automatically through this rite. This would be denying their personhood. Basically, we are concerned personally with the spiritual well-being of each youth in our midst.

Stan Freeberg in his satirical record album *The United States of America* has a marvelous parody on commonplace attitudes toward Brotherhood Week. One of his songs begins "Take an Indian to lunch this week. Show him we are a regular bunch this week . . ." Far too often, the church's policy toward its teenagers gives them the impression that the adult congregation is just going through the motions of making them feel necessary and wanted. It's the Christian thing to do! But if there be only token warmth and sincerity in the adults' acceptance of confirmed youth as part of their church fellowship, the whole purpose of confirmation crumbles.

Youth are too canny to be taken in by noble sentiments that have little basis in reality. If they fight "the establishment," it is often because they feel they are not wanted as themselves. And yet the only way they can sense that the life and mission of the church involves them personally is by knowing that the congregation respects them as individuals, that the people of God expect them to make valuable contributions to the effectiveness of the Christian witness in their day. This means that the ministry of the congregation to its baptized youth must always be on a personal basis. The educational process, the pastoral concern, the rite itself should give each young person the feeling that through these channels God is addressing him personally.

Back of the commission's recommendations for changes in confirmation practices is a plea for a ministry to persons. This means that, while formalized programs and procedures and rites need to be developed for the sake of good order, these are guides rather than rules. As Paul points out, the letter of the law kills; the spirit alone gives life (cf. 2 Corinthians 3:6). The basic question before each congregation should always be how we can help Jim and Diane and Tom and Kathy feel a part of the adult congregation. Even though all four of them may be confirmed together, the route each takes to that significant celebration may be slightly different—and should be if those adults doing the counseling and guiding are alert to individual needs.

Actually what confirmation is all about is helping youth become responsible Christian persons, not only in their congregation life but also in their everyday involvements. The old expression, "ambassadors of Christ" is just a whisker away from becoming a cliché. But it still has some meaning. As members of the people of God, youth are charged with the responsibility of carrying the gospel with them, each in his own way, wherever they go. Then whether they are gathered with their fellowship of Christians or scattered on their own, the church will grow. If, as someone has said, the church is always just one generation from dying out, there are few more important demands upon a congregation's energy and time than developing an effective pastoral and educational ministry to its youth to help them accept the life and mission of the adult Christian community as their own.

10

Evaluations and Decisions

In a midwestern town the superintendent of schools has a sign on his office wall, "In the event of enemy air attack, praying will be allowed in this school." A gag sign! But perhaps there is more truth than humor in those words. Emergencies make us come to the place where we make decisions about what is important and what is not. There is little time for frivolous speculation.

If you listen to the pessimists, you can come to the conclusion that the modern church is on the edge of passing out of existence as a vital force in society. Who needs it, they say; it is a moss-back, an anachronism from the past that offers little of value to people today confronted by contemporary problems. The optimists, on the other hand, feel that there are no problems that the church of Jesus Christ cannot conquer. It has done so in the past, surviving twenty centuries of human problems. "We have Christ's own promise and that cannot fail," wrote Sabine Baring-Gould in his famous old hymn, "Onward Christian Soldiers." In other words, the pessimist sees only Good Friday; the optimist sees only Easter. The sensitive Christian, however, realizes that the gospel includes both experiences.

The church exists as a collection of very human people caught up in the business of living in the midst of change. Constantly, it must make its message and its programs helpful to people where they are. New demands require reassessment and new ideas. The burning question always is: Where do we go from here?

There are many ways to answer that question. The best way is to study the problems thoroughly and to gather the pertinent facts that need to be considered in making decisions. This is the way the commission has proceeded with its task of studying the nature and the practice of confirmation. But what do people do with facts? Actually, there is only one procedure for living comfortably with facts: weigh them carefully and make a thoughtful, responsible judgment.

You now have in your hands all the evidence that the commission feels is important in shaping the church's decisions about what to do with admission to first Communion and confirmation. These are critical steps to take. A number of other areas in church organizations and practice are involved. Let's look at two areas.

Revision in the Rite of Infant Baptism

To follow the commission's recommendations for establishing a new concept of confirmation will necessitate a careful revision of the rite of infant Baptism. Theologically, we are vulnerable. We have allowed the language presently used in that rite to remain fuzzy. By trying to make infant Baptism identical with adult Baptism, we have confused the issues of what God does for us and how we accept his gifts. Read through the commission's comments on pages 208-09.

As Lutherans, we do not think that we must apologize for baptizing infants and young children. This Baptism is God's free act mediated through his people, announcing publicly that these are his children, that they belong to his family, the church.

Dietrich Bonhoeffer, however, called our attention to one element that must not be overlooked. In *The Cost of Discipleship,* Bonhoeffer wrote, "As far as infant baptism is concerned, it must be insisted that the sacrament should be administered only where there is a firm faith present which remembers Christ's deed of salvation wrought for us once and for all." Bonhoeffer, the German theologian who died a martyr's death in a Nazi concentration camp, positively identifies the locus of that faith. "That can only happen," he continues, "in a living Christian community."

Therefore, the congregation should have a larger part in the rite, confessing the faith in which they have been baptized and into which these children are baptized. In short, they are accepting the children into their fellowship and share the responsibility for their "growth in grace." The child then comes to accept his church family quite naturally in much the same way that he comes to accept the human family into which he was born.

Some critics of infant Baptism think it unfair to the child to baptize him into Christianity without his consent. But family life and citizenship in his country are conferred upon him also without his say-so. Why should a baby be excluded from the greatest gifts adults can give him, membership in the family of God, citizenship in God's kingdom?

Baptism for adults is the same Baptism offered infants, bringing the full range of God's gifts, forgiveness, love, and eternal life to the individual. There should be the same warm expression of support offered by the congregation receiving them. But there is a difference in the mode of acceptance. The adult accepts Baptism by his own free will, turning away from his former life and in Paul's words, "putting on Christ." The rite for adults then legitimately can ask the mature candidate for Baptism if he indeed is willing to become a member of the church, to take God's gifts as his own.

By straightening out current baptismal rites, we will move toward establishing an evangelical concept of confirmation.

Receiving Adults into Church Membership

The second area of current practice that will need revision concerns the reception of adults into church membership. Since the commission has defined confirmation in terms of the congregation's ministry to its baptized youth to help them identify with the adult Christian community, it will no longer be necessary nor desirable to confirm adults.

There has generally been a great deal of confusion, anyhow, in how to use confirmation with adults. Some congregations have insisted on confirming baptized adults even though they come from other denominations where they had participated in similar rites. Others only confirmed young adults, evidently assuming that older adults were, by their age, beyond the need of the rite. Actually, a simple rite of profession of faith would serve as well, without the complications.

The commission, therefore, recommends that adults not be confirmed. They should be received into church membership by Baptism or, if they have been baptized, by profession of faith. Since our faith relationship with God should be renewed daily, it probably would be advisable to have those coming into a congregational fellowship by letters of transfer from another congregation participate also in a rite of profession of faith. If the commission's recommendations are accepted, these matters will need to be studied thoroughly.

Along with a new rite of infant Baptism the church needs a new rite for profession of faith. Both would enable the church to minister more intelligently and effectively to persons on their appropriate age levels.

Other Changes

It is obvious that if the three Lutheran churches which engaged in the intensive study of confirmation and first Communion adopt the commission's recommendations a number of changes will be required in present organizational patterns beyond the rites themselves. Some of these changes will be minor; others will demand a thorough overhaul of current procedures. But if we accept the task of the church to let the full power of the gospel shine through whatever we do in the name of Jesus Christ, changes to meet the needs of each new age are perfectly in order. In fact, change is essential even though it may be uncomfortable for some in the days when it is initiated. Essentially, we can classify the necessary changes into four areas: liturgical, constitutional, statistical, and educational.

Nothing much more need be said about liturgical changes. Most of this book was concerned with these possibilities. Functional and evangelical rites for Baptism (both infant and adult), admission to first Communion, confirmation, and profession of faith are involved. The three churches united in the present study are also participating in a joint commission on worship. The task of this group is to develop a common liturgy for the majority of Lutherans in North America. In harmony with their assignment, the new rites could be planned as part of their production of a new service book and hymnal.

The constitutional changes required to reflect church-membership status will be relatively minor. Since none of the three churches has really defined confirmed membership, there are no definitions to replace. What should be added is a careful distinction between communing and confirmed members where this is essential in constitutional documents for legal purposes.

Constitutional changes lead to statistical changes where the most work will need to be done. The present categories used in reporting various degrees of membership and as a means of determining apportioned benevolence among the congregations will need some revamping. This is not a serious alteration in keeping records although it may make comparisons with the past more difficult. Those who are record-minded can make the adjustments.

When major league baseball increased both the National and the American Leagues to ten teams each and the season to a hundred and sixty-five games, many moaned about what would happen to the record books. Surely baseball has produced more statistical fanatics than any other sport. But in time they found it possible to talk about Babe Ruth's home run record of sixty in a hundred and fifty-four games and Roger Maris' total of sixty-one homers in a hundred and sixty-two games. Did Maris break Ruth's record or not? Baseball fans can have a lot of pleasure arguing that point for years to come. Incidentally, both major leagues are considering expanding now to twelve teams each and perhaps even more games in a season. The whole question of records will start all over again.

But, really, the only value in keeping records is to ascertain where people are and what they are doing. Records look backward; they should have little function in controlling what lies ahead. If the church feels that it should make policy changes, then it should do so on the basis of its best judgment and worry about record-keeping chores afterward.

By far the most radical changes will need to be made in the church's educational program. The development of a new curriculum, however, is always a current task. Experts say that at best any curriculum is obsolete in about seven years. Congregations deserve the most sufficient and efficient educational courses and programs that can be devised. New educational media, classroom methods, insights into the ways people learn challenge the church constantly to put God's message of love in Jesus Christ into "new wineskins." Making adequate provision for admission to first Communion in the fifth grade and having confirmation in the tenth grade will come not by adding a few concentrated, select courses at appropriate spots in current curricula but by building a solid series of educational experiences for children and youth along the continuum of their growth.

Toward Unified Practice

With our highly mobile population moving regularly to new neighborhoods or to new communities, it is essential to help

Lutherans feel at home in the parishes to which they go. One way of encouraging their ready transfer from one congregation to another is by developing a unified approach to such key Lutheran practices as admission to first Communion and confirmation. Instead of a move disrupting a child's catechetical experiences, for instance, he ought to be able to pick right up in his new congregation the studies he had in his former one.

As the Lutheran churches in America take seriously their responsibility to their children and youth, they will find no alternative to establishing common standards and procedures. Already they have accepted a common translation of Luther's *Small Catechism in Contemporary English.* Now they have the opportunity to go a great deal further in their work together. Is it too much to imagine an enthusiastic Luther saying, "Why not"?

What Do You Think?

We have come a long way together, through the tangled undergrowth of church history and the rarified atmosphere of theology, to look at the church's concern for its young persons. We have examined the commission's definition of confirmation in detail and noted its suggestions for changing our current practices in confirmation and first Communion. Where do we go from here?

First of all, maybe you would like some time to think about the commission's recommendations in the light of your study of the issues involved. Take time now to reread the commission's report, this time straight through to see how each part of that document fits together in a model program for the church's planning in developing an effective ministry for the future.

The commission is eager to hear from you and from your congregation when you have completed your study of confirmation and first Communion. The opinions and suggestions you offer through your congregation's report will help the commission members frame the final report on the nature and practice of confirmation to be submitted to the churches for action at their national conventions, the Lutheran Church in America and The American Lutheran Church in 1970, The Lutheran Church— Missouri Synod in 1971.

Your concern, your interest and, most of all, your prayers can aid the church in developing the kind of effective ministry our children and youth need in today's changing world.

Anglican William Temple, at one time the Archbishop of Canterbury, wrote in *Christian Faith and Life* some stimulating thoughts that Lutherans could profitably think with him:

> *Remember, the supreme wonder of the history of the Christian church is that always in the moments when it has seemed most dead, out of its own body there has sprung new life; so that in age after age it has renewed itself, and age after age by its renewal has carried the world forward into new stages of progress, as it will do for us in our day, if only we give ourselves in devotion to its Lord and take our place in its service.*

A REPORT FOR STUDY

from the Joint Commission
on the Theology and Practice of Confirmation

to the
HONORABLE PRESIDENTS
of
THE AMERICAN LUTHERAN CHURCH,
LUTHERAN CHURCH in AMERICA, and
THE LUTHERAN CHURCH—MISSOURI SYNOD

DECEMBER 28, 1967

Introduction

The report is presented in five parts. The first part deals with the definition of confirmation as the commission finally formulated it, stripped of its nonessentials and set forth in a manner most suitable for the Lutheran churches in the United States and Canada. This is followed by a brief historical sketch of confirmation through its various stages of development in the church prior to the Reformation and particularly since then in the Lutheran church throughout the world.

The third part deals with the theological aspects of confirmation especially as it relates to the means of grace and the biblical and confessional concept of the church. The next section deals with the practical implications for the Lutheran churches in this day and age with express reference to the age of first Communion and confirmation, the significance which the proposed changes have for educators, and what is implied in the development of the necessary rites. The last section of the report offers a series of recommendations for adoption and implementation.

Contents

A Definition
of Confirmation

I

Preamble

Confirmation is the church's own creation invested with meanings that the church seeks to communicate to its members. Since the practice of confirmation is not biblically ordained, its meaning and form may change as the needs of the church for this particular practice change from time to time and place to place. In fact, flexibility need not indicate a haphazard, ill-considered approach by the church but rather pastoral care and congregational concern for individual persons and situations.

We are faced, therefore, with the question of the most useful purpose a practice of confirmation may serve as the church seeks to fulfill its mission in the pluralistic society of North America in this century. Such a purpose will, or course, also reflect historical context, because the present situation is related to its heritage and origin.

Both historic practice and present need indicate that confirmation can best serve the church today as a practice designed for baptized children. Adults should not be confirmed but following adequate instruction should be received into membership in the congregation by Baptism or, where they have already been baptized, by profession of faith.

Definition

Confirmation is a pastoral and educational ministry of the church that is designed to help baptized children identify with the life and mission of the adult Christian community and that is celebrated in a public rite.

The pastoral ministry expresses the loving concern of the parents, sponsors, and all agencies of the church for the welfare of the child.

The educational ministry is that phase of a lifelong catechumenate which nourishes in the child his particular gifts so that he can know and confess as his own the Christian faith, live his role as a child and servant of God, and grow in the life of the Christian community.

In the public rite the people of God recognize the confirmand as capable of identifying with the adult Christian community and its mission. They recall with him the event of Baptism through which God, by grace, received them into his church, and they testify to the strengthening they receive through the Word and Holy Communion. The confirmand gives assurance that he believes the Word and promises of God and affirms his commitment to the Christian life. The people pray God to sustain the confirmand and to strengthen him further in Christian life. This prayer may be individualized by the laying on of hands.

Commentary

• The practice of confirmation has become distorted through accretions and misunderstandings. This applies particularly to the rite and calls for further definition by exclusion. The church cannot regard the rite of confirmation as a sacrament in the sense that Baptism and Holy Communion are called sacraments. The rite of confirmation does not complete Baptism. The word "confirmation" does not mean a ratification of promises made by sponsors at Baptism, but it means "a strengthening," a work which God performs. Thus, the rite of confirmation does not make a person more fully a member of the church than he already is by virtue of his Baptism. It does not infuse any special grace or by its nature confer special privileges. It is not a prerequisite for Holy Communion. The rite of confirmation, helpful as it may be, is therefore in no way essential to the Christian life.

• The ability to identify with "the adult Christian community" denotes a level of Christian maturity rather than an age reference. The initial boundary of such maturity cannot be defined precisely, for there are wide variations in personal growth, development, and achievement. Nevertheless, there is a point at which the adult community recognizes that the young person has developed elements of maturity, such as stability, independence, and self-confidence, that enable him to identify with and to accept a more responsible role in that community.

• The "mission" of the adult Christian community with which the young person identifies is as broad as the gospel and as specific as a cup of cold water given in Jesus' name. While the essential mission of the church remains the same, the situation in the world is constantly changing. The church must therefore equip the young person with the ability to recognize the need to adapt that mission to his own time and to accept his responsibility to it, using the resources which the church has received from the Holy Spirit.

• It is recognized that there are public occasions other than confirmation when stages of Christian growth, such as admission to first Communion, may be celebrated.

II

The History of Confirmation in the Lutheran Church

It is generally agreed that the current problems facing the Lutheran church in reference to confirmation are deeply rooted in its history. Since confirmation, unlike Baptism and the Lord's Supper, lacks scriptural authority and is a practice that has arisen in connection with the observance of the sacraments, its tradition has developed as needs and conditions changed. This was particularly true of the Lutheran church, which had rejected the practice current in the sixteenth century and yet had difficulty in agreeing whether a substitute for confirmation was needed and what its function and form should be.

Confirmation has been correctly described as one of the unsolved problems of the Lutheran church, lacking both a consistent approach and a universally accepted definition. The judgment expressed in the report to the Helsinki Assembly of the Lutheran World Federation (p. 18) "that the whole problem of confirmation must be discussed thoroughly in the light of its historical development," requires thoughtful attention. If the Lutheran church is seriously concerned with a reconstruction of confirmation, it must study its history in order to understand the rationale behind present-day practices and be prepared to examine them in the light of its theology and current needs.

REFORMERS' VIEW

Lutheran confirmation is usually, though not necessarily, associated with both sacraments. As far as its relation to Baptism is concerned, Lutheran confirmation traces its heritage directly to the early church where confirmation was part of the initiation rite. In so far as the practice is associated with the Lord's Supper, it has only little in common with confirmation as it was practiced in the early church and as it was found later in the Greek Orthodox and the Roman Catholic churches.

The rite for the sacrament of initiation in the early church developed in separate ways in the East and the West. In the East initiation rites were developed after instruction and prior to Baptism, which included a renunciation, a vow of obedience to Christ, a confession of faith, and the anointing on the forehead. In the West the anointing usually followed Baptism as a sign of "sealing" and of "confirmation" connected with the confession of faith. A remnant of this early practice of confirmation has survived in liturgical form in the present post-baptismal prayer still in use among some Lutherans. In both the East and the West participation in Holy Communion was the concluding event in the initiation rite. When infant Baptism became more general, the church continued for some time to include infants in the celebration of the Eucharist.

With the growth of the Christian church, especially with the universal practice of infant Baptism, emphasis began to be placed on post-baptismal instruction in the West. The right to baptize was delegated by the bishop to the priest. This, in time, permitted confirmation and with it the baptismal Eucharist to be separated from the initiation rite. Where the Roman liturgy came into use, Baptism and confirmation gradually became distinct and separate rites. Confirmation came to be regarded as a complement to Baptism, at first as an added gift of the Spirit and, later, as necessary for salvation.

Already in the first half of the twelfth century, confirmation was referred to as a sacrament, and at the Council of Florence in 1439 it was declared to be a sacrament. The Council of Trent in 1547 fixed this as a doctrine, affirming confirmation to be a sacrament which was effective *ex opere operato*, not necessarily associated with a period of instruction. The council fixed the age for confirmation some time between the seventh and the twelfth years.

Concurrently, a second view of confirmation which regarded it as catechetical was prevalent in the West. Accordingly, confirmation marked the close of the catechumenate and the acceptance into the worshiping congregation. This was the view of Erasmus and was adopted by the Bohemian Brethren. The catechetical emphasis receded in Roman Catholic circles after the Council of Trent had fixed the doctrine and anathematized the Evangelical substitution with its emphasis on instruction.

IN THE SIXTEENTH CENTURY

The Roman concept of confirmation as a supplement to Baptism, conferring grace and the added gift of the Spirit was vehemently rejected by Luther, Melanchthon, and the Lutheran Confessions, as well as by Calvin. The Reformers regarded the Roman confirmation as a blasphemous abridgment of Baptism.

Luther

In spite of Luther's strong criticism of the Roman confirmation, he was not opposed to the idea of an evangelical confirmation, disapproved of by some in the Reformation movement, though he was insistent that any proposed practice dare not detract from the sacraments. Luther was, however, not personally interested in reforming medieval confirmation and therefore he did not directly contribute to a reformation or the development of a substitute. Because of his high regard for Holy Baptism and the Lord's Supper, Luther did stress the element of instruction in connection with both sacraments. The importance which he attributed to confession and absolution underscored his concern for a proper preparation for the Lord's Supper. This emphasis became the first step toward a restructured confirmation which later was associated not merely with Baptism but also with the Lord's Supper. The need for religious instruction rising out of both sacraments was appreciated by all Evangelicals and created a natural situation which, in time, led to a Lutheran type of confirmation. In most instances, however, Lutherans were not consciously developing a new kind of confirmation. In fact, the very name "confirmation" was long regarded as a Romanizing offense. The gradual development of a restructured confirmation which began in the sixteenth century followed no uniform pattern, and it is for this reason that we find no consistent approach today.

The Development of a Lutheran Practice

Out of the tangled mass of influences and counter-influences which affected the practice of confirmation, six major emphases may be discerned in its gradual development: catechetical, hierarchical, sacramental, traditional, pietistic, and rationalistic. The first four made their appearance during the sixteenth century, the latter two in the seventeenth and eighteenth centuries. When speaking of six emphases, there is the risk of oversimplification. One must understand that these types were rarely found in their pure form. Several strands may often be detected in a single rite. In the latter part of the nineteenth century and particularly in the twentieth, it is not unusual to find the impact which four or even five may have had on a particular area. This is true especially in the United States.

The so-called *catechetical* type of confirmation in its initial stage was actually only a prototype of confirmation for there was no conscious thought of developing the practice. The catechetical type grew out of the need for instruction and preparation for the Lord's Supper, though not necessarily limited to those preparing for first Communion. No formal rite was necessarily associated with the practice at first, though a simple ceremony might be performed when it marked the occasion for first Communion. The ceremony was usually limited to an intercession on the part of the congregation, led by the pastor. This type of "confirmation" was the most common form in the Lutheran church during its first 150 years, particularly among the Scandinavians and most of the Gnesio-Lutherans of Germany.

The *hierarchical*[1] type of confirmation had its origin with Martin Bucer who introduced it in the Hessian churches in 1538-39 through the Ziegenhain Order of Church Discipline. He combined the pedagogical and subjective concerns of Erasmus with the disciplinary pastoral emphasis of Luther in a type of confirmation which became most familiar in the Lutheran church. In many respects Bucer may actually be regarded as the father of Lutheran confirmation. Bucer's form has been referred to as hierarchical because he introduced a vow wherein the child pledged to surrender himself to Christ and to submit himself to the discipline of the church. With

[1]The term "hierarchical" is used in its elementary sense to denote the rule of the parish clergy in a local congregation.

this emphasis a subjective element was introduced through the rite.

The *sacramental* tendency appeared usually with some other type of confirmation. It placed the emphasis on the laying on of hands, often with a sacramental interpretation. Bucer's ambiguous wording in the Hessian rite offered the occasion to interpret the laying on of hands as an actual imparting of the Holy Spirit. Though this interpretation was not widely accepted, the sacramental element continued to be felt in different parts of the Lutheran church.

Because of the disciplinary emphasis which Bucer placed on confirmation, it became necessary to emphasize that confirmation placed one under the church's discipline and marked the beginning of one's membership in the church. While originally this was intended to mean the church as an organization, it was often associated in the mind of the clergy and the laity as marking the beginning of membership in the Christian church, giving confirmation a sacramental overtone which it has not been able to lose over the centuries.

Occasionally efforts were made to retain the *traditional* form of confirmation without the Roman Catholic abuses. Accordingly, confirmation was practiced independent of the Lord's Supper with first Communion occurring some time later—anywhere from a few weeks to several months. In the seventeenth and eighteenth centuries, where the traditional type was practiced, first Communion might be postponed as much as one or two years. The traditional form of confirmation emphasized the laying on of hands and the instruction which preceded it. The Brandenburg church order of 1540 is an early example. This type of confirmation was commonly practiced in Pomerania (as early as 1545, and in some instances, as late as the middle of the nineteenth century). It was vehemently opposed as romanizing especially after the Leipzig Interim in 1548. In recent years modifications of the traditional type have been incorporated in some of the changes proposed among Lutherans.

Areas of Agreement

A study of the varying practices of confirmation in the sixteenth century among Lutherans permits very few generalizations except when stated in very broad terms. Regardless of the type of confirmation in vogue, there was general agreement in a number of areas: (a) universal rejection of the Roman Catholic doctrine of confirmation as a sacrament supplementing Holy Baptism; (b) all Lutheran confirmation forms either assumed or specified Christian instruction before a catechumen was presented for confirmation or first Communion; (c) except in the case of the traditional type of confirmation, Lutheran practice was associated directly with both sacraments; (d) the usual age of the catechumen at the time of his first Communion was quite early when compared with present-day practice. In fact, age was not regarded as important since the major criterion was the catechumen's readiness to partake of the Lord's Supper. In practice, the age was rarely higher than twelve.

IN THE NEXT THREE CENTURIES

The four types of confirmation originating in the sixteenth century continued during the period of orthodoxy, though the development of the practice with a distinct rite attached to it was slowed down considerably in most Lutheran churches. Parish life in Germany generally declined during this time due to the ravages of the Thirty Years War, the French invasion, and the losses effected by the Counter-Reformation. The breakdown of parish life in many communities was paralleled by a deterioration of catechetical instruction. As a reaction to this decline a *pietistic* influence was brought to bear on confirmation, particularly through the influence of Philip Spener.

Using the Hessian confirmation as a model, Spener restructured confirmation to serve his conversion theology. The vow became the occasion for a renewal of the baptismal covenant. The confession of faith became subjective in nature. Similarly, subjective elements permeated the examination, preparation for the Lord's Supper, and the confirmation blessing. Since it was important that the catechumen "feel" his new life, the age for confirmation was advanced, allowing for greater maturity. It was this type of confirmation which became official in Norway and Denmark in 1736.

The sixth type of confirmation was a reaction to Pietism. Under the influence of Rationalism with its de-emphasis on the sacraments and its stress on understanding God's witness to mankind in Holy Scripture, confirmation became a cultural hallmark which served the conventional Christian who summed up his Christianity as a series of virtues to be respected and which he might emulate. The *rationalistic* type of confirmation was regarded as the event which gave meaning to Holy Baptism. With this emphasis confirmation became the great festival of youth in which the candidate made his dramatic decision, marked by a vow and now elevated to an oath, to become a member of the church. Great stress was placed on the examination which was to show that the catechumen understood the meaning of the confession he was about to make to the world.

This drama of confirmation became the occasion for long addresses by pastors. Sentimentalism was allowed free reign on the part of parents and friends. Because of the importance attributed to confirmation, totally unrelated acts were usually attached to the event by law (e.g., enforcement of school laws, eligibility to guild membership, voting and majority rights, and such church privileges as baptismal sponsorship and the privilege of marriage in the church). In short, confirmation became necessary if people wished to have the rights of first-class citizenship. In this manner confirmation became part of the social and national fabric.

By the middle of the nineteenth century, the harmful effects of confirmation were evident to many of the religious leaders. In spite of their anxious attempts to bring about changes, nothing of importance happened. The drift of discontent away from the church due to economic, political, and social causes prevented any real reforms in confirmation from being effected. Even after Neo-Pietism arose, the effects of Rationalism continued to influence confirmation practices and rites.

CONFIRMATION IN THE NEW WORLD

It was only natural that this "Lutheran heritage" was transferred by immigration to the New World. Though Rationalism as far as doctrine is concerned had little influence among Lutherans in the United States, the mark of Rationalism on the prevailing Pietism was clearly evident in confirmation. Even when the "Old Lutherans," who were protesting laxity in doctrine, arrived in the 1830's and 40's, they did little to correct the unwholesome accretions which by now had attached themselves to the practice everywhere. There was even less positive influence by later Lutherans. In fact, the exaggerated esteem which confirmation enjoyed in Europe because of Rationalism became a major obstacle for any real reform among Lutherans in North America. What little differences did exist among the various groups of Lutheran immigrants were largely assimilated in practice though variations in degree continued regionally and ethnically.

What was the prevailing pattern for confirmation among the Lutherans in the New World? Generally speaking, the central feature of the practice was its emphasis on the renewal of the baptismal covenant and preparation for first Communion. Great stress was placed on the solemnity of the vows and their lifelong effect. The confession of faith was regarded as subjective in nature. It was said that in the rite the catechumen was assuming the promises which his parents or sponsors had made for him in infancy. Confirmation marked the event in which the child joined the Lutheran church or a local congregation. The examination was intended to give evidence that the catechumen understood the meaning of the solemn moment. The handclasp was interpreted in one of two ways, either it formalized the vow or the transmission of the rights and privileges which were said to come with confirmation. One of these privileges was usually assumed to be the right to partake of the Lord's Supper. The laying on of hands gave dignity to the occasion but was not given a sacramental meaning. It symbolized the gift of the Holy Ghost working through the Word and, in the minds of many of the people, through the importance of the rite itself.

Many of the secondary associations with Rationalism continued. As long as graduation from the elementary school marked the end of formal education, confirmation was closely linked to that event. For this reason the customary age for confirmation was about thirteen or fourteen. Concomitantly, confirmation marked also the end of formal religious education.

Palm Sunday, which in Europe had normally fallen about one week before spring graduation from school, continued to be observed as the popular day for confirmation, even after school-closing and graduation were no longer connected with the rite and were held late in spring. One reason for the retention of Palm Sunday no doubt lay in the fact that it made it possible for the catechumen to partake of his first Communion during Holy Week, since the Lord's Supper was celebrated only occasionally in most of the Lutheran churches in America.

TWENTIETH-CENTURY DEVELOPMENTS

Though efforts at reform continued to be made in Europe, little actually happened until the close of World War II. The waning influence of the church in the life of the people called for drastic action. The serious inroads of Communism in previously strong areas of Lutheranism served to show that the *Jugendweihe* of the Communists had, in fact, become a real threat where confirmation had become merely a civic event with religious overtones. Several commissions were appointed in Germany and the Scandinavian countries to study confirmation. As a result, a number of plans were proposed at different times and several were adopted. Some recommendations suggested a division of the catechumenate into several stages. Confirmation and first Communion were at times separated and variously placed. New curricular materials were developed by Lutheran educators in all parts of Europe to meet the changing needs of the churches. A major contribution was the examination of confirmation rites to eliminate un-Lutheran emphases. The United Lutheran Church of Germany (VELKD) adopted a new rite restoring the Lutheran theological accent.

At the urging of its member churches the Lutheran World Federation called for a thorough study of confirmation. Two important seminars were held in connection with the study. The Hofgeismar (Germany) seminar in 1955 was national in scope and the Loccum (Germany) seminar in 1961 was international. Papers and study documents of these two seminars were the main sources of the report made to the Lutheran World Federation in 1963 at Helsinki (Document No. 16).

Reform plans in North America were until recently primarily concerned with the improvement of curriculum and teaching methods rather than with the theological issues and historical problems involved. More recently an important intersynodical seminar was held at Racine, Wisconsin (1954) at which most Lutheran churches were represented. The study seminar gave lengthy consideration to a broad scope of the problems facing the Lutheran churches in America. Subsequent confirmation workshops were held in 1957-1960 by the antecedent bodies of The American Lutheran Church, reflecting historical, theological, and practical concerns. In 1961, the Lutheran World Federation seminar on confirmation raised the question of confirmation on an international level, and in large measure, stimulated the present intersynodical study herein reported. At its initial meeting in 1962, the Lutheran Church in America reviewed a report on confirmation which stressed also the theological issues, especially the association of confirmation with the Lord's Supper. Other Lutheran bodies have done little officially to bring the theological questions to the attention of their constituencies, though all Lutheran churches have prepared more and better curricular material.

III

Theological Aspects of Confirmation

Lutheran theology declares as its central doctrine that the sinner is justified alone by God's grace, for Christ's sake, through faith. To impart the free gift of justification to mankind, the Holy Spirit employs the gospel, using preaching and other forms of proclamation as well as Holy Baptism and the Lord's Supper as instruments of conveyance. Through these means of grace, God reveals and declares to men that he is fully reconciled to all the world, and through them the Holy Spirit creates, sustains, and strengthens faith in the forgiveness merited by God's Son, Jesus Christ.

Thus, "all this is from God, who through Christ reconciled us to himself and gave us the ministry of reconciliation," (2 Corinthians 5:18). This ministry is the determinative goal for the church's message under which the church is to perform all of its functions. It is in the light of its gospel ministry that the church must appraise the validity of all its activities, including its ritual heritage. This applies also to a consideration of the theology and practice of confirmation.

CONFIRMATION AND THE MEANS OF GRACE

The Word

The Word of God is creative. It is the source of all life. "In the beginning was the Word . . . the Word was God. . . . All things were made through him and without him was not anything made that was made" (John 1:1,3). The same Word that initially brought all things into being has ceaselessly spoken and variously wrought God's purposes ever since. God has entrusted the Word of the redeeming Christ to the church, so that the force of Christ's death and resurrection is brought to all believers of every age and place (2 Corinthians 5:18-21; Romans 5:1-16). The Word is the origin and source of the church, called by the Spirit into being under the lordship of Christ.

The church is not only the result or the expression of the Kingdom come in Christ but also the means of furthering its coming among men. As Luther put it, "God's Word cannot be present without God's people, and God's people cannot be without God's Word." It is the purpose of the church, God's people, to produce and maintain sons of God by means of the Word (*Augsburg Confession*, VII).

Proceeding on the premise that infant Baptism is the normal practice in the established church, the regenerating Word in Baptism brings the child into the life in Christ, and into the community of faith. But all life, and this includes the life in Christ, is dynamic. The grace completely conferred in Baptism is yet a grace within which the child of God grows and changes (1 Peter 2:2).

Because this life must be sustained, the church is concerned that the life-transforming power of the Word may be effective in human lives and that its authority be recognized and accepted. This must not only be known as truth but realized as experience both in individual lives and in the collective life of the church. It takes shape in worship, education, and moral living (Colossians 3:16-17; 2 Timothy 3:16-17) as these reflect the "whole counsel of God," that is, the proclamation of law and gospel, to those who *are* the children of God.

The Spirit's strengthening, or confirmation, takes place daily in the Christian life and must cover the whole life span. Yet, in the process of nourishing and encouraging growth, it is possible that there is a stage at which it will be particularly advantageous for the Christian community to provide for a special memorializing of a person's Baptism, some sort of confirming through the Word that accords with his maturer consciousness. This confirming occurs normally within the context of a pastoral and educational ministry. Understood in this way, confirmation is not a terminal experience. It is simply a stage in what may be termed a lifelong catechumenate. Confirmation, with its instruction and public rite, becomes then one of the many events or experiences in the Christian life by which the nature and character of the Christian individual receives encouragement and finds expression without an attempt to complement or supplement a holiness which is the gift of God through faith in Christ.

Holy Baptism

As a Means of Grace

The simple act of Baptism, which the church performs in obedience to its Lord's command, is indeed a stupendous miracle in his name. In this sacrament God lays his claim upon the sinner and makes him his. By this act God establishes a new relationship: the old man of sin who is under the wrath and judgment of God dies, and the new man of faith who is under grace and forgiveness is born (Romans 6:4).

Holy Baptism imparts the grace of God. It is a means to awaken and sustain life. It is "a washing of regeneration" (Titus 3:5). It imparts forgiveness of sins (Acts 2:38, 22:16). It saves (Mark 16:16; 1 Peter 3:2). It incorporates fully into the church and makes the baptized one fully a member of that church, the body of Christ (1 Corinthians 12:13), and it bestows the gift of the Holy Spirit (Titus 3:5).

Thus, Baptism is complete in itself. Confirmation may, therefore, in no sense be regarded as a completion of an unfinished act. To assert or even to imply that the saving power of Baptism is in any way contingent on any subsequent event is to deny its status. It is, therefore, theologically indefensible to elevate confirmation to a position in which it either complements or supplements the sacrament of Holy Baptism. It can be properly regarded neither in the pietistic sense of a conversion experience and an act of decision nor in the rationalistic sense of a free choice. At the same time, however, there is a relationship between confirmation and the saving nature of Baptism. For in the public rite the confirmand, in company with the congregation, recalls his Baptism together with the benefits given him in the sacrament. This remembering is not a one-time response but a celebration of what is actually taking place regularly in the life of each baptized child of God.

As a Covenant

Closely related to the saving power of Baptism is the covenant which God here establishes. This is in every sense of the word a covenant of grace and therefore outside the ordinary covenant concept. It is a unilateral covenant, an act of God that is complete in itself, solely prompted by his mercy and grace. It is therefore not conditioned by an act or promise of man whether it be by his parents, sponsors, or in later years, by himself, through a rite or a vow. Man merely accepts the promises and gifts of Baptism and thereby enters into a covenant relationship. Even this acceptance is the result of the regenerative work of the Holy Spirit.

Furthermore, this baptismal covenant cannot be broken by man. God alone made the covenant; he alone can negate it. But God never breaks his covenant and therefore it needs no renewal. He never withdraws his promises. As Luther said, "Baptism remains forever. Even though we fall from it and sin, nevertheless we always have access to it so that we may again subdue the old man" (The Large Catechism, IV, 77).

In this covenant it is God who holds the child in a new relationship in which he is the son and heir possessing all the blessings of salvation. There is thus an unconscious, hidden relation, the depth of which no man can plumb.

Thus the function of the confirmand with respect to the covenant of Baptism is not to reaffirm a possible contractual agreement he has made with God. Any vow committing the confirmand to a lifelong faith in Christ and loyalty to him contradicts the nature of the faith relation which is in need of constant renewal, and such a vow is beyond the capacity of any man to keep. Where included in the rite of confirmation, the promise should not be regarded as a condition of the covenant but as part of the covenant relationship in response to the God who keeps the covenant.

As an Event in Spiritual Growth

In the Great Commission the Lord commands Baptism and then adds the command to teach the baptized. To every baptized Christian God says, "Grow in the grace and knowledge of our Lord and Savior Jesus Christ" (2 Peter 3:18). The life bestowed in Baptism needs to be nurtured by the Word. The nature of the baptized person is such that he requires instruction in the significance of that sacrament and in the Word of God in order that he know who he is and what he may become. In this process confirmation makes a distinct contribution, not in a terminal sense, but as part of the lifelong process in which the believer is to grow in Christ.

Holy Communion

As a Means of Grace

The spiritual and eternal gifts of God are received and appropriated exclusively by faith. God does not demand of those whom he would bless a measure of achievement in the performance of his will or a period of probation in his service or a level of status in the membership of his church. His gifts are ours by faith alone.

Nor does God impart his grace in a piecemeal manner, as though the fullness of his salvation were to be approached only through successive stages as in a process of gradual progress from poverty to wealth. All is received by faith, and faith receives all.

That the total gift of grace is given to all Christians by faith, whether they are infants or mature, becomes significant for an understanding of Holy Communion in its distinction from Holy Baptism as a means of grace. There is, of course, a similarity between the two sacraments. Both give forgiveness of sins, life, and salvation. Similarly faith appropriates the blessings and benefits offered in both sacraments.

Nevertheless, there is a distinction between the two sacraments that is both scriptural and confessional. We may distinguish between them from the point of view of the specific effect of each. Holy Baptism grants sonship; Holy Communion carries it forward. The former is the initiating, the latter, the sustaining sacrament. The distinction is one of emphasis. The relationship is not exclusive or supplementary but collateral.

By way of further distinction, we note that Scripture makes no prerequisite demands for the administration of infant Baptism. Concerning the Lord's Supper, however, the Lutheran church on the basis of Scripture understands that whoever participates in that sacrament must be competent to examine himself. This competence can be said to include understanding and faith with respect to the essential elements of this sacrament.

The following desirable prerequisites for participation in the Holy Communion are not a divine prescription but reflect pastoral and theological concern. As such they can be adopted in the practice of the church to make possible a meaningful participation in Holy Communion.

1. Holy Communion is a memorial of the event of Calvary which occurred in history at a specific time and place (1 Corinthians 11:24). Without a reference to the divine act of atonement there is no sacrament, and to celebrate a memorial of an unknown event is meaningless. This implies for those who receive the sacrament a knowledge of the event of Calvary and faith that what happened there was for them.

2. Holy Communion is the sacrament instituted by Christ himself in which he gives us his body and blood under the bread and wine (1 Corinthians 10:16). This implies the recognition that the Savior is present in the sacrament and that he gives his body and blood to the believer for the forgiveness of sins.

3. Holy Communion expresses expectation and anticipation of the Lord's return to receive his believers into eternal life (1 Corinthians 11:26). It is a forward look to an event as it is a backward look to an event. This implies knowledge of the Lord's promise of his return and faith to trust his promises.

4. Holy Communion is the pledge and assurance of the promise of God of forgiveness, life, and salvation in place of sin, death, and damnation (Matthew 26:28). This implies a recognition and acceptance of God's grace.

5. Holy Communion is the communion of believers with their Lord and through him with each other. This implies that the communicant acknowledges Christ as Lord and fellow believers as brethren in this one Lord (1 Corinthians 10:17).

In the light of these prerequisites the church must address itself to the task of education to provide an opportunity for persons who are to commune to acquire these understandings so that their participation in Holy Communion can be meaningful. This learning is not merely an intellectual matter even though it requires certain basic historical and theological information, but it involves attitudes and conduct responses as vital parts of the educational process.

As a Covenant

In Holy Communion, as in Baptism, the function of a covenant is given a significant place. This is the sacrament of the new covenant, the covenant of the gospel in contrast to the law, of the acts of God in contrast to the acts of man, of grace in contrast to justice. In this sacrament, moreover, as in Holy Baptism, the covenant is unilateral. It is not a contract between God and man with mutually binding stipulations of fulfillment for its validity. It is truly a sacramental covenant, in which the communicant, by faith, personally accepts God's grace on his behalf and expresses his commitment to let that grace express itself in the Christian life.

The covenant aspect of the Lord's Supper has some important implications for the practice of confirmation. What happens in Holy Communion should not be an attempt to prepare or predispose the communicant to offer a worthy sacrifice as an obedience of merit in fulfillment of contractual obligation. Confirmation can contribute to the blessings of communion by instructing the Christian believer to commune with understanding and to offer a sacrifice of thanksgiving for Christ's atoning sacrifice.

As an Event in Spiritual Growth

In Holy Communion, as in Baptism, the Christian partakes of a sacrament of forgiveness, a free gift from the gracious hand of God. But the Lord's Supper has an added element of value. Partly because it presupposes a measure of understanding of God's plan of salvation and partly because of its repeated occurrence, Holy Communion assists the baptized believer to remain within the baptismal covenant of grace.

Moreover, Holy Communion is the sacrament of fellowship, not only with Christ, but also with all the saints. As such, it encourages spiritual growth and maturity and becomes a significant event in the edification of the Christian believer.

But these experiences of Christian growth do not happen as by magical infusion. The groundwork must be laid. To receive Holy Communion without understanding would be to perform a meaningless act that would contribute nothing to the process of growth. For this purpose the church must provide the necessary Christian instruction for the preparation of the young Christian's first experience at the Lord's Table. Such instruction does not, however, impart a lifetime competence for a blessed Communion, for each individual Communion is an event in itself and to each Communion there applies the

Apostle Paul's insistence on self-examination. The instruction preceding first Communion will normally be continued in order to provide a further base from which the growth of the believer can proceed and which can offer the resources for an increasing maturity in Christ. Confirmation instruction during adolescence will provide an enlarged supporting base with additional resources for the maturing Christian.

CONFIRMATION AND THE CHURCH

The practice of confirmation in the Lutheran church is closely associated with the doctrine of the church, often in such a manner that the practice has impinged on that doctrine as set forth in the New Testament and the Lutheran Confessions. The various ways in which church membership and the special privileges, rights, and responsibilities have been associated with confirmation, and the various shades of meaning attributed to these elements, have had a tendency to skew the Lutheran teaching of the doctrine of the church. A similar impairing influence arising out of the practice of confirmation may at times be detected when the objectives and the curriculum of confirmation instruction are reviewed. For this reason it is necessary in a study of confirmation to re-examine its relationship with the doctrine of the church.

The Nature of the Church

Biblical Meaning of "Church"

In spite of the many popular usages of the term "church," the New Testament restricts the term to but one meaning. On the basis of Scripture (e.g., Ephesians 5:23-30) we speak of the church as being sanctified, cleansed, holy, and without blemish. According to the *Augsburg Confession*, Lutherans say that, "the Christian Church, properly speaking, is nothing else than the assembly *(Versammlung—congregatio)* of all believers and saints" (A.C., VIII).

Though the New Testament limits itself to but one meaning of "church," it uses the word in two different ways. In the Ephesians passage already referred to, "church" means the sum total of all believers throughout the world—past, present, and those yet to be called by the Holy Spirit. A study of Acts 9:31, 1 Corinthians 1:2, and 1 Corinthians 16:19 makes it clear that "church" in these passages refers to believers at a given place, the Christians that are there. Paul refers to the Corinthians as "those sanctified in Christ Jesus, called to be saints."

Clearly the letter is addressed to every last Christian at Corinth, both the weak and the strong, but only to the Christians. Thus the word "church" in the New Testament always means the total number of believers, either at given localities or throughout the world in every age.

A further New Testament characterization of the church is that it is the body of Christ. This characterization must not be regarded in some idealistic, Platonic way but as a powerful and true figure denoting a living reality. Every member of the church is in truth a member, deriving his function, purpose, and life within the body from its head, which is Christ. Thus Christians are not an assembly of individuals, like so many beads in a box, but with Christ constitute a living body with him as head and Lord (Ephesians 4:1-16; 5:21-32; Colossians 1:21-23).

Membership in the Church

Membership in the Christian church is bestowed upon an infant or a young child through Holy Baptism. When the church, in obedience to its Lord, baptizes a child, it makes him by that very act a member of the church (1 Corinthians 12:13). The membership begun in Baptism is thereupon experienced in the Christian life (worship, teaching, the Lord's Supper, and service). Membership in the church is not conferred by this later experience nor by a special rite, such as confirmation, but in the way commanded by Christ, through Holy Baptism.

When a young child is baptized by the church, he is baptized in the Name of the Father, and the Son, and the Holy Ghost according to the faith expressed in the Apostles Creed, the ancient baptismal confession. Baptism is normally administered by a minister of Christ who has been called by a particular group of Christians assembled about the means of grace, that is, by the church at a given place. Also when a layman performs an emergency Baptism, he does so by virtue of the command which Christ gave to his church. In such cases, the child's newly created membership in the church is normally inscribed in the records of a community of Christians who recognize him as a fellow member.

The baptized child's membership in the holy Christian church may be expressed and may be made more evident through the confession of the congregation which authorized or accepted his Baptism. By virtue of his Baptism a child becomes a member of the local congregation. The pastor who baptizes such a child therefore immediately assumes a pastoral relationship with him. The congregation that authorizes the Baptism assumes likewise a relationship of fellowship with such a baptized person, prays for him, and otherwise expresses its concern that the child be "strengthened," i.e., confirmed, in the grace of the Almighty God unto life everlasting.

In the case of older children and adults who request to be baptized, the church accedes to their request when it has been assured that they have already been made one with Christ through the power of the gospel. By their faith the candidates for Baptism already share in the death and resurrection of their Lord. The subsequent Baptism clearly signifies the new relationship which is theirs by faith, confirming their personal share in the redemptive work of Jesus Christ. For this reason they do not have a need for the congregation's rite of confirmation.

Through the sanctifying power of the sacrament and the nurturing, sustaining, and refining power of the Word, the church is what its members confess it to be in the Nicene Creed, "one holy, catholic, and apostolic church." Each of these attributes has far-reaching and compelling implications for confirmation.

The Mission of the Church

God did not call the church into existence for its own purpose, to serve itself, or to remain a pious aggregation of people satisfied with their own existence. God created the church for his holy purpose, to serve him. He called the church into existence ". . . according to the purpose of his will, to the praise of his glorious grace which he freely bestowed upon us in the Beloved" (Ephesians 1:5-7). God's purpose set forth in Christ was "to unite all things in him, things in heaven and things on earth" (Ephesians 1:10). This is the mission of the church (John 20: 21-23).

In order to carry out its mission, the church is a teaching community bringing the Word of God to bear upon itself and to others. In this way the church becomes more and more what it already is, a living fellowship, sharing the fellowship with the redeemed world in the hope that all may partake of the inheritance purchased with Christ's blood.

The Lord has not left the church unequipped for its mission, to continue alone in its life and struggle. He has given the church such resources as worship, fellowship, witness, ministry, and an eschatological hope. These rich resources are generated and undergirded by the Spirit who created the church. The Spirit of God unleashes his power through the means of grace, Word and Sacraments, which serve as the divine dynamic through which he empowers and sustains the church.

Confirmation and Church Organization

God has not prescribed to the church how it should organize itself. Therefore its choice of structure is part of the church's liberty. Whatever action it takes will be for the sake of mutual edification through Word and Sacrament and in order to carry out the church's ministry in an effective manner. In a derived, though in a nonbiblical sense, Christians may refer to their organization as a church. Membership, however, in such an organization gets its meaning and validity in the sight of God only because of the group's membership in the holy Christian church.

The different types of membership, which an organization may devise for the sake of order and efficiency, are merely convenient tags to indicate various levels or rights or responsibilities that the members may have accepted within the organization. But the Scriptures do not speak of various kinds of memberships. Baptism makes us members of the Body of Christ, the only church of which the New Testament speaks. Thorough study of such significant passages as Romans 12:4, 5; 1 Corinthians 12:13; Galatians 3:26-27; Ephesians 5:25-27 leads inevitably to this conclusion.

Whatever polity a congregation may choose as its pattern, the choice will be governed by the purpose for which God called the church into being. Christians will organize themselves in a manner in which they can serve God most effectively and in a way pleasing to him, making certain that in the chosen structure they are not in danger of denying the essence of the church. Confirmation will therefore serve to prepare confirmands to minister effectively in the organizational structure of their congregation and beyond it.

Conceivably the congregation may in the public rite of confirmation attest to the fact that the confirmand can now exercise certain privileges and responsibilities which the congregation is prepared to give him within its particular organizational structure. However, the congregation must recognize that in doing this it runs the risk of confusing the rights and responsibilities which the confirmand already has by virtue of his being a member of the church with those that are part of the church's polity.

Current practices in the rite in various parts of the Lutheran church evidence such confusion. The handclasp between the pastor and the confirmands may serve as an illustration. Under given circumstances a handclasp could correctly symbolize that the confirmand is assuming certain organizational privileges and responsibilities, such as voting membership, willingness to accept appointments to certain offices, readiness to serve as a sponsor, and similar duties. The handclasp, however, may not be identified, as it sometimes is, with the conferring and acceptance of rights and privileges which the Christian already has by virtue of his fellowship in the Christian church, as for example, membership in the church and the right to participate in the Lord's Supper. However, though the right to partake of the Lord's Supper is conferred on every baptized Christian, the congregation in a pastoral concern for the individual Christian may determine when a Christian may exercise his God-given right. This may be at the time of his confirmation or it may be at a prior occasion.

When the nature, mission, and resources of the church are correctly understood in the light of the New Testament and the Lutheran Confessions, many of the unwholesome emphases associated with confirmation will disappear. There will be no reference, either in the instruction or in the rite, to becoming a "member of the church" or to entering into "full communion" with the church or to the granting of rights and privileges inherent in one's adoption into the family of our Lord Jesus Christ. Instead, the process of confirmation will be regarded as part of the normal life-long strengthening through Word and Sacrament, that takes place in the church, by the church under the blessing of the Spirit. The instruction will prepare the catechumen for the privileges and responsibilities which he is expected to assume as a maturing Christian.

197

Confirmation in the Church's Mission

Though membership in the church begins with Baptism, even baptized children must experience their fellowship by being told of it. They must learn to know who and what they are: redeemed individuals in community. The spiritual life begun in them must be nourished by the Word. As they mature, they must further learn what their responsibility is as children of God. They must learn to know their particular identity and that while they are in the world they are not of it. They are sojourners on the way. Because the church is under the cross and in tension, this confirming of faith and life must continue throughout the life of the Christian.

The nurturing of the Christian must furthermore include his total life. There dare be no compartmentalism between the spiritual and the secular as though the Christian's ministry were reserved for certain isolated pockets of his life.

What then is the relationship of the practice of confirmation and the church's preparation for its mission? The confirmation rite punctuates a formal stage within a lifelong preparation or strengthening that takes place within the church. It represents a stage, and only a stage, in the normal life of a Christian who, having previously been nurtured by the Word and having become more fully aware of the lifelong power of his Baptism, now at his level of spiritual maturity makes a personal statement of his faith.

Because the congregation has a personal interest in the welfare of the confirmands, the members intercede in the confirmation rite in behalf of the confirmands, petitioning God to impart the gifts of his Holy Spirit. The prayers of the congregation are individualized by the laying on of hands, whereby the confirmand is blessed and all are reminded that the sustaining help must come from God.

Since confirmation instruction is the occasion when the church concentrates much of its efforts to equip its members for their mission, the instruction will impress on the catechumen his responsibility to use the resources which the church has received from the Spirit. The instruction will further equip him for his task by deepening his Christian understanding and by cultivating proper attitudes and wholesome action patterns suitable to his level of maturity.

The church would seriously inhibit its responsibilities and opportunities if it regarded its function merely to minister to itself. Because Christ came to redeem all mankind, he bids his church to extend itself through the proclamation of the gospel so that all may share in the living fellowship of his church, and "serve him in everlasting righteousness, innocence, and blessedness."

In meeting its responsibility to pursue its mission, the church will regard the world as its parish. For this task confirmation too must live up to its responsibility.

The congregation's pastoral and educational ministry should involve confirmands in significant relationships and in meaningful responsibilities in the extension of the church, not at some indeterminate future date, but during the very time in which they are being confirmed in their faith and life. Equipped for that period of their lives, they will learn that the process of becoming equipped must continue throughout a lifelong ministry.

IV

Practical Aspects of Confirmation

As confirmation is currently practiced in the United States and Canada, it is associated with both sacraments, Holy Baptism and the Lord's Supper. In relation to Baptism the church has used confirmation as the occasion for meeting a major portion of its obligation to instruct the young person in what it means to be a Christian. At the same time and with the same instruction, the church has prepared the child for his first Communion. This has created a tension. Where parents, pastors, and congregational members recognize that Holy Communion may be taken in a worthy manner prior to age fourteen or fifteen, there has been a tendency to observe confirmation at a much earlier age, as for example, ten or twelve. Such a shift, however, does not fully meet the educational and pastoral concerns of the church unless thereafter an unusually strong educational program is maintained by the congregation, especially during the critical early adolescent period of the child. On the other hand, where the congregation emphasizes a longer range educational and pastoral responsibility rising out of the baptismal obligation, the tendency has been to postpone confirmation instruction until the mid-adolescent years and with it postpone first Communion for so long a portion of the child's life that the delay can no longer be theologically justified.

SEPARATION OF CONFIRMATION AND FIRST COMMUNION

Because of the tension between the educational demands of Holy Baptism and the Lord's Supper within the present practice of confirmation, the commission is unanimously moved to recommend *that first Communion and confirmation be separated as two distinct acts.* This separation will allow children to partake of the Lord's Supper at an earlier age and then permit the church to carry on its pastoral and educational ministry through confirmation instruction at a time when

Christian children are more mature. This recommendation, however, does not imply that confirmation may then be regarded as a final step in the church's concern for its members, but rather that confirmation may continue to serve as one of several stages in the life of a maturing Christian.

While in the past the dominant practice in the Lutheran churches in North America combined confirmation with first Communion, there is the beginning of a difficult practice and a growing pressure to separate the two. After carefully weighing the pros and cons for an earlier first Communion and a later confirmation, the commission believes that separation is the appropriate recommendation that it can make for our times. The separation will permit eligible young Christians to partake of the Lord's Supper at an earlier period of their life and also make possible a more effective experience of confirmation at a more mature age.

Important Considerations

In coming to its decision, the commission carefully evaluated all considerations bearing on the separation of confirmation and first Communion.

Traditional Confusion of New Definition

The configuration of special instruction directly under the pastor culminating in a rite in which the child publicly affirms the faith into which he was baptized and receives a confirmation of God's promises and which is coupled with first Communion is deeply ingrained in the life of the people, and has been one of the formative influences in Lutheran piety. Any change in past practice will meet resistance because of the fear that the Lutheran church will thereby lose values which will be difficult to replace.

The very significance which the present practice of confirmation has needs careful assessment. The confirmation configuration,

199

in popular thinking, is coupled with mis-understandings and superstitions to a point where the practice, and particularly the rite, replaced Baptism in significance. New practices that commend themselves may also become deeply significant. This is a time of change and experimentation. Lutherans should be free to exercise their evangelical freedom and adapt their practices to the best interests of the church and its mission.

The joining of confirmation with admission to first Communion and the status of full church membership has tended to make all instruction, if not all of church connection, terminal with confirmation. One of the main reasons for continuing instruction to a later age of confirmation is to encourage the habit of lifelong education. This is the reason for stressing confirmation as only one phase of a lifelong pastoral and education ministry.

Although psychological, sociological, educational, and ecclesiastical considerations do favor a later age for confirmation as it has been defined by the commission, the nature of Holy Communion as a means of grace by no means warrants pushing off the age of first Communion to that point. The need of children for spiritual nourishment through the Lord's Supper should not be denied. This makes a separation inevitable.

Ecumenical Considerations

By separating first Communion from confirmation, the Lutheran church would be departing in its practice from most of the Protestant churches which require confirmation (or some similar rite) prior to first Communion. Curiously a separation would be approaching the Roman Catholic practice on the one hand and the Baptist practice on the other by allowing Communion at a relatively early age. There are thus serious ecumenical considerations at stake regardless of the action taken.

If a practice commends itself for the upbuilding of the children of the church, Lutherans should not hesitate to go their own way, as long as it is in harmony with the Word of God. In any case the rationale for confirmation in the Lutheran church would differ both from that of Roman Catholics and Baptists—and most other Protestants.

Dropouts

A later confirmation may make it difficult to keep pupils in instruction classes once they have been admitted to Communion. The church faces the possibility that the practice of confirmation may disappear entirely and Christian education be confined for most persons to early childhood.

This difficulty is no greater than the present dropout problem after confirmation. In any case the preadolescent child is much more amenable to parental influence than the older youth. There is need also for firm parental discipline of the right kind.

The instruction itself should be of such kind as to meet the need and hold the interest of the pupil.

If participation in Holy Communion is meaningful it should, as a means of grace, strengthen the child's God-relationship, encourage him to faithfulness, and increase the desire to grow in understanding.

Demands on Adolescents

The practical difficulties involved in continuing instruction beyond the present age, especially in view of the greater demands made upon the high school student's time and interests and the difficulties in transportation from more remote schools will be serious obstacles for a later confirmation. Add to this the loss of strong parental discipline, and the church will face even greater difficulty in holding a teen-ager in instruction until mid-adolescence.

The preparation before confirmation need not involve specific instruction as traditionally conceived. The present concentration of instruction during the seventh, eighth, and ninth grades may well continue. Besides, the additional years would provide opportunities involving enrichment courses of various kinds connected with the church school and youth work, weekend retreats, and active involvement in religious and social issues. As the time for confirmation approaches, there could be special retreats involving sponsors, teachers, and the pastor. This would encourage imagination, creativity, consecration on the part of the entire congregation.

The psychological observations show that there are at this time strong family ties along with the forming of other relations. There is respect for parents who show understanding and a desire for guidance. The difficulty in holding them in some kind of instruction is no greater than holding them in the church at all. The goal of confirmation at a more mature age may prove an added incentive.

Sophistication of the Mid-Adolescent

The increased sophistication of the youth in secondary school together with his predominantly scientific training may prove a stumbling block for any later confirmation. High school curricula today include subjects previously deferred until college.

Such sophistication is all the more reason for providing especially meaningful instructional and fellowship experiences during this formative period.

A Right Understanding of Holy Communion

An early Communion may create a possibility in which children will participate in the Lord's Supper without proper appreciation, understanding, and awe, and without being capable of the necessary serious self-examination. The Lord's Supper may either be trivialized, or become a species of magic.

With the right blend of instruction, as indicated above, this threat can be obviated. There is also a proper appreciation on the part of the whole person that is not merely intellectual. Children may have a depth of feeling and appreciation denied to the more mature whose ratiocinations get in the way. A profound sense of sin and appreciation of forgiveness and of self-giving, suffering, victorious love is not foreign to childhood. Proper pastoral judgment should exclude those not yet prepared. At no time, however, is there any *real assurance* of any person's readiness, be he child or adult.

Problems in Emphases

By allowing earlier Communion there is danger that the Lord's Supper will become the center of Christian worship instead of the life-giving Word of God itself in the many forms which it takes. Furthermore, the separation of first Communion from confirmation could encourage the notion that confirmation is a sacrament requiring episcopal blessing.

This possibility depends upon the instruction given also for the congregation. In actual practice the celebration of the Lord's Supper will come to have whatever meaning, significance, and power it is in actual, living proclamation declared to have. The mere recitation of the right words does not have a magic effect. The whole context is important. Inclusion of younger persons in Holy Communion will call for more thought, consideration of meaning, and explanation among family members, not less.

Pastoral Care

It will be very difficult to differentiate between those children of the parish who are deemed sufficiently prepared for participation in the Lord's Supper and those who are not. This will create friction among the parents as well as the children.

This is a burden of pastoral care which a pastor should be willing to assume, but which should be shared by the parents, the church school staff, and the entire congregation. It is also possible to choose sponsors for the child specifically to share this responsibility, to replace the now almost meaningless baptismal sponsors.

Problems of Uniform Practice

The proposed separation of first Communion from confirmation will result in a confusing diversity of practice throughout the church precisely at a time when the mobility of population demands greater uniformity.

In spite of the general impression of uniformity, there is at present a great diversity of practice with respect to the age of confirmation and the number of years of specific catechetical instructions. A measure of greater uniformity for a new commendable practice could be achieved by concerted effort. This was one reason why the Lutheran Church in America did not make any changes on its own but pressed for a uniform action on the part of all Lutherans. In any case there should also always be freedom for adaptation to individual circumstances. A variety of practices would be evidence of genuine pastoral concern.

Administrative and Statistical Adjustments

A redefinition of church membership, the basis for many administrative procedures, will be required if the proposed change is adopted. This will add confusion compounded to the present statistical turmoil.

To be sure, the necessary work of the church cannot be done without efficient organization and accurate statistics. The statistics on the church register should, however, never be mistaken as the statistics of the true church that is always hidden. The present method of counting church members is not satisfactory in any case. The basic figure is that of those baptized in the Triune Name. Then it should not be too difficult to proceed from there to some other categories. Where a separate category of those who have communed at least once a year is employed, there is a definite reflection of Roman Catholic canon law which makes it a mortal sin not to commune at least once a year during the Easter season. A proper attitude toward the Lord's Supper should eliminate this once-a-year fetish.

Schedule of Worship and Education

Attention is called to the practice of having Sunday school at the same hour as The Service. This tends to make Sunday school a substitute for The Service or The Service a substitute for Christian education. This is a practice against which the commission must speak. Church school teachers as well as the children of the church should be regular in church attendance. This is the reason why lengthy worship has been eliminated from the Sunday school session. At the same time, adults need continuing Christian education. If confirmation instruction is to be conducted at a later period, it is crucially important that the Sunday school period should not be in competition with The Service or vice versa. This is even more important if the younger children are to be admitted to Communion. Worship and education are twin needs.

Conclusion

Recognizing the real difficulties which are involved in a departure from a time-honored practice, the commission nevertheless feels that our particular time and place in mid-twentieth–century North America, will be best served by a separation. The history of confirmation shows the variety of practices that have prevailed in the past. The review of the present situation shows the dissatisfaction with it and the variety of experimental procedures. Since, as Lutherans, we do not hold ourselves bound by any one specific God-given church polity but only by such polity and practices as are required by the nature of the church and its mission, we should be free and flexible for new creative ventures under the Word of God. We should strive for a uniform polity which is nevertheless flexible to different situational needs. The whole educational procedure demands change and flexibility.

At this juncture of growing Lutheran unity a joint new creative venture that reflects our heritage along with full ecumenical participation today would be most encouraging. A changing society needs a unified approach.

AGE FOR FIRST COMMUNION AND CONFIRMATION

Admitting Children to First Communion

The church's practice on admission to Holy Communion has varied through the centuries. In the early church participation in Holy Communion was the concluding event in the initiation rite. When infant Baptism became the universal practice, the church continued to include infants in baptismal Eucharists.

In the Western church baptismal Eucharist for infants began to decline for various reasons, especially with the popular acceptance of the doctrine of transubstantiation. When in the thirteenth century Communion was administered through the species of bread only, the baptismal Eucharist had practically disappeared. During the period of decline of the baptismal Eucharist, the church was concerned to preserve the sanctity of the sacrament by guarding against its possible desecration as the infant might reject or regurgitate the elements. With the acceptance of transubstantiation, the church placed greater emphasis on the concern for spiritual competence to receive the sacrament and, in its practice, delayed admission to Communion until the baptized child could understand and believe the gospel presented in this sacrament in the larger context of the Christian faith.

The Lutheran church, though for different reasons, followed the later tradition of the Western church and has historically delayed admission to Holy Communion until the child has been instructed. (Refer to page 188.) Although at the beginning admission to Holy Communion was not usually related to confirmation, later it was. The association of these two observances resulted in even further delay of the child's admission to Holy Communion, as the age of confirmation was raised from twelve or less in Reformation times to as high as eighteen.

Today there has developed in the Lutheran church a greater emphasis on the power of the sacrament as a means by which the Holy Spirit strengthens God's children and less emphasis on man's reason and ability to achieve as prerequisites for admission to Holy Communion. Moreover, a careful study of age level characteristics indicates that the baptized child may be ready to participate in Holy Communion much earlier than he is ready to identify with the adult Christian community as he does at confirmation.

The Recommended Practice

Admission to first Communion is an invitation of the Lord Jesus Christ to his Supper, presented through his church to its baptized children when they are ready to participate in the sacrament in a worthy manner. This readiness involves the understanding, attitudes, and action patterns necessary to receive the sacrament with benefit.

The church will therefore invite to Holy Communion those children who have been instructed in preparation for the sacrament and who then in the pastoral judgment of the congregation possess the competence to partake of Holy Communion in a worthy manner.

An examination of the prerequisites for participation in the Lord's Supper indicated above would imply that *the latter part of the fifth grade* would normally be the most strategic time at which children should be admitted to Holy Communion, provided they have been brought up within the church (Christian home, Christian fellowship, church-school) and have received instruction for first Communion.

Admission to first Communion would have to be deferred for those who have not had these advantages. This will put the burden of decision and of pastoral care upon the pastor which, however, he should be able to share with the home, the church school teachers, and the entire congregation.

Characteristics of the Fifth-Grade Child

Age group characteristics that commend the latter part of the fifth grade are the following:[1]

The average fifth-grade child "has reached the prime of childhood—a plateau of growth, an emotional balance, and the peak of childhood capacities. It is a period of rest before the sudden change of adolescence." . . . This period of calm commends itself rather than the somewhat later period of greater turmoil and distractions.

The child at this age normally possesses an agreeable balance of his emotional self, is happy to be what he is, friendly, agreeable, amenable, cooperative, sincere, poised, unselfconscious, easy-going, quick to admit his errors, and seems to have found himself as a child and is content. All this would indicate

[1] W. Kent Gilbert, *The Age Group Objectives of Christian Education* (Philadelphia: LCA, Board of Parish Education, 1958), pp. 49-52.

that he is ready to join in the fellowship meal at the joyful celebration of the Lord's presence without overemphasis on the fears of unworthy participation that have come to disturb so many. He is concerned with the specific and concrete and he is not yet ready to conceptualize or generalize very widely. He likes to assimilate facts and to memorize. He acquires some of the time concepts needed for the study of history. The child is therefore capable of appreciating the historic facts on which the Christian faith and, specifically, the celebration of the Lord's Supper is based.

The child at this age is more aware of what is wrong than what is right and, therefore, needs help in making ethical decisions in the face of his impulses. The proper preparation for participation in the Lord's Supper would provide occasion for such help.

"He is particularly open to close family companionships and activities." This would indicate the advisability of sharing in the Communion with his family. At the same time he will learn that one shares one's life with the larger family of the church, with all people, and not only one's own kind.

He "is not as distrustful of his abilities nor as concerned about his status as in later years." This would be a good time for him to accept all who join with him at the Lord's Table.

"He is increasingly able to make responsible contributions to group activities and he enjoys doing so. He feels closer identification with other groups beyond the family and enjoys participating in their activities." This indicates that this is a propitious time at which to balance the emphasis upon the *individual-in-community*, which participation at the Lord's Table demands.

"This seems to be a most strategic time for Christian education to utilize the influence of the family and the active participation of the child in family life. He needs to see Christian faith and worship as a natural part of his family life." This would indicate making participation in the Lord's Supper a natural part of his family's life of faith and worship.

"He is educationally amenable and responsive, hence this is an important age for dealing with basic facts about the Bible and for completing a general factual framework in understanding the Christian heritage." This can be applied particularly also to facts of the cross and the resurrection as the basis of the celebration of the Lord's Supper.

203

"He can be helped to understand more fully the meaning of Christian stewardship and to assume more stewardship responsibilities." This can be related meaningfully to participation in the Lord's Supper, by which he is moved to serve the neighbor with his gifts as he has been served by the love of God.

"Since he is able to think more deeply, he needs to develop a concept of God as an invisible Spirit and to gain a Christian understanding of the tragedies and evils of life." Since in Holy Communion it is the invisible, hidden Lord, who is present together with the visible, tangible vehicles and pledges of his presence and who brings joy and confidence in spite of sin and wrong and tragedy, this can contribute to the child's Christian growth. God never appears directly but always in a hidden way in the common things of life. Faith is always "in spite of." The joy and assurance of the Christian life are bought at the price of the suffering love of God in Christ.

"He can be helped to feel more and more a part of the church family," particularly by his participation in the Lord's Supper.

These characteristics are only illustrative of the readiness of the child for a meaningful participation in Holy Communion. Each of the understandings, attitudes, and action patterns considered a requisite for the Lord's Supper should be matched against the particular child and pastoral assurance gained that he is meeting these requirements. If he is not, then participation in the Lord's Supper should be postponed until such time when in pastoral judgment he is ready.

This allows for both a measure of uniformity and also the necessary flexibility to meet individual instances.

It should be very clear that the instruction necessary for first Communion is not a matter simply of a few stage directions and familiarity with the ritual. Nor is it a matter of instruction in this sacrament in isolation from the large context of the Christian faith. If the sacrament, as Luther said, is the gospel, then the gospel must be understood.

All this is not to say that admission to first Communion imparts a lifelong competence for a blessed Communion. Each Communion is an event in itself, and to each Communion there applies the apostle Paul's insistence on self-examination.

The instruction preceding first Communion will therefore normally be supplemented by instruction for confirmation in adolescence in order to offer resources for increasing maturity in Christ.

Age for Confirmation

Since the commission has defined confirmation as "a pastoral and educational ministry of the church that is designed to help baptized children identify with the life and mission of the adult Christian community and that is celebrated in a public rite," it is necessary that the commission suggest also an age most suitable when confirmation can achieve the purpose for which it is designed. A review of the age group characteristics and the kinds of learning of which a person is capable between the ages of ten to seventeen, points to grade ten as the period most suitable for confirmation. This designation of a specific period in a person's life is not, however, to be considered the termination of the pastoral and educational ministry of the church. Rather, it is to mark the attainment of a certain stage of development within a lifelong process. This does not preclude the celebration of other such events marking other stages of development should the church so see fit.

Characteristics of the Tenth-Grade Youth

Some of the important and pertinent age group characteristics for a person in the tenth grade which led the commission to this age designation are the following:[2]

The average tenth-grade youth continues to grow "toward maturity at a slow, gentle pace with no dramatic change" from that of the previous year. By this time a degree of wholesome self-confidence has been achieved. "A growing sense of independence, a feeling of greater ease with the opposite sex and with adults" is characteristic of this age. "The youth now gives the impression of being more grown-up and dependable. Having better emotional balance he no longer evidences the tensions within himself and with others" that he did previously.

At this grade level most youths have found an emotional perspective. The many disquieting forces of the ninth grade seem to have disappeared. "No longer is he so impulsive or such an extremist. Rather he has become a more affable, easy-going individual, better adjusted to life's situations. He realizes that his own happiness involves that of others."

[2]Ibid., pp. 73-76.

Authorities on adolescent psychology agree that the tenth-grader "is conscious of his own responsibility in handling emotions. He tries to control his anger and cover up his emotions by keeeping his feelings to himself or by appearing to be insensitive to remarks of others. Some even welcome criticism as a means toward self-improvement. His good sense of humor helps him accept criticism in a more positive manner. He is more willing to see another's point of view and takes a broader outlook on things in general." He is slowly maturing.

Because the tenth-grader "has an alert mind, and his intellectual capacities for thinking and reasoning have reached new heights," confirmation instruction at this period of the young Christian's life offers splendid opportunity for stimulating discussions. The young adolescent "is able to plan more logically and carry out plans which extend over a longer period of time. His sense of historical time is no longer subject to foreshortening. Although he has nearly reached mental maturity, his judgment is not yet mature." Tenth-graders are "willing to assume responsibility but want and need more guidance than they are willing to request."

At this age youth has a special interest in people. "His newly acquired sense of independence and his greater self-reliance give him a freedom and ease in his social relationships" which he did not have previously. "He seeks to cultivate friendships of both sexes. He may have one or two special friends with whom he is very close, but the boy still enjoys the 'gang' and the girl, her 'bunch-of-friends.' "

Whereas the tenth-grader may prefer "the company of friends to that of his family, parent-child relationships are generally good if his parents treat him as a grownup."

It should not be surprising that at this age an apparent disinterest in church or church activities may be present. This "should not be taken as a lack of interest in religion but rather as an indication that the church has not met the needs of the youth." They want help in thinking through their problems "and straightening out their beliefs."

"Both boys and girls are intensely interested in achieving a personal religion. They are very sensitive to an atmosphere of worship and usually respond deeply to a liturgical form of service. Many are interested in discovering what prayer can mean to them and knowing how to pray."

The tenth-grader is usually "able to distinguish between right and wrong. Problems of decision and conscience which were of great concern earlier have lessened because of his sense of independence, self-confidence, and self-assurance."

"The church needs to give these teenagers the help they want and need in order that they might experience an increased interest in religion."

Hence the conclusions of the commission seem warranted. Its working definition puts emphasis upon a level of development, commitment, and responsibility which is more characteristic of middle adolescence than it is of later childhood.

If the child is to become aware of what happened to him in Baptism to the degree that he (a) understands his fellowship in the body of Christ, (b) can appreciate the life-sustaining Word by which God builds faith, and (c) is ready to assume the responsibilities his faith entails, then he must have lived long enough to have had the need to make decisions for himself independent of his parents and teachers. In making decisions in his relations to others, he must tend to the consequences of trial and error all by himself.

By the tenth grade the young person usually has achieved the combination of stability, independence, and self-confidence which enables him to accept a role in an adult community and to be accepted, in turn, by that community.

A voluntary affirmation would seem most likely at the tenth-grade level. At that age the young person is likely to be ready to speak out of an independence with emotional balance, an informed interest in religious expression, and an appreciation for the people, the beliefs, and the devotional practices of the church.

The public aspect of an affirmation would seem most fitting at this grade level, when family ties have lessened; a greater interest in and an appreciation for people are more likely than in earlier years; and readiness to be seen as an adult is pretty well established.

He is capable of the level of understanding of his faith and expression of it which are inherent in the commission's definition. Personal acknowledgment of the Triune God seems most appropriate at this age level, after the growth in the realm of abstractions at fourteen and the reorganizing of concepts at fifteen. The greater belief in divinity and the need to do things "on their own" at Grade

10 also point to this grade level as most fitting. Under the circumstances Grade 10 seems to be the level which holds most promise of fulfilling the described role of the confirmand in the most meaningful way.

EDUCATIONAL IMPLICATIONS FOR THE CHURCH

For First Communion

Participation in the Sacrament of Holy Communion is to be viewed as part of a Christian's total life in the Word as a means of grace.

Education necessary for first Communion will aid the fifth-grade child to know and appreciate Holy Communion as a sacrament instituted by Christ, as his means of grace.

Objectives of Instruction for First Communion

The objectives of the instruction are to help the baptized child of God as a member of the body of Christ:

1. To understand and appreciate the nature of the Sacrament of Holy Communion,
2. To accept his place as a communicant in the fellowship of believers, and
3. To examine himself, to make confession of sin, and to receive the absolution of his sin for Christ's sake.

Expanding the Objectives

These objectives can be expanded as follows:

1. To understand and appreciate the nature of the Sacrament of Holy Communion.
    a. Understanding of the Lord's Supper as instituted by Christ, as an act of great love as recorded in Scripture.
    b. Understanding that the Word of God, Holy Baptism, and Holy Communion are all means of grace by which God loves man through Christ.
    c. Ability to tell in his own words the story of Jesus' birth, life, death, resurrection, ascension, coming again.
    d. An assurance that in this sacrament the church believes and celebrates the life, work, and presence of Christ in its midst.

    e. A developing sense of awe and wonder before the mystery of Christ's presence and love.
    f. The expectation that in eternity he will see the Savior face to face and be with him and God's family forever.

2. To accept his place as a communicant in the fellowship of believers.
    a. Understanding the fellowship and communal aspects of Holy Communion, as instituted by Christ, and as recorded in the history of the Christian church.
    b. Participating in the worshiping and teaching life of the congregation with its evidence of closeness and fellowship.
    c. Recognizing and responding to ways in which members of the congregation have shown their acceptance and concern for him.
    d. Desiring to receive Holy Communion as a way of joining with others around the same Christ and for the same purpose.
    e. Accepting others as relatives in the family of God.

3. To examine himself, to make confession of sin, and to receive the absolution of his sin for Christ's sake.
    a. An understanding of the connection between forgiveness of sin and Holy Communion.
    b. A knowledge of Bible stories about sinners brought to repentance and a love for Christ who forgives.
    c. A desire and willingness to join others in asking for forgiveness and receiving forgiveness together.
    d. A knowledge of the seriousness and of the joy of the Christian life, as interpreted in Scripture, prayers, hymns, and practices of the congregation, and a willingness to face the reality of evil and tragedy.
    e. An indication of sorrow for sin and thankfulness for forgiveness with regard to self and others.
    f. A desire to be open and honest with the pastor and other members.
    g. A willingness to share his life, feelings, and abilities with all kinds of people, even with those whom he does not really appreciate or like.

Implications for Christian Education

1. The child should be instructed for first Communion during the fifth grade, through the normal curriculum provided in the parish education program of the congregation.

2. Learning experiences for the child should include such things as observing actual demonstrations of Baptism and Holy Communion, individual and group prayers within the communion of believers, and participating in the worship services of the congregation.

3. The experiences of self-examination and confession should be provided for the child within the fellowship of believers.

4. Flexibility of instruction should respect differences in children due to such factors as the inner city, suburbia, unchurched homes, and the normal range of educational experiences.

5. The child should be given the opportunity in the latter part of the fifth-grade year to indicate his readiness to receive the first Communion.

6. Guidance should be provided to those responsible for judging a child's readiness for first Communion.

7. The rite of first Communion should be in the language and experiences appropriate to the child's world.

For Confirmation Instruction

While confirmation is only a part of the lifelong instruction of the Christian, it has, under the Spirit's power, a special pastoral and educational function for the maturing young Christian, as set forth in the commission's definition of confirmation: "to help baptized children identify with the life and mission of the adult Christian community."

Objectives of Confirmation Instruction

The objectives of the instruction are that the confirmand, as a baptized child of God and as a member of the body of Christ:

1. Know and confess as his own the Christian faith,

2. Live his role as a child and servant of God, and

3. Grow in the life of the Christian community and its mission.

Expanding the Objectives

These objectives can be expanded as follows:

1. To know and confess as his own the Christian faith.
   a. Understanding of the central teachings of the church as expressed in Luther's *Small Catechism*.
   b. Appreciation of the way in which these Christian doctrines are based on the Holy Scripture.
   c. Willingness and ability to confess this Christian faith as his own.

2. To live his role more fully as a child and servant of God.
   a. Understanding of his Christian vocation and the responsibility that this entails in carrying out the mission of the church in the world.
   b. Acceptance of himself and his relationship to God which influences him in his dealings with fellowman.

3. To grow in the life of the Christian community and its mission.
   a. Understanding that the church is the people of God and that it has the following God-given functions: worship, witness, education, service, fellowship.
   b. Understanding that Christian growth is a lifelong process and that the Christian is never in a state of completion but always in a process of becoming.
   c. Understanding that all believers in Christ are members of the body of Christ and are joined in a fellowship that transcends race, nationality, age, and time.
   d. Feeling that he is genuinely a part of the body of Christ and experiencing the fellowship which this implies.
   e. Finding those tasks within the church for which he is fitted and accepting responsibility to fulfill them.

Implications for Christian Education

1. Pressures on the tenth-grader from school work and activities make it unlikely that he will be able to attend a regular weekly class in Christian education. It would appear, therefore, that:
   a. Regular weekday instruction should be confined to Grades 7, 8, and 9.
   b. Every effort should be made for the youth to continue in Sunday school.
   c. Several short-term opportunities should be provided during the year for the

tenth-graders to explore with the pastor their coming confirmation and their religious concerns. These opportunities may be in the form of discussion groups or weekend retreats.

2. In order that ample time can be given for further educational development of tenth-graders, the confirmation rite should come in the latter part of the school year or subsequently.

3. Because of the importance of family influence on the young person's continuation in an active relationship with the church after confirmation, it is essential to involve parents in the educational process whenever possible.

4. If confirmands are expected to assume a more mature role in the congregation, genuine opportunities must be provided for them to do so.

5. Because of the mobility of population today, at least the core program and its objectives should be similar in the three Lutheran churches.

6. Confirmation instruction should be built on previous instruction in the schools of the church.

7. Major attention should be given to helping the confirmand become involved in a lifelong concern for his Christian education instead of viewing confirmation as a terminus to learning.

RITES OF ADMISSION TO FIRST COMMUNION AND CONFIRMATION

While the commission does not have the responsibility to draw up a series of rites for first Communion, confirmation, and other possible stages of growth in a lifelong catechumate, the commission is constrained to suggest for consideration the following guidelines to the commissions on worship of the participating churches.

General Guidelines

The language of the rites should be contemporary for the intended age levels. This will make them meaningful and teachable.

The rites, being occasions for joy, should communicate the note of celebration as well as responsibility.

The observance celebrated with a rite should serve to extend the role of the sponsors in a sound and positive way—to function in the rite of admission to first Communion and from then on to and including the rite of confirmation.

The rubrics should be sufficiently flexible to allow a variety in practice.

It is not precluded that there may be other public occasions when other stages of Christian growth are celebrated in a special way by the congregation.

For Holy Baptism

Because confirmation is so closely related to infant Baptism, the church will not be able to invest confirmation with a meaning that is free of distortions unless the language of the rite of infant Baptism expresses and describes the Baptism event precisely. There is a need for a baptismal rite specifically intended for infants and cleansed of all those elements which are proper only in an adult Baptism.

There is serious question whether the language addressed to sponsors and the degree of their involvement in the orders for infant baptism currently in use communicate what the church believes or does in infant Baptism. The rites for infant Baptism in current use continue to make an ambiguous witness to the gospel because the sponsors are still asked to answer in the stead of the infant candidate for Baptism (*Service Book and Hymnal*, p. 243). This ambiguity is heightened when in the rite of Baptism the sponsor is asked, "Wilt thou be baptized into this Christian faith?" ("The Order of Holy Baptism: The Baptism of Infants," *The Lutheran Agenda*, p. 7). As long as the questions addressed to sponsors remain in essentially the form originally addressed to adult candidates for Baptism, it will be difficult to guard against the impression that sponsors mediate in behalf of the infant candidate for Baptism.

The renunciation ought not appear in both the rite of infant Baptism and the rite of confirmation, however it is interpreted. For it does not appear that the renunciation can mean the same thing in both rites. If in Baptism it refers to reception into the church, it cannot mean this at confirmation. If in confirmation it means to purpose leading a holy life, this is clearly an intent that the child cannot consciously have at Baptism.

The Baptism rite should be designed to make it clear that the confession and renunciation is that of the church and that by Baptism the child is made a member of the church. This could be done by asking the congregation to renounce the Devil and confess together the faith into which the child is being baptized.

Admission to First Communion

A rite for the admission to first Communion ought not to be considered as marking the occasion for a kind of sacramental infusion of a special grace or a mystical bestowal of the Holy Spirit, through either or both of which the baptized child suddenly becomes worthy to receive the Lord's Body and Blood with blessing.

In this rite recognition should be given to the fact that the use of the Lord's Supper is a means of nurturing the young communicant.

The rite should make it clear that when the church proclaims the gospel and administers the sacraments, it is utilizing not two different means of grace but one. For the Word alone is the bearer of God's grace. When preached and taught, it is the audible Word in which God offers his own righteousness by the hearing of the Word. In Baptism and the Lord's Supper it is again the Word, through visible actions and elements, by which God offers, bestows, and covenants his grace.

The commission suggests that it should be made clear in the rite that the candidates presented for first Communion have been instructed in the meaning of Holy Communion and of confession and that their candidacy has previously been approved by the pastor and the church council. It is further recommended that each candidate have a sponsor or sponsors who are themselves communicant members of the church, and who shall, if possible, be present for the rite. In the event that the baptismal sponsors or the parents cannot assume this duty, another sponsor or sponsors may be appointed by the pastor in consultation with the candidate and the family.

It is assumed that the rite will follow the Gospel for the Day in The Service and that Holy Communion will be celebrated.

The rubrics should suggest that at the confession the candidates about to be admitted to the sacrament may receive absolution at the Communion rail, accompanied by the laying on of hands.

Questions should be addressed to the candidate regarding his belief that in Holy Baptism God accepted him as his child; and his belief that in Holy Communion Christ comes to him, with his body and blood, forgives his sins, and strengthens the fellowship of believers to trust and love one another.

The candidate should be asked to accept the responsibilities associated with admission to the Lord's Supper and to continue to receive instruction in the Christian faith.

The congregation, and particularly the sponsors, should be reminded of their responsibilities to help the candidates in fulfilling their promises.

The Rite of Confirmation

It is difficult to overestimate the psychological impact of a religious rite, such as confirmation, when it has the weight of approval by the Christian community and its meaning is perceived by the participant. Much has been learned in recent years about the influence of the group on the individual. The climate of the congregation, the attitude of parents, and the values held by the peer group combine to have a profound effect upon the way a confirmand views the event. The rite of confirmation must reflect the church's convictions. The language, structure, and action involved in the rite should, therefore, be examined carefully by the commissions on worship in the light of the definition of the purpose of confirmation as set forth in this report.

Some General Considerations

As stated in the definition of confirmation, both historic practice and present need indicate that confirmation today can best serve the church as a practice designed for baptized children. Adults shall therefore not be confirmed. They shall be received into the membership of a congregation by Baptism or, where previously baptized, by a profession of faith after adequate instruction.

The church must prevent an exaggeration of the volitional and individual aspects of decision at the expense of the response of faith within the community of believers. The Holy Spirit alone is able to "confirm," not the candidate, nor the pastor, nor the church. Therefore, throughout the rite the emphasis must be placed on God's active confirming through the means of grace rather than on the confirmand's confession of faith, much less on his promises.

The church must avoid giving a quasi-sacramental significance to confirmation which, in effect, desacramentalizes Baptism by making it a provisional means of grace.

The rite of confirmation must make it clear that it does not mark the end of the catechumenate or of learning experiences which must be a part of the lifelong process in which the believer is to grow into Christ.

For evangelical confirmation two things are essential:

1. That both instruction and the confirmation rite be fully determined by and also be effective channels of the Word.
2. That both be recognized and structured as part of the church's whole educational program of post-baptismal nurture.

More Specific Considerations and Rite Elements

1. *Relation to Baptism and to the baptismal covenant*

As set forth in the commission's definition, the confirmand with the adult Christian community recalls, in the confirmation rite, the act of Baptism through which God, by grace, received him into his church. The confirmand gives assurance that he believes the Word and promises of God he received in Baptism and states his intention to make faithful use of the means of grace and live as a responsible Christian. In turn, the congregation prays God to sustain him and strengthen him further in his Christian life.

As stated earlier (p. 193), it would be "theologically indefensible to elevate confirmation to a position in which it either complements or supplements the sacrament of Holy Baptism. It can be properly regarded neither in the pietistic sense of a conversion experience and an act of decision nor the rationalistic sense of a free choice."

Baptism is a unilateral covenant. It is complete, fully bestowing the gifts of salvation. Baptism is not conditioned by an act or promise of man. The covenant needs no renewal. God never withdraws his promises. Man may spurn the covenant but should he, by the grace of God, return to his baptismal covenant, he would not be renewing it. It was never made by him nor can he break it, though he may lose his covenant relationship. When man returns through the Spirit, he places himself under God's covenant and again receives its precious benefits.

Nevertheless, there may well be a relationship between confirmation and the saving nature of Baptism, for confirmation may call Baptism to remembrance.

The relation in which confirmation should stand to Baptism can be expressed thus: Negatively, it is not to contradict evangelical understanding of Baptism as a means of grace, as a covenant, or as an event in spiritual growth. Positively, it is to affirm further and serve that understanding. It cannot do more; it should not do less.

2. *The vow*

Any "vow" committing the confirmand to a lifelong faith in Christ and loyalty to him contradicts the nature of the faith relation which is in need of constant renewal, and such a vow is beyond the capacity of any man to keep. The confirmand is simply to assert and affirm, in his declaration of faith, his personal acceptance of God's acts of grace and his resultant personal intent to express that grace in a Christian life. No formal vow is necessary.

3. *The blessing*

The blessing of confirmation is not an episcopal bestowal of graces or supernatural powers but the intercession of the congregation for the bestowal of God's gracious favor. The gift of benediction is nothing other than that of the spoken Word and of intercessory prayer on behalf of one who stands in the full and complete faith already received in Baptism.

There should be, in the confirmation rite itself, an appreciation of the life-sustaining Word by which God builds faith. Through this Word in response to prayer God confirms the child in his faith and strengthens that which Baptism has already granted him.

4. *The laying on of hands*

The laying on of hands serves to personalize the prayers of the congregation as they intercede for the confirmands in prayer and petition God to impart to them the gifts of his Holy Spirit.

5. *Privileges and responsibilities*

If the rite attests to the fact that the confirmand may now assume certain privileges and responsibilities which the congregation is prepared to give in its particular organizational structure, these rights and responsibilities must be clearly stated lest the confirmand be led to believe that he is receiving through confirmation those rights and responsibilities which he already has by virtue of his Baptism.

6. *Church membership*

No statement should be made in the rite that the confirmand, by virtue of confirmation, is now a "member of the church" or entering into "full communion" with the church.

Further Recommendations

The commission suggests that the rite for confirmation should make clear that candidates for confirmation were instructed in the faith and life of the church as it finds expression in the Lutheran Confessions and that the candidates were approved in such manner as was deemed satisfactory by the pastor and the church council.

Confirmation should normally be administered at a public service of the congregation. Where this is impossible in an individual case, confirmation may be administered in the presence of members of the congregation privately. Such confirmation should subsequently be publicly announced to the congregation.

It is further recommended that each candidate for confirmation be accompanied by a sponsor or sponsors.

Questions should be addressed to the confirmand regarding his belief in one God, Father, Son, and Holy Spirit; and regarding his acceptance of Jesus Christ as his lord and as savior of the world.

Following the confession of faith, the candidate should be asked his intention in regard to his faith and the covenant which God made with him in his Baptism and whether he intends to be regular in the study of God's Word, in worship, and in the use of prayer. The commission believes that the candidates should be asked also to declare their intention concerning their Christian life, whether they intend to live it in harmony with the gospel of Christ and to accept as their own the mission of Christ's church in the world.

To emphasize the role of sponsors, where these have functioned, as well as the parents and teachers, an address may be provided in the rite. The address should emphasize that, when the candidates were first admitted to the fellowship of the Lord's Table, parents and sponsors promised that the children would be further instructed and one day be brought to the altar for the rite of confirmation. The presence of the confirmands at the confirmation service is evidence that parents, teachers, and sponsors have been faithful to their obligations. In turn the church, in whose behalf they have acted, voices its hope that all who have assisted in the educational process will be rewarded through the lives of the young people whom they have brought to the day of their confirmation.

V

Recommendations to the Presidents of the Lutheran Church Bodies

The Joint Commission on the Theology and Practice of Confirmation herewith respectfully submits its report for study, together with a number of recommendation, to the Honorable Presidents of The American Lutheran Church, the Lutheran Church in America, and The Lutheran Church —Missouri Synod.

The report of the commission is accompanied by a supplement, "Current Concepts and Practices of Confirmation." The supplement is submitted primarily for illustrative purpose and is not a part of the report. (It is not included in this study book.)

In making its report, the commission recognizes full well that the report, should it be adopted, will have far-reaching implications within the church bodies represented. The commission's survey, "Current Concepts and Practices of Confirmation," makes it very clear that the recommendations of the commission will need to be carefully considered in the light of the practical realities existing within the churches that are asked to make the changes. The commission is further conscious of the fact that many of the present practices concerning confirmation within the Lutheran churches are not only diverse, inconsistent, and harmful to the welfare of the Lutheran church but that they at times run contrary to the very theology which the Lutheran church publicly confesses.

Practically viewed, the commission recognizes also that there is a diversity of opinion and considerable confusion among Lutherans as to the manner in which the present dilemma may be solved. For this reason the commission believes that before the respective churches are confronted with a final report for action by conventions, it will be necessary to draw on the synods' full resources through a study program which can provide thoughtful and considered reaction toward improvements in the commission's final report and at the same time prepare the

constituencies for the needed changes. Because there is further danger that misinformation and unwarranted judgments may inadvertently be disseminated prior to a careful study of the entire report in its present form, it is necessary that utmost discretion be exercised in the publication of excerpts and summaries of the report or the accompanying supplements.

The commission therefore respectfully recommends to the Presidents—

1. That each president provide, by whatever means is appropriate to his church, for authorization of a program of study and reaction to this report as follows:

   a. That the president announce the program in his church at the time that seems most strategic.

   b. That the program be conducted by each church under the direction of its board of parish education beginning early in 1969.

   c. That responsibility be assigned to the executives of the boards of parish education of the three churches to develop plans for the program and arrange for the preparation of necessary study materials and instruments for reaction to implement these plans.

   d. That the program include—

      1) Briefing sessions for leaders, such as seminary professors, who will conduct one-day area seminars for pastors.

      2) Study sessions on a local level to be conducted by pastors for congregational leaders, such as church councilmen and teachers

   e. That this report and the study materials be furnished through the president of each church to any appropriate boards, commissions, or committees of that church for study and reaction at the same time that the study program is begun early in 1969.

f. That each church allot by whatever procedures are appropriate the necessary funds to cover the cost of—
1) Preparing and distributing a copy of the study material to each of its pastors.
2) The costs of briefing sessions for leaders and their expense in conducting area seminars for pastors. (It is assumed that the expenses of pastors attending such seminars will be borne by their congregations.)
g. That the study program be completed and reaction submitted to the commission by August 1, 1969.

2. That, in view of the commission's effort to accomplish widespread discussion of the "Report for Study" in an orderly and well-planned way, from which reaction and comment can be systematically gathered and a final report be prepared by the commission for action by each church body, the "Report for Study" not be released by the presidents until the study program is begun early in 1969.

3. That a news release concerning the work of the commission and the report being prepared for church-wide study in 1969 be issued by the presidents, preferably in concert, February 1, 1968.

4. That church publications be provided with advance copies of the "Report for Study" March 1, 1968—with the specific request that the release date for publication be January 1, 1969.

5. That a copy of this report be given to the president of the Synod of Evangelical Lutheran Churches at the time that the study program is begun.

6. That pastors and congregations be urgently requested not to initiate major changes in their practice of confirmation until the final report has been adopted by the conventions of the respective churches.

7. That the commission be authorized to prepare its final report after having had an opportunity to examine reactions to the study report and submit the final report to the presidents by March 1, 1970 for consideration and action by their church conventions.

8. That each president indicate to the chairman of the commission his response to these recommendations.

JOINT COMMISSION ON THE THEOLOGY AND PRACTICE OF CONFIRMATION

Herbert Brokering (TALC)
C. Richard Evenson (TALC, *Chairman*)
Francis Gamelin (LCA)
W. Kent Gilbert (LCA)
Martin J. Heinecken (LCA)
Arnold H. Heumann (TLC—MS)
A. L. Hock (TALC)
Edward T. Horn, III (LCA)
Theodore Liefeld (TALC)
Robert J. Marshall (LCA)
Arthur L. Miller (TLC—MS)
Alvin W. Mueller (TLC—MS)
Daniel E. Poellot (TLC—MS)
Arthur C. Repp (TLC—MS)
Alton S. Rogness (TALC)
Frank W. Klos, (*LCA, Recorder*)

PRESTUDY
Questionnaire

Name_____

Name of Congregation_____

City or Town_____

State or Province_____Zip Code_____

In addition to filling in the information requested above, be sure to fill in the spaces for your name and congregation at the top of the last page of the Prestudy Questionnaire.

PRESTUDY
Questionnaire

1. Which of the following statements is closest to your own understanding of the *central purpose* of confirmation? (Circle *only* one number in the column at the right.)

11:

To prepare for reception of the Lord's Supper 1
To receive the Holy Spirit through the laying on of hands 2
To identify with the life and mission
       of the adult Christian community 3
To renew the baptismal covenant .... (4)
To commit oneself to Christ 5
To become a member of the church 6
To complete the covenant which was begun in Baptism 7
Other (Please specify.)_____ 8

1, 5 ꝸ 3 ꝸ 7

2. The process through which the central purpose of confirmation is accomplished may include several elements. (Circle the numbers of the following elements you regard as *essential*.)

A program of instruction for a specific period of time .... (12:)
An ongoing pastoral ministry to young people .... (13:)
A public ceremony or rite of confirmation 14:
Admission to the Lord's Supper following the rite of confirmation (15:)
A public examination of confirmands 16:
A private examination of confirmands .... (17:)
Official approval of the confirmands by the church council 18:
Testimony by the confirmands to their faith in Christ .... (19:)
Other (Please specify.)_____ 20:

3. To achieve the purpose of confirmation as I understand that purpose, confirmation instruction should be conducted over a period of— (Circle only one number after reading both columns.)

21:   *21:*

1 year 1   4 years 4
2 years 2   Six months 5
3 years .... (3)   Other (Specify.)_____ 6

PRESTUDY
Questionnaire

4. On the basis of my understanding of confirmation, I think the best time for the confirmation rite is in the latter part of— (Circle *only* one number.)

	22:		22:
Grade 5	1	Grade 10	6
Grade 6	2	Grade 11	7
Grade 7	3	Grade 12	8
Grade 8	4	Other (Specify.)_____	9
Grade 9	(5)		

5. The baptized child may be able to participate meaningfully in Holy Communion earlier than he is able to participate meaningfully in the rite of confirmation. (Circle *only* one number.)

	23:		23:
I agree strongly	1	I disagree somewhat	4
I agree somewhat	2	I disagree strongly	(5)
I am uncertain	3		

6. Admission to the Lord's Supper should come at an earlier age than the rite of confirmation. (Circle *only* one number.)

	24:		24:
Yes	1	Uncertain	3
No	(2)		

7. If children are admitted to the Lord's Supper before the rite of confirmation, this should be in the latter part of— (Circle *only* one number.)

	25:		25:
Grade 3	1	Grade 8	6
Grade 4	2	Grade 9	(7)
Grade 5	3	Grade 10	8
Grade 6	4	Other (Specify.)_____	9
Grade 7	5		

PRESTUDY
Questionnaire

*Name*_____

*Name of Congregation*_____

8. My answers to questions No. 5, 6, and 7 are based *primarily* on my concern for— (Circle numbers of those that apply.)

Practical problems involved in changing present practice .... (26:)
Strong tradition in our congregation 27:
Adherence to the doctrines of the church 28:
The child's right to receive the sacrament 29:
Other (Please specify.) _____ 30:

Child should understand their own feelings about faith before receiving communion

9. Adults should not be confirmed, but following adequate instruction, should be received into membership in the congregation by Baptism or, where they have already been baptized, by profession of faith. (Circle *only* one number.)

	31:		31:
I agree strongly	1	I disagree somewhat	4
I agree somewhat	(2)	I disagree strongly	5
I am uncertain	3		

10. It is desirable that there be uniformity among all North American Lutheran church bodies in regard to the age of confirmation and admission to the Lord's Supper. (Circle *only* one number.)

	32:		32:
I agree strongly	1	I disagree somewhat	4
I agree somewhat	(2)	I disagree strongly	5
I am uncertain	3		

11. Additional comments about confirmation:_____

_____

_____

_____

_____

POST
STUDY Questionnaire

Name_____

Name of Congregation_____

City or Town_____

State or Province_____Zip Code_____

In addition to filling in the information requested above, be sure to fill in the spaces for your name and congregation at the top of the last page of the Poststudy Questionnaire.

POST
STUDY Questionnaire

1. Which of the following statements is closest to your own understanding of the *central purpose* of confirmation? (Circle *only* one number in the column at the right.)

11:

To prepare for reception of the Lord's Supper 1
To receive the Holy Spirit through the laying on of hands 2
To identify with the life and mission
     of the adult Christian community 3
To renew the baptismal covenant 4
To commit oneself to Christ 5
To become a member of the church 6
To complete the covenant which was begun in Baptism 7
Other (Please specify.) _____ 8

2. The process through which the central purpose of confirmation is accomplished may include several elements. (Circle the numbers of the following elements you regard as *essential*.)

A program of instruction for a specific period of time 12:
An ongoing pastoral ministry to young people 13:
A public ceremony or rite of confirmation 14:
Admission to the Lord's Supper following the rite of confirmation 15:
A public examination of confirmands 16:
A private examination of confirmands 17:
Official approval of the confirmands by the church council 18:
Testimony by the confirmands to their faith in Christ 19:
Other (Please specify.) _____ 20:

3. To achieve the purpose of confirmation as I understand that purpose, confirmation instruction should be conducted over a period of: (Circle *only* one number after reading both columns.)

21:		21:
1 year 1	4 years 4
2 years 2	Six months 5
3 years 3	Other (Specify.)_____ 6

POST
STUDY Questionnaire

4. On the basis of my understanding of confirmation, I think the best time for the confirmation rite is in the latter part of: (Circle *only* one number.)

22:

		22:	
Grade 5 1	Grade 10 6
Grade 6 2	Grade 11 7
Grade 7 3	Grade 12 8
Grade 8 4	Other (Specify.)_____ 9
Grade 9 5	

5. The baptized child may be able to participate meaningfully in Holy Communion earlier than he is able to participate meaningfully in the rite of confirmation. (Circle *only* one number.)

23:

	23:
I agree strongly 1	I disagree somewhat 4
I agree somewhat 2	I disagree strongly 5
I am uncertain 3	

6. Admission to the Lord's Supper should come at an earlier age than the rite of confirmaiton. (Circle *only* one number.)

24:

	24:
Yes 1	Uncertain 3
No 2	

7. If children are admitted to the Lord's Supper before the rite of confirmation, this should be in the latter part of: (Circle *only* one number.)

25:

	25:
Grade 3 1	Grade 8 6
Grade 4 2	Grade 9 7
Grade 5 3	Grade 10 8
Grade 6 4	Other (Specify.)_____ 9
Grade 7 5	

POST
STUDY Questionnaire

Name_____

Name of Congregation_____

8. My answers to questions No. 5, 6, and 7 are based *primarily* on my concern for: (Circle numbers of those that apply.)

Practical problems involved in changing present practices 26:
Strong tradition in our congregation 27:
Adherence to the doctrines of the church 28:
The child's right to receive the sacrament 29:
Other (Please specify.)_____ 30:

9. Adults should not be confirmed, but following adequate instruction, should be received into membership in the congregation by Baptism or, where they have already been baptized, by profession of faith. (Circle one number.)

	31:		*31:*
I agree strongly 1		I disagree somewhat 4	
I agree somewhat 2		I disagree strongly 5	
I am uncertain 3			

10. It is desirable that there be uniformity among all North American Lutheran church bodies in regard to the age of confirmation and admission to the Lord's Supper. (Circle one number.)

	32:		*32:*
I agree strongly 1		I disagree somewhat 4	
I agree somewhat 2		I disagree strongly 5	
I am uncertain 3			

11. Additional comments about confirmation:_____

_____

_____

_____

_____